Penguin Books

# PAVLOVA PARADISE
REVISITED

*E*nglish-born Austin Mitchell arrived in New Zealand forty years ago as a young university lecturer to teach history at the University of Otago. In the next decade he also became a well-known television current affairs frontman, interviewer and commentator. His bestselling book *The Half-gallon Quarter-acre Pavlova Paradise* was published by Whitcombe and Tombs in 1972. After returning to Britain Mitchell became a Labour Member of Parliament for the electorate of Grimsby and he is still an MP.

# PAVLOVA PARADISE
### REVISITED

A Guide
to the Strange
but Endearing Land
where Kiwis Live

## AUSTIN MITCHELL

PENGUIN BOOKS

PENGUIN BOOKS
Penguin Books (NZ) Ltd, cnr Airborne and Rosedale Roads, Albany,
Auckland 1310, New Zealand
Penguin Books Ltd, 80 Strand, London, WC2R 0RL, England
Penguin Putnam Inc, 375 Hudson Street, New York, NY 10014, United States
Penguin Books Australia Ltd, 250 Camberwell Road, Camberwell,
Victoria 3124, Australia
Penguin Books Canada Ltd, 10 Alcorn Avenue, Toronto,
Ontario, Canada M4V 3B2
Penguin Books (South Africa) (Pty) Ltd, 24 Sturdee Avenue, Rosebank,
Johannesburg 2196, South Africa
Penguin Books India (P) Ltd, 11, Community Centre, Panchsheel Park,
New Delhi 110 017, India
Penguin Books Ltd, Registered Offices: Harmondsworth, Middlesex, England

First published by Penguin Books (NZ) Ltd, 2002

1 3 5 7 9 10 8 6 4 2

Copyright © Austin Mitchell 2002

The right of Austin Mitchell to be identified as the author of this work in
terms of section 96 of the Copyright Act 1994 is hereby asserted.

Designed and typeset by Egan-Reid Ltd
Printed in Australia by McPherson's Printing Group

All rights reserved. Without limiting the rights under copyright reserved above,
no part of this publication may be reproduced, stored in or introduced
into a retrieval system, or transmitted, in any form or by any means
(electronic, mechanical, photocopying, recording or otherwise), without
the prior written permission of both the copyright owner and
the above publisher of this book.

ISBN 0-14-301826-4
www.penguin.co.nz

# Contents

| | | |
|---|---|---|
| Preface | | 7 |
| Chapter One | Welcome to God's Own Country | 11 |
| Chapter Two | A Pavlova Pilgrimage | 27 |
| Chapter Three | Kiwis Come from Lilliput | 46 |
| Chapter Four | Dunedin | 76 |
| Chapter Five | Southland | 94 |
| Chapter Six | Central Otago | 114 |
| Chapter Seven | Christchurch: A Godley Land | 131 |
| Chapter Eight | Absolutely, Positively, Wellington Dunnit | 149 |
| Chapter Nine | Wellington: Women Rule – OK? | 172 |
| Chapter Ten | Maori | 185 |
| Chapter Eleven | Auckland | 203 |
| Chapter Twelve | Ringing the Changes | 233 |
| Chapter Thirteen | Back to the Future | 253 |
| Chapter Fourteen | Global Kiwis | 271 |

# Preface

It's forty years since I first arrived in New Zealand, thirty since *Half-gallon Quarter-acre Pavlova Paradise* was published. The anniversaries are a good reason to reassess what's changed. Even better to come back to the beloved country to see, experience and attempt to understand the new New Zealand.

Second comings to paradise are a unique privilege, given only to the dead or the drug-addicted. So this preface can only be a long gibbering paean of gratitude to all who have made my return to the land of the long white pavlova possible. It's been such a wonderful experience. I wanted to prolong it forever rather than actually writing the book or finishing the film, but my delaying tactics generated as much suspicion as one of Helen Clark's paintings, or a pair of Tuku Morgan's underpants, to mix the sublime and the corblimey. Sadly, delay had to be finite, particularly at my age, and both jobs had to be finished but I couldn't have done either without a lot of help from a lot of people. Particularly those who went to so much trouble to explain the new New Zealand to Rip Van Mitchell. They'd lived it, I'd only read about it and watched at a distance. I envy them. They helped me.

The idea for the film came from the late Neil Roberts and was picked up by Shaun Brown, both of TVNZ. It was accepted and funded by New Zealand On Air and the Television Corporation. The idea of a book about the pilgrimage was then taken up by Geoff Walker of Penguin, who not only ran with it but extracted it from me forcibly by long distance bullying via the Internet. He saw it edited and prepared with Penguin's consummate skill.

New Zealand can be very proud of its film and television technicians, particularly the experts who worked with us: Wayne Vinten, Jonathan Mitchell, Michael Monton and Warren Bradshaw. As well as providing wonderful pictures and sound, they were infinitely patient when I carried on asking more and more questions long after they'd packed up equipment and wanted to go because it was past their bedtimes. Jackie Hay organised the interviews, planned the troop movements around the tens of thousands of kilometres we covered, and did the research.

My old friend, the Rt. Hon. Jonathan Hunt helped, guided and gave me the benefit of his enormous wisdom. He's been my guide and friend for so long, I can't work out how I've

PREFACE

managed to fail so disastrously at so many careers. My way was made easier by several other friends, Stan Rodger and his son Craig, and my former colleagues and older friends, Bob Chapman and Keith Jackson with whom I first worked on our 1960 book – *New Zealand Politics in Action* (last two words separate). Both were patient in explaining the changes since then to me. The NZ-UK link helped too, bringing me out to New Zealand for a debate which first prepared me for the changes in the New Zealand meat industry, because I was ritually slaughtered and chopped into small pieces.

Production and editing were huge jobs for a technical Luddite like me but Joyce Benton, Pat Murray, Emma Sandler and Mark Meilack saved me from my own incompetence, turning scribble into text and worked above and beyond the call of duty to finish the manuscript. The errors are mine, the achievement that of this devoted team.

Most of all I should thank my wife Linda who made sense of my ramblings on film and pushed me into finishing the book almost in time. She also kindly excused me my usual heavy household duties and transferred me to a light schedule to give me time to write it.

'Linda makes things happen,' as Bryan Gould once said. Mainly to me, but she did make all this happen and without her none of it would have been possible. Except the photographs, for which I alone and unaided am responsible. Unfortunately, having turned photography from a hobby into a disease, working on the principle that ten million monkeys with ten million typewriters can eventually write Shakespeare, and applying that to cameras in the hope of taking a Cartier-Bresson, the result was a hundred thousand pictures. Regrettably Penguin declined to publish all of them in this book. I was reduced to thirty happy snaps.

It's all been a wonderful experience. Which makes me wonder why the hell I left New Zealand in the first place.

Except that if I hadn't I'd never have been able to come back and catch up on the change, the excitement and the misery. I've missed out on a lot of good times and some bad, but now I've seen the future and it works. For New Zealand. It has become exciting and dynamic in a way I could never have thought and, if the truth be told, never expected it to be back in those dim and distant sixties. Good on yer youse Kiwis.

Austin Mitchell
Somewhere Else
May 2002

# Chapter One

> **KIA ORA!**
> **RULES OF BEHAVIOUR FOR THE SMOKE-, NUCLEAR- AND ALMOST GM-FREE, WORLD-CLASS DEMI-PARADISE (ALL MAJOR CREDIT CARDS ACCEPTED)**

# Welcome to God's Own Country

She's sorry She can't be here Herself to greet you in person. Air fares from Dunedin are so high these days and it's difficult to get time off from Her 'Adjusting to Retirement' course at Otago University. So She doesn't get north much and doesn't like Auckland in any case. Particularly since John Banks became Mayor. It's more like Australia, where She's not at home, than Otago, where She's retired to.

So many visitors now come to see God's chosen country – two million a year – that benediction would be like the baptism by hose pipe that missionaries in China used to administer rice to thousands of Christians at a time. Besides, doing that would compete with the Department of Agriculture's own spraying requirements. It would also counter the purpose of bringing visitors here in the first place, which is to get them out into the shops, the *bureaux de change* and the car rentals to spend as much as possible, as quickly as possible. Providing for eternal salvation would hold all that back too much.

So She's delegated the welcoming role to those friendly little cocker spaniels who sniffed your feet at the airport to see if you'd been treading grapes for French wine, and your suitcase for fruit, drugs, pornography, and other rural fare. If you need any further blessing or divine contact, the Auckland Airport Authority and the Auckland Port Authority have powers delegated by God regarding everything north of the Bombay Hills, the land where Mammon has co-dominion. You can see why as you look around the airport: it could be anywhere, even Australia – airport staff dressed like Canadian Mounties, hordes of overweight Islanders, their luggage crushing the trolleys, well drilled parties of Japanese jogging through like an invading army, overburdened backpackers blocking every door, and the occasional Pom trying to find people to condescend to. Auckland isn't New Zealand, but don't alienate Kiwis by asking if you're in Australia. Just head South quickly.

So welcome, but remember that it's not total acceptance. If visitors stayed and bred, New Zealand would soon have the population of India. Enjoy. But leave promptly, and if you do want to multiply, don't do it here. Kiwis are secular saints and naturally friendly, but niceness and patience can be tried by the sheer numbers of foreigners who insist on visiting rather than simply staying home and sending their money. Because of this influx, great hulking lumps of lads, bred for the rugby field, buxom lasses built for breeding, and youths who'd rather live the aesthetic life followed by New Zealand's patron saint, Barry Crump, have to take servile service jobs as waiters and recite incomprehensible homilies in blank verse about the food they're serving. That's no manly role, and if New Zealand didn't need their money and if the lads and lasses working in the hospitality industry didn't need the jobs to save up enough to get overseas, tourists would be about as welcome as asylum seekers (or Kiwis) in Australia.

In the Good Old Days (which means any time before reviled former Finance Minister Roger Douglas) New Zealand had fewer visitors and a higher percentage stayed. Indeed, they couldn't go back and had to experience New Zealand by living it, which is the best introduction to this wonderful land, since being Kiwi is a way of life rather than a national identity. Once lived the identity sticks.

New Zealand's proud identity is unique, and highly respected, particularly by New Zealanders. Its biggest and best export is locally produced and assembled Kiwis who ship themselves (sometimes 'Completely Knocked Down', but never 'Free On Board' as the shipping statistics put it) overseas to form a huge Kiwi Diaspora, a worldwide net of the Second Chosen People (Third Division South), differing from the Jews – the prematurely chosen people – in that Kiwis have always had a national home but don't all want to stay there. At the top of every tree in Australia, and even in civilised countries, there is a little arboreal coterie of Kiwis recognisable by their mateyness, their informality and obsession with sports most of the world don't play so as to avoid brain damage, and a niceness that puts Paul McCartney to shame. Kiwis are World Citizens, humanity's finest flowering, and serve the world well by running the World Trade Organisation, the Commonwealth or Queensland, or by doing the really messy jobs like marrying Rod Stewart or Karitane nursing upper-class children.

You'll need this guide to the lifestyle – your cram course in Kiwi studies – to ensure you enjoy your visit and introduce you to what is agreed by its inhabitants to be the best country in the world, living what they know is its most wonderful way of life, enjoyed by the world's best people, in its finest, if least convenient, location. It will initiate you into the full richness of New Zealand life, right down to its dark inner sanctums: the male misogynist shed (Kiwi equivalent of the Taliban caves of Afghanistan), the bedroom (unpenetrated so far by the media), and the Kiwi wife's last retreat, the kitchen. First though, a little housekeeping, as the tour guides say. You now need the basics of survival for those few wonderful days before your ship or plane returns to Overseasia.

## Rule One

New Zealand is a country of rules. In an intimate society everyone knows each other. Indeed, they're probably related by some remote act of incest or, at the very least, grew up together, programmed in the schools and in the home to basic Kiwi-ism. This makes everyone their own policeman, enforcing rules they've personally had to observe for years on lesser breeds like you. Do something off-code and people will sprint across dangerous roads, shinny down ladders or bellow from hundreds of yards away to put you right. In friendly and helpful fashion, of course, but that can't conceal their strong conviction that you must conform, because if you don't it could destroy their faith in living. Don't resent any such correction. It's in your best interests.

## Rule Two

Be seemly in behaviour. Don't spit, pee, smoke or fornicate in the street. These activities may be OK back home, and even in the native bush, but New Zealand is a carefully sanitised, spotlessly clean and smoke-free world with more fresh air per capita than any other country, particularly in Wellington where it's changed by gale-force winds every five minutes. The atmosphere mustn't be polluted by the merest drag. If you're addicted to nicotine then stay on the boat (not the plane, Air New Zealand is smoke-free too) or get out of town. All cities have nearby hills: in Auckland One Tree Hill (where the one tree was killed by passive smoking), in Wellington Mount Victoria, in Dunedin Signal Hill, and the Port Hills in Christchurch. These are the heights of depravity, set aside for smokers, junkies, and courting couples attempting interesting exercises in the back seats of cars. Take to the hills and take your filthy habit with you. Otherwise butt ends discarded in the streets will be returned to you by pursuing joggers. If you manage to make a getaway, they'll be DNA tested so that you can be hunted down, x-rayed for cancer and possibly sentenced to death under new legislation now being considered requiring smoking diners to eat outside – whatever the weather.

Please leave New Zealand as tidy and lovely as you found it. Take your litter home with you. That's what suitcases are for. Eschew all violence, however slow the service in restaurants. You won't be robbed, raped, thumped or mugged – quite a change for Australians – but please be nice back. Most of the world's niceness reserves are in New Zealand, and the nearest equivalent to America's Angry Brigade is the Slightly Cross Brigade with only two members. Avoid road rage, however meanderingly bucolic the habits of most New Zealand drivers. In turn you won't get any directed at you, because in New Zealand the syndrome is merely Road-Temporary-Loss-of-Niceness. If you manage to produce that in a New Zealand driver, rest assured you're well in the wrong.

## Rule Three

Walk and drive on the left at all times to avoid accidents. Lane discipline extends to jogging lanes, where you could be trampled, and to pavements, where painful injuries await those who cross an oncoming lane to gaze into a window. To avoid this, window displays on the right are kept deliberately dull so that no one crosses the flow to look at them. To ensure a level playing field, those on the left must be the same. Look people coming towards you in the eye. To flinch is to show you have something to hide. Look where you're going, summary punishment by elbows, gumboots or knocking down awaits meanderers. This rule does not apply to Auckland because Queen Street is inhabited by foreigners who aren't here long enough to learn the rules.

## Rule Four

Don't tip. It causes embarrassment. Not to you, or the service provider (most of whom will accept anything), but to the rest of the population who don't want to have to tip when you've gone. The natives won't be servile. Your waiter likes to pretend to be another diner, dressed for the cheap end of the market but just helping out. Your bus guide likes to be treated as just another passenger. To the great regret of their employers, the government requires both functionaries to be paid. Spoiling them further by offering tips is bad in a country where wealth is resented and the heads of tall poppies are there to be knocked off. Don't expose anyone to the temptation of not reporting tips to the taxman. This can cause the appointment of expensive Royal Commissions.

The same advice applies to taxi drivers. Perhaps even more so, because since deregulation they aren't required to know where anything is. So in Auckland you are likely to be asked, 'Do you know the way to the bridge?' This is also the only country in the world where taxi drivers ask passengers where they can get a woman.

## Rule Five

Don't be fooled by the sheep-like docility and niceness of the people. Dress Kiwis in khaki or All Black uniform and they're killers. Indeed, in every documentary about the British SAS the people disguised by balaclavas usually speak with Kiwi accents. Take the bras off the women and you're at major risk. These are fierce people, they'd much rather be in the bush killing small animals, or overseas killing people like you. Since they can no longer fulfil that destiny by travelling abroad to kill Germans and Japanese, or to Vietnam to kill Australians, they now entice them to New Zealand and kill them there on mountains, in the rapids, in helicopters or in the unexplored bush. Death is a marketable commodity and New Zealand's Unique Selling Proposition. It could be yours.

## Rule Six

The great unmentionable, as far as visitors are concerned, is sex. You're here to see, not to participate, whatever aspect of life it may be: from Maori challenges to Scottish Country Dancing or nude bathing. If sex is your need, it is available – grudgingly – because the market is now supreme. But go to the professionals. Sex is in its infancy in New Zealand and misunderstandings frequent because of the difficulty in distinguishing between general niceness and flirtation. To enter the professional market you need a credit card, a mobile phone, and *Truth* newspaper – the illustrated server guide. However, on no account be seen carrying or consulting it. Strict discipline is also available for passing public school chaps, but be extremely cautious or you may well find yourself floating down the appropriately named Huka Falls, trussed and naked, before the video cameras of bemused tourists.

Never approach any New Zealand woman directly. If one approaches you in the street don't view it as a sexual advance or a tribute to foreign virility compared to rugby-obsessed Kiwis. It could be a transvestite, a passing MP or an undercover cop. This is a country where androgyny by hairstyle, build or dress is more common than any country outside Androgenina. So you never know. More likely it's an ordinary Kiwi lady anxious to ask how you like the country or if you'd like her to take a photograph of you and your group. Let her. This is the service most frequently demanded of natives by tourists. They like giving it because it allows them to helpfully explain the theory and practice of photography and the workings of their own cameras to the visitors and, more importantly, New Zealand is the only country in the world where the volunteer won't run away with the camera. Since the liberalisation of the economy, everything is for sale: farms, businesses, degrees, qualifications, landscapes, livestock, and even the vulva, but never offer cash immediately. You could get the last for free.

## Rule Seven

New Zealanders are a very polite people but not over-articulate, which is why quotes such as 'bugger the polls' (Sir James Bolger), 'get off my fucking boat' (Sir Peter Blake), and the WRU has 'shitted on us' (Sir Colin Meads) are normal, but ensure that your own public communications and conversations are polite and Politically Correct. Avoid criticisms of women, who run the country and should not be provoked. Defer to Maori, whatever rubbish they talk, and whether they're wearing grass skirts or Mongrel Mob death's head jackets with Nazi helmets. Treat them all as the original owners – which they are. Say nothing about them being overweight, drunk, or in bad health.

Never swear at Islanders, a deeply Christian people. As

for the whites (called Pakehas), wear a Rotary badge, give Masonic handshakes and offer any other forms of reassurance that come to mind. Particularly money. Don't stand out or try to be fashionable. It won't be noticed. Ignore their casual eccentricities as they do each other's. They know you're a visitor because Kiwis have automatic tourist detectors, but there's no point in drawing attention to such an ignoble status. Standing out makes everyone uncertain, and being a tourist stranger in paradise makes you some kind of scrounger imposing on them. So don't presume.

## Rule Eight

Don't expect to see Hobbits, monsters or any other Tolkien grotesques. Australians were brought in to model for them then sent back under plain cover. All you'll see are other tourists and tall, often blond and usually handsome Kiwis of both sexes. Although you may not see too many of them because most go overseas in the huge national effort to keep Air New Zealand flying. The hospitality industry is manned by Australians and owned by Americans and Japanese, but if you do spot any Kiwis, don't clutter their place up or obstruct them going about their daily business, but talk to them. With men in suits talk about the rugby, with women about cuisine, décor or how useless men are.

New Zealand depends on tourism to finance the flood of Kiwis, more per capita than any other country, pouring abroad. Which is why so few of them are here to greet you, particularly in Auckland, now a Chinese city, and Christchurch, as Japanese as English. In summer, New Zealand would be like the *Marie Celeste* if it weren't for tourists, since more Kiwis go to Overseasia than tourists arrive from it. Ministers, MPs, generals, businessmen and most young people are overseas. It would be the best time of year to invade, but since the only people likely to do that – the

Australians – are also on holiday, there's no danger of a hostile takeover. Be unobtrusive, spending to the maximum without flashing your dosh. Be numerous, not noticed. The best appreciation you can show for New Zealand's generosity in allowing you to be here, is to leave the maximum money behind. Since New Zealand is no longer eligible for US overseas aid and the IMF's intense admiration for its economic policies resolved it to stop all financial support, you're helping the world to pay its dues.

# Rule Nine

The natives are more extrovert and noisier than they used to be, but compared with Americans they'd make good Trappist monks. The women have turned positively aggressive. Yet this should not conceal the fact that all Kiwis are basically insecure. They need your approval. Representing the outside world, you are here to give that. In the old days they would ask 'how do you like New Zealand?' several times before you'd even got off the tarmac, whereas now Kiwis need to be assured that everything is 'world class'. Having put up with all sorts of abuse, punishment and sado-economics to make them world class they're damn well going to be it. Thousands of costly reports have been commissioned from accountancy houses, think tanks and astrologers to grade companies, departments, churches, sports teams and massage parlours as 'world class', 'lower world class' 'incompetent' or 'Tranz Rail'. A vast reassurance industry has developed to tell them how world class they are, so don't even hint that they're not.

In fact, only the toilets are truly world class – anal neuroticism being a national disease. The airline could be regarded as world class because it's as bankrupt as all the others, and one or two companies have been better at looting and asset-stripping than Enron or Long-Term Asset Management. World class is not an unqualified accolade, yet

New Zealanders are still desperate to attain it because it gives institutions, companies and people something to live for. Besides, it's cheaper than an ad in *National Business Review*.

So murmur seductively at every available opportunity about how impressed you are to see that cake decorating, Tuatapere sausages, Havelock mussels, Plunket babies, Kaikoura whales, Taumarunui lattes or anything else that comes to mind is 'world class'. It costs nothing, brings a lot of happiness and may even make people think the economic lunacy of the last two decades has been worthwhile. In fact, it was several major steps backward but what's the point in telling children there's no Santa Claus?

If you can't rise to reassure, say something vague like 'It's better than Australia'. Never confuse Kiwis with Australians or say their country is like that continent – particularly Tasmania. There New Zealanders are jealously regarded as 'half-baked Poms' except for those like Russell Crowe who became famous and are immediately claimed as Australian (along with pavlova). In Britain, New Zealanders face the unpleasantness of being thought to be Aussies, even of having to associate with them, fed up with explaining to the ignorant English that they're quite different. Here, in New Zealand, Kiwis are themselves, the masters. So at the very least say 'It's a lovely country you've got here', if only because it is. It's got a huge variety crammed into its thousand-mile length.

## Rule Ten

Get out of the cities as quickly as possible. Head for the lakes, the mountains and the sea but remember that the countryside is not a welcoming pastoral landscape, like Constable's, but an outdoor factory for the practical purpose of feeding exportable animals. You can buy large chunks of it but can't litter, light fires, or live in it; and remember the environmentally aware hiker in the Wye Creek near Queenstown, who conscientiously burnt his toilet paper after using it and set off a major bush fire requiring ten fire-fighting helicopters. Take a portaloo.

## Rule Eleven

You are a neophyte, possibly worse, and New Zealand Police would make it an offence if they knew what it meant. You've come to paradise to see and be seduced by it, a reaction which isn't optional. Before you came you may have regarded New Zealand as a distant place, cheaper than the real world. Now you'll discover that it's unique. You've come from a richer land, to a better one with more wonderful scenery crammed into a smaller space, a country turned into an outdoor pleasure plant. Enjoy! But be humble and admire. That's why you've been allowed in.

## Rule Twelve

Don't touch! New Zealanders are reserved. They're not a touchy-feely people. Except on the rugby field. Auckland has gone a bit kissy-kissy under continental influence, but the continent in question is Australia so it can be slobbery. Wellington is shakey-handy and Maori nose-rubby, but don't touch the other body parts or invade Kiwi personal space unless invited in. Uppity Maori would claim it as an infringement of the Treaty of Waitangi, feminists as rape, the repercussions could go right up to the Privy Council (until they got around to abolishing this last link to colonialism).

## Rule Thirteen

Beware the women. The Kiwi bird is a fierce creature, terrifying when roused, which she is by assumed slights, anti-feminist remarks and male condescension, but not prolonged sexual foreplay. Women must never be referred to as 'birds', as they have hackles, which rise easily. A Parliamentary secretarial agency calls itself 'Loose Women'. However, refer to any one of its members in those terms and you're dead. Respect!!!

## Rule Fourteen

Take it easy. Slow down. You'll find service in restaurants about as fast as rigor mortis. This is a) because it takes time to drizzle everything in pesto and b) because all eateries are understaffed. It's no use trying to attract attention by shouting, setting fire to the table-cloth or having sex on the table. If you try to get a reaction by lighting a cigarette in a non-smoking section to bring a waiter, it won't. Your fellow diners will chastise you for smoking in a smoke-free area/restaurant/street/city, all loudly quoting half-remembered articles from the *New Zealand Woman's Weekly* about the dangers of passive smoking. In Christchurch I read once of a young student trying to get attention in a Manchester Street bar by nailing his foreskin to it. The ambulance and fire brigade duly arrived to free him but he still didn't get his drink. Don't grumble at the service you don't get. They're doing you a favour by admitting you, and their intentions are the best. So why not practise transcendental meditation?

The same is true at traffic lights. Particularly in Auckland, where fortunes are made by fast food franchises at intersections, because motorists have time to queue up, order their food, take delivery and sometimes eat it before the lights change. New Zealand is bang up to the minute but gets there more slowly than other countries, because longer-lived Kiwis must pace themselves differently and consequently the nation has a more downbeat tempo. Remember, this is the country that invented jogging as an alternative to running, and whose trains are the slowest in the world but still so fast that Tranz Rail had to slow them down even more for safety. Where else do people take days to read newspapers with nothing in them or does the national news last an hour when nothing significant happens?

## Rule Fifteen

Don't be pushy or demanding. Appeal to their better instincts and New Zealanders will do anything for you. Push them about and they become bureaucratic and obstructive. They aren't there to serve but to help. This is the only place where shop assistants try to persuade you that you don't need what you came in to buy, or direct you to a competitor store to get something cheaper. I called in at Pelorus supplies in Havelock, which boasts of being run by 'three wise women', to buy a map of the road to Nelson: price $5.50. 'Oh you don't need that,' said the duty wise woman. 'I'll show you the way.'

## Rule Sixteen

Try to learn more about this people's paradise than you can on the segregated tourist circuit. It's an example to the world, which deserves to be far better known than its modest inhabitants can make it. So get to know them so you can tell the world what they can't. You're a pilgrim as much as a tourist, and New Zealand offers a better life and grows better people than anywhere else on this overcrowded, polluted, strife-torn planet. It may be Down Under, but Down is the new Up. You're privileged to be here in the peaceful Pacific not the dirty Atlantic; the harmonious South, not the war-torn North, though there's only penguins to fight down here and Kiwis can't take on anyone their own size any more because they've killed all the moa.

## Rule Seventeen

Don't try to be smart. Greeted by 'kia ora', don't reply, 'No, I'd prefer lemon squash.' Asked vacuous questions like, 'How's your day been?' don't go on about how your mother-in-law fell accidentally on the carving knife in your hands, your wife has committed suicide, and you're on your way to the psychiatric ward. No answer is expected beyond 'fine'. To add 'How's yours been? You don't look too good' is superfluous. New Zealand has less sophistication, more niceness per acre than big societies. Its people aren't natural Smart Alecs, they're Serious Waynes. Sarcasm or trying to be funny unnerves them and could even demoralise because they lack the wit and malevolence which are the symptoms of impotence in Britain. When oldies answer your telephone call by saying, 'Are you there?' don't ask 'Where the hell do you think I am?' Remember, too, the New Zealand gift for abbreviation: 'Postie', 'Footie', 'Puddie', 'Bikie', 'Bikky,' etc. In the case of www, it becomes 'dub-dub-dub'.

After your visit you will want to become a Kiwi. Unless you're some kind of snob or pervert. You can't. The Demi-Kiwi grade is available, but only to foreigners with large sums of money who've thoroughly repented of their foreignness and haven't come to draw social security. Beneath that is the Semi-Demi grade, which you could aspire to by coming back enough times to gain frequent visitor status.

Which is why you must read, learn and thoroughly digest this book because visitors generally don't have the time to absorb the ambience or talk to the natives as they're whipped round on the principle of, 'if it's Tuesday it's Mount Cook'. Even if the bloody thing isn't visible. Nor is it any use turning to the enormous outpourings of New Zealand books, which are an illiterate-literature for those who like to read colour photos. About a hundred different photo books, that year's crop, are on sale at any one time; showing a New Zealand you'll not have seen, because even if you had managed to get there after several days' trek, you would have found it raining. Sadly, all these lovely volumes are excessively heavy because of a secret agreement between the New Zealand Publishers' Association and Air New Zealand designed to ensure that one will tip you into excess baggage charges and then require you to travel by

Hercules. So that most get abandoned at Auckland airport to be resold. If any did get overseas it could well turn entire populations into asylum seekers trying to get into New Zealand.

You could talk to the local experts: Winston Peters on consistency, John Banks on compromise, Bill English on population control, Jonah Lomu on ballet, Tim Shadbolt on meditation; but won't have time to penetrate the inner sanctums of New Zealand life: the pubs, the RSA, the New Zealand Cake Decorators Guild, the front row of the Otago scrum; your tour being restricted to McDonald's, plastic hotels (mostly French owned), Queenstown or other highly polished gems of the closed circuit entrepreneurs have created as a tourist preserve. All that is as unrepresentative of the real New Zealand as it's expensive. Kiwis must keep out, unless allowed in as cleaners, waiters, medical staff to treat injured thrill seekers, or other menial positions usually reserved for underpaid foreigners and students.

Which is why I offer this Rip Van Winkle Kiwi tour. Your visit will whet your appetite and this book provides a graduate course for those who want to move to higher level New Zealand studies or even become Real Dinkum Kiwis. It will acclimatise you and demonstrate that, though New Zealand may no longer be a unique paradise, it's still pretty good as paradises go: the best bit of a shrinking world far better than bigger more crowded bits – and a great place to bring up children as well as conceive them. It's also the perfect place to drink the best wine in superb scenery, with no snakes to bite as you slump drunkenly to the floor, while the sound of the bellbird rings through the night sky and the stars, brighter and more numerous than in polluted European skies, twinkle down on God's Own Country. Look after it until She comes back.

Chapter Two

# A Pavlova Pilgrimage

Old men don't forget. They remember and regret but embellish the past in the heritage museum of the mind. That process takes me back to New Zealand, where I arrived on 6 August 1959 on one of the first 680,404 ships, the *Rangitiki*, bearing a passport ten years' old in which 'We Ernest Bevin, His Britannic Majesty's Principal Secretary of State' requested and required the natives to give this particular Pom every assistance and generally not mess him about. Under threat of a gunboat or the King-Emperor's displeasure. No one read it, let alone obeyed it, but coming out (in national, not sexual terms) with delusions of superiority as the English usually go anywhere (except home) I'd stumbled on a better world.

New Zealand was one of the few forms of escape permitted to the British working class – apart from drink. Taking the Kiwi road out of tired, drab, Pomerania was the wisest decision I ever made. Like most of my decisions, it was made by accident. I'd applied for jobs at universities in Australia, Canada, New Zealand, and a few British kindergartens. The University of Otago, which no one in Oxford had heard of, was first to reply, because the most desperate. So I was employed at a salary of £900 a year, which rocketed to £1045 in weeks, and despatched free and First Class along the Panama route of empire, frantically reading up what I was supposed to know already as we sailed.

Arrival was the prelude to the happiest years of my life. Fellow students in Oxford, most of whom had never seen a sheep, farewelled me with loud bleats and predicted brain death and boredom, as if New Zealand was an Antipodean Wigan. In fact, it made me a real person, the nearest thing to a human being an Oxbridge chap can become, and contributed more to my development than Oxford's attempts at cerebral hand polishing. Those years in New Zealand changed me from a pedantic, Pommy prig – possibly even a Pongo – the clinically diagnosed version, into a human being of sorts. A Semi-Demi-Kiwi.

Arriving meant not the Shock of the New but the comfort of the familiar, like moving to an outshed in the same imperial house. Along with several other newlyweds, my wife Pat and I travelled out by ship in, what I thought of as, imperial style but what would now be called a love boat. First Class on the *Rangitiki* was an overawing experience for raw northerners.

The ship was populated by British Naval chaps going to show the Kiwis how to run a Navy, by teachers to improve them, a stray missionary, returning farmers (who I assumed must be rich, so impressed was I by anyone who could pay their own fare), and white collar and manual workers on their way to start a new life. The six-week voyage along the umbilical cord of empire made us feel British, imperial, even empire builders; instincts and a conditioning which were no preparation at all for the life we were going to.

Hunter and Maureen Howe, a Southland farmer and his young Scottish bride, were our fellow passengers. Unlike we poor paid-for Poms they paid their own fares, making them unique in the *Rangitiki*'s First Class. We became friends and regularly visited them in Southland, usually for Hogmanay where we always had to hide the bottles when neighbours came to first-foot. Forty years on, I met them again, now exiled from Southland and living in Alexandra.

## Maureen Howe

*Leaving London was the worst bit about the whole trip. Some of my family had come down to London to see us off. There was a stream of us going from the ship to the side onto the quay, and they were playing 'Now is the Hour'. It was terrible. People on both sides crying – my brother and sister-in-law still say they'll never again see anybody off. It was really heart-wrenching. There were 150 places in First Class and only fifty people to fill them and we had a full crew complement for 150, so we had all of the service and attention. It was wonderful. It was just one big party all the time. Wonderful relaxation and a great holiday.*

*I used to look round and think how many of these people have paid their own fares? There were only the Carsons, the judge and his wife. But it actually didn't cost us all that much, I guess, £140 each; only £12 dearer to come via Panama than to go Economy Class through Suez. And we had fewer stops so we wouldn't have spent as much. I'd never been on a ship before and never been across the equator and I wanted to have a porthole, that's why we came that way. I dreaded it, though, because I thought it would be lots of old people with lots of money, dripping in diamonds, that kind of thing. But it was such a friendly group. It was wonderful.*

## Hunter Howe

*We were met when we arrived and spent a day or two in Auckland with an aunt and an uncle. Then we flew down by DC-3 with stops at Wellington, Christchurch, Dunedin and on down to Invercargill. I think Maureen wondered where she had arrived in Invercargill.*

## Maureen Howe

*Well, it was so long and so far away and I couldn't believe that planes so old could fly either. Then we had to drive out to the farm and I thought that was just so far away from anywhere.*

*I always knew I could go back if I had to, if there was any reason that I had to, and I went back in less than two years because my mother was ill. But I felt for the people who came out fifty, sixty years before that and knew they'd never get back.*

*I missed home. But I'd made the choice to come here. And it was easy for me really because it wasn't as though we'd both come out and didn't know anybody. There was all of Hunter's family and all of his friends, and it was very easy to fit in. I couldn't believe that they still had gravel roads and the only kind of furniture you got was Formica and chrome. Things to buy in the shops were so limited in what they had available. That's all changed now, of course. It was all import controls.*

## Hunter Howe

*If you wanted to buy a car you had to have overseas funds. That was the only way you could get one. Earlier on, farmers had been able to get them as a crucial industry. But by 1959 it was starting to get hard to get the overseas funds to get cars in.*

## Maureen Howe

*Getting overseas funds was a racket. We needed a new car so I wrote to my mother and said, write that you have missed my birthday and Christmas for the last two years. So here is x-number of pounds as a birthday present. That gave us overseas funds to put towards a car.*

*We didn't even have hotels in the area at that stage. It was a dry area so you had to go to Invercargill to get your beer and hotels were closed at six o'clock. I didn't think I'd come to an uncivilised country but it was just so short of what I was used to. Lots of things were lacking that we had in Britain. But one just adjusted. I never had a moment's regret. Never a moment's regret at all.*

Nor did I. I discovered such modern devices as showers and soap, things previously glimpsed only in games periods (which I went to as infrequently as I could), or once a week on family bath night. Englishmen think their poop doesn't stink and assume that a bath a week is enough. Which is why I wandered lonely as a cloud, unaware of my own smell, which in those days was in inverse ratio to social class. I was unaware, too, of the mundane realities of life, the things the English leave to wives or hot and cold running servants. I had no discriminating palate but didn't need one as New Zealand food was the same stodge I'd been brought up on, though servings were bigger, fish smaller, and chip shops sold oysters at 2/6 a dozen. Yet I did discover such exciting new dishes as saveloys, hogget (though I never found out what animal that came from), and pavlova (preferably by the tonne – or ton, as it was in those less-greedy days). All these delights had been precluded back home on grounds of class, cost or sugar rationing.

So I took up my post at the University of Otago to win an enduring and undeserved reputation as a raving sex maniac when I observed in my very first lecture that the nineteenth-century Romantics viewed the state not as a mechanism but as 'an orgasm', a slip received in stunned silence. Several women students have told me since that they knew it was dirty but didn't want to show it. But it made my reputation as someone to be avoided at parties.

The University of Otago was the oldest and best in New Zealand, and almost as good as it proclaimed itself to be. Yet compared with Oxbridge it was a dullard's dungeon, a pedant's preserve. It recruited staff from Britain, which restricted it to also-ran academics who couldn't get a job anywhere else – the white tile universities and the polytechnic demi-varsities not yet having opened. Otago academics had to be both serious and pedantic to be accepted. All were, which made the university boring. Many of my fellow searchers for truth didn't know enough about their subject to risk talking about it, and had no opinions on anything else. Except sex. Which they were against. And students. Which they hid from, as if fearing being bitten.

The University of Otago was dedicated to cutting itself off from Dunedin to be part of a worldwide community of scholars dedicated to the higher levels of boredom. So New Zealand left little trace in this Edinburgh of the South. Otago didn't speak or teach Kiwi. No New Zealand history, politics or literature, though lots of opportunities for English pedants to read out lectures they'd copied down in their own student days to be taken down and regurgitated by uncomprehending classes: 'It's hot in here, open the window' becoming 'Hot open window' without passing through any human brain. Shorthand was more useful than the search for truth, though no doubt today's students take better notes given their dexterity at text messaging.

This Pom pedantry ensured that I got to know New Zealand by forcing me to look outside the university for interest. There I discovered New Zealand's great virtues. Boredom with my assigned lectures on Europe in the sixteenth and seventeenth centuries strengthened my interest in the real world and in a New Zealand which academic colleagues professed to find crude, anti-intellectual and insufficiently respectful to them. I began to carry out opinion surveys, though I had neither training nor expertise, and to do radio and later television commentaries because the NZBC preferred commentators who could be dropped at any sign of trouble, rather than employees who couldn't. To do either in Britain would have needed a diploma, years of waiting, relatives who'd been presented at court and testimonials from ten Oxford dons. New Zealand was fascinating to study: a working democracy but small enough to understand.

I'm not sure anyone understood what I was saying. Producers were too diffident to produce and in awe of academics assumed to know what they were talking about. I was allowed to go too fast for comprehension, thereby saving them the trouble of editing and cramming more words into the allotted space than the natives ever attempted. It looked good printed. Which it wasn't. Incomprehensible in delivery, listeners and viewers naturally assumed it was brilliant coming from an educated Englishman, even if a Yorkshire accent added an exotic touch usually taken for Dutch. New Zealanders assume anything they don't understand is important and are far too nice and polite to criticise. They lack standards by which to judge performance and confidence to sort rubbish from real. So I quickly became a respected pundit, able to punditify on anything I was paid for. All was wonderfully well received except by the few who knew anything about anything, which was usually only Professor Bob Chapman.

Poms back home then, as now, were sorted into classes

and categories and supposed to stay there. In New Zealand I found myself able to move up, down, left or right; to develop, widen my interests and expertise and do anything I wanted; without the condescending, superior criticism which inhibits the English, particularly the inarticulate lower orders supposed to know their place and able to find it even pissed out of their brains. In New Zealand, no one cared.

Career development in British universities was the opposite to New Zealand, centring on knowing more and more about less and less and jealously defending your specialism against all comers. 'Historians are like a lot of bloody women. Always on about their periods,' Kingsley Amis remarked, but it applied to any discipline, from nuclear physics to deep fat frying. At Oxford the history of the Labour Party was being doled out in two (later reduced to one) year stretches but the two I was offered were so boring I've forgotten which they were. So I grabbed a twenty year stretch of the early nineteenth century left lying around, unnoticed since they were actually lived in, and became a world expert. I never needed it in New Zealand.

As I said, in Britain you know your place, your subject, your class, your town, and stick to it. In New Zealand the world is your oyster. You can do anything you want, well or badly, no one will know. There are no middle-class intellectuals carping and sneering as a way of life. Soon I was the expert on New Zealand politics because no one else in the country, apart from Bob Chapman, was interested. The same on the USSR, Japan, Africa, the USA, South-East Asia and even Australia. I knew little about any, but had the Oxford knack of talking at length on any subject I knew nothing about, where a self-respecting Kiwi would have kept quiet until he knew something. No one contradicted me. Journalists didn't know enough, and External Affairs staff who did weren't allowed to talk lest they give away New Zealand's location and military capacity to Russian spies, then assumed to be thronging the streets and toilets everywhere. Except, possibly, Pahiatua.

Opportunity was in greater supply than the ability to seize it, which sorted the aimless from the active. You succeeded, coasted or mouldered at your own discretion and on your own efforts or the lack of them, and it didn't matter much with no pressures to publish or get promotion. The universities, like New Zealand, were a competition-free zone. You did what you wanted and no more, for this was before the balance shifted from employee to employer and universities brought in performance measures and short-term contracts. Once in you were secure for life and New Zealand was much the same.

So we were free to follow up any interest or none: politics, culture, gardening, plagiarism, sex (where I was too naïve to seize the opportunities offered in the one area in which students were genuinely enthusiastic) and religion (where I was amazed on going to an Evangelical Union event to find them all lying around necking). Brutish men invited you to seek death on the rugby field or a heart attack at basketball. 'It's casual, of course,' they would say, meaning the death rate was lower.

None of this was my bag, but I wanted to be accepted so pretended to love sport so as not to be viewed as effeminate, homosexual, a security risk or possibly all three. I bought a fourteen-foot Idle-along as protective cover and could have been a challenger for the America's Cup, had it ever hit the water. Which, after three years of occasional caulking, sanding and painting, it didn't.

This was the golden age for New Zealand universities. They were expanding, pay increased to keep pace with salaries overseas and government – then Labour – appeared to like us rather than regarding us as a branch of the Comintern, likely to indoctrinate the lads and impregnate the lasses. Life was made even better by access to Dunedin's secret garden: Central Otago, then largely Dunedin's exclusive preserve. The flood of tourists was only a trickle but several university staff had baches or caravans, so bach swapping was inevitable, wife swapping not yet having been thought of, and wonderful Otago images were dubbed onto the subconscious of everyone who went there. When I close my eyes now, what comes to mind is neither the rugged landscapes nor the dark satanic mills of Yorkshire, but the colour of Central Otago's lakes and mountains and the landscapes immortalised by Grahame Sydney. Heaven will look like Central Otago. If Warren Cooper doesn't get there first.

My Otago days became a course in New Zealand studies. I failed the practicals but became good at the theory; infinitely preferable to the British constitution, which bored me as much as the students. Compared with dead Poms in wigs and tights, Keith Holyoake was fascinating and New Zealand, historical and actual (much the same thing in Dunedin) offered the excitement of discovering a new world while living among the natives, though Margaret Mead got closer than I ever did, judging by her description of casual sex in New Guinea. I never stumbled across that even at the Woolstore hops, which legend made a wild debauch of bonking behind the bales, but which were really as harmless as a Country and Western evening run by Lloyd Geering.

So I took up New Zealand studies in their pure, i.e. South Island, form, to end up neither an in- nor an outsider, reliving the fifties through the sixties while Britain began to swing. If you can remember the sixties you weren't there. I was, but in New Zealand, and doomed to catch up in the seventies.

I saw the good society, and it worked, and concluded that Britain's salvation was to be more like New Zealand, as distinct from making New Zealand more like the rest of the world, as New Zealand's grumbling academics and 'intellectuals' wanted. Many of New Zealand's élite aped England, but for me its strength resided in being egalitarian, open, and pragmatic; New Zealand wouldn't have recognised an ideology if it arrived in a tank. There weren't any until Roger Douglas freed the imports. The New Zealand *Weltanschauung* was an ambience imbibed by living easily with others, relating to people as individuals not stereotypes. It made me a pragmatist and a populist, attitudes construed as a form of brain rot in Britain. I became an advocate of the Third Way before it was invented, though in my version the 'h' wasn't silent. It was Kiwi pragmatism.

Living for an equivalent period in America, Japan or Russia might have been more interesting, stimulating and exciting, but much less beneficial. Mass societies nurture resentments, differences, intense emotions and dislikes, and feelings of impotence because the individual has so little influence and scale diminishes. Big nations lack the intimacy, the friendships and the opportunities. You climb by conforming in the big world. In Lilliput everyone's a Gulliver.

Leave other countries and they fade in the mind. Not New Zealand, because its attitudes leave with you. I didn't intend to go back to Britain, but my career moved from accident to accident like an ambulance-chasing panelbeater, so I took an offer proposing only a short stay to show off my Kiwi credentials. Then, further accidents, such as going into TV for which I'd been trained in New Zealand, and then being elected to Parliament for Grimsby, a place difficult to represent from Dunedin, combined to prevent return.

I should have stayed in New Zealand, become an MP, retired at forty-five on a good pension with world travel benefits, too old for sex, too young for the RSA, commuting between Dunedin and Surfers, plugged up to a catheter in the luggage rack.

I was neither Pom nor Kiwi. In New Zealand I'd even gone to a rugby match (one was enough) and occasionally asked how the All Blacks were doing, queries usually received with blank amazement that anyone couldn't know. I could neither mend cars nor take pleasure groping for the soap in sports club showers. So naturalisation was out but I was unfitted for England because I was conditioned to knock the head off any available tall poppy and unable to take Britain seriously again. I became an exile in both countries, ferrying to and fro, but not at home at either end.

In 1972 I summed up my impressions of New Zealand in *The Half-gallon Quarter-acre Pavlova Paradise*, an affectionate look at Kiwi quirks and characteristics sentimentalised by distance. Everything is romanticised in the heritage museum of memory. Even Rob Muldoon. Since then though, the gulf between my happy vision and the realities of a New Zealand changing more rapidly than I'd ever thought possible has widened and deepened.

Had I been smart enough to see it, the era of change was just beginning as I arrived in 1959 in the last days of the staid, tightly cosseted, Grundyistic society. Grundy was something more than an Australian media company. Grundy lived next door watching through lace curtains and listening on the party phone-line, though that daft Kiwi introduction 'Are you working?' was meant to clear it. The Grundy of last resort was the Security Service, where all abominations, from reading *Lolita* on the bus, to the untidy garden next door and masturbatory stains on sheets at Curious Cove could be reported. Grundy was killed by the pill, pop and youth culture. As soon as kids became a group rather than an awkward part of the family carted round sulking in the back of the car.

Distance was also being abolished. Mass air travel came in, building to today's mass exoduses and incursions and replacing a floating isolation ward by a twenty-four hour dose of oblivion, relegating past lives and countries to a fitful dream world, ensuring that arrivals are half doped, fully quiescent and ready to be reprogrammed. New Zealand was being plugged into the world.

Particularly by TV, which arrived in Dunedin in 1961, the same night as Governor General Bernard Fergusson's reception at the Town Hall, the Bolshoi Ballet, and an open lecture of mine which nobody turned up for. That brought instant access to fashion, pop culture, the quickening pace of change, and world events (which became New Zealand news by dint of the fact that there was so little going on here). TV also boosted the consumer lifestyle among a people who up to then had thought that consumption was something requiring treatment in a TB sanatorium rather than a form of retail therapy.

Import controls were the norm when I arrived. No colour film. No instant coffee. No cars. All records locally pressed, and often badly. One friend tried to replace a lost button on his raincoat to be told: 'We've sold our button quota. But we've got an import quota for raincoats coming in next week. You should order one.' As the controls went, variety appeared in the shops, though not price competition. Although the consumer eventually became king after a long, slow walk down the aisle to final enthronement in the Warehouse. Where everyone gets an import. Now the ultimate consumer triumph has come in seven-day shopping, where once Saturdays and Sundays were exempt, and still are for anyone with any sense.

I was living through the beginning of the end, not of settler society but of settled society, built round the dream of a better Britain in the South Seas. Protest, which became so vigorous in the seventies and eighties, first flowered against the Vietnam War, an agitation which began a decade and a half of the demos which were an essential part of growing up.

People had not come to New Zealand because they were sent like convicts to Australia (as in the joke of the visitor asked by Australian immigration if he had a criminal record who replied, 'Why? Is it still necessary?') 'They can change the sky but not their hearts who cross the seas', and New Zealand's immigrants wanted land and jobs unavailable at home in order to live the lifestyle of those above them in the British hierarchy: the solid middle class. Their dream of a comfortable, middle-class life open to all and lived by most was attractive and closer to being realised than at any time before or since. But this was the end of the golden weather, the pay-off for the years of struggle, for in the seventies it began to disintegrate. The world became colder and harder. Panicked by a long, comparative decline, which eventually became absolute, Britain went whoring after Europe. New Zealand, long loyal and profitable, was bamboozled, betrayed and dumped with less grace, help and dignity than the imperial withdrawal from some miserable African colony which had been a nuisance and a burden ever since annexation. Never be nice to the Brits. They'll dump on you.

In 1950 New Zealand had one of the highest standards of living in the world. By the sixties it was slipping down the scale because Britain, its main customer, was growing so slowly. In the seventies and eighties slip became fall. Abandoning the long effort to be different and better, the politicians threw the country into an economic Outward Bound course and took the axe to the established structures of welfare, public services, economic management and labour relations. The old deal between capital and labour always overseen by government, which served the agreed purposes of both, was abrogated forever. With it went the one feature which had made New Zealand unique: absolutely full employment. The base of equality was kicked away.

I anticipate. *The Half-gallon Quarter-acre Pavlova Paradise* was a portrayal of that quaint society in its happiest era. The cracks were beginning to appear, the pavlova to deflate, but the decades of disintegration came later when the dream was vandalised, change became a norm and the world lost interest in a small, remote, former paradise (retired) whose products were such a glut on its markets that butter had to be sold as a sex aid in Japan and scientists tried to make wool edible and milk into a material.

Everything changed. The one-time enemies of the people, gambling and booze, are now idolised with casinos up every mountain, and Sky the most profitable company in New Zealand, with its symbol dominating the Auckland skyline. The wine industry, which once produced a full range from red to red then went on to undrinkable müller thurgau, has ripped its rubbish out, replanted and become a new religion with producers and masters its high priests, and pilgrimages to wineries a national devotion. The honest advertising slogan 'McBlogg's wine – makes you drunk' can't now be hinted at, so a whole literature has to be invented. Swill and spit priests litanise about hints of loganberries, oak, pig swill, or 'delicious herbal, gooseberries and tropical fruit flavours. Generous and soft mouth feel with lively acidity' or 'Fragrant lime and stone-fruit flavours, developing honey nuances from botrytis'. If they wanted all those flavours they could buy them separately from Foodtown, but a new chair endowed for wine lyricism might come cheaper.

Eating was once compulsory, cooking an optional skill. Then Graham Kerr discovered God in food and Alison Holst made 'fush fungers'. Their heirs and disciples have transformed it into an obsession, with star chefs pouring out of New Zealand and bestriding the planet before they can even whip up a pavlova, then pouring back again to set up overpriced eateries only Hawke's Bay residents can afford.

'Home' closed its doors to the descendants of those who'd died for it and New Zealand society became multi-racial in a way no one who's lived through the old days can quite believe. The old racism is still there, but silent except on redneck talkback radio. Even the sacred trinity of rugby, racing and beer has become a plurality, with two brands of rugger – Union and League – soccer and other sports, from basket and netball to hockey, water polo and squash; so that now there's All Blacks, Tall Blacks, Black Caps and Sox, Silver Ferns, Sharks, Bulls, Dinosaurs and a long list of other beasts and bullies.

Once no one would wear anything that might make them stand out, except Keith Holyoake's platform heels. Now fashion has naturalised, and pop, once cover versions of overseas hits by Ray Columbus or Howard Morrison, with such immortal lines as 'I want to be in a Maori car' or 'No moa no moa. In Aotearoa' became melodious originals such as Greg Johnson's 'Ball Gowns and Small Towns', 'It's Been Too Long' and 'Cut to the Chase'. The quality is so much higher and the scene exciting.

*Tout lasse, tout casse, tout passe.* So much has changed, but has everything or do fundamentals of the old New Zealand remain? Has the whole pavlova changed or merely the topping? The simple pleasures of life are always simpler and more pleasurable in New Zealand than anywhere else: basking at the bach (preferably someone else's), cooling at the beach and in the sea, sweating along some of the world's loveliest tramps, fishing, sailing, cooking are all the same, even if you can't dig up a few pauas and cook them and keep the shells for ashtrays any more. All these pleasures are accessible to everyone from cities built by the sea, as all should be.

Lotus eating is still possible as a way of life, but there's less of it, the pace is faster, the pressures greater, the restaurants, wine bars, cafés and theatres more numerous and far livelier, even though the population is older. What's froth and bubble and what's fundamental? Has New Zealand caught up with a world which is changing fast anyway, or does it still lag, as a poorer, shabbier version of the universal, American, suburban lifestyle? Are the people living it the same easygoing, egalitarian, pragmatic Kiwis they once were, or has change changed them to create a new national identity?

Such questions are posed by a return to Pavlova Paradise. The original book was claimed by some to be out of date as soon as published, like the phone book. A book which didn't mention New Zealand's ten miles of motorway, the transformation of the Chinese gooseberry into the kiwifruit and the tree tomato into the tamarillo, which made no allowance for the possibility of All Black defeat or assumed that Aunt Daisy and Walter Nash were as immortal as they seemed at the time, clearly needed some revision. Particularly when the old staples of New Zealand life and humour – the six o'clock swill, the rush to the buffet as trains stopped 'with ten minutes for refreshments then they carts you off again' which made Kiwis such good rugby players, the instruction 'Ladies a plate' (now too obscene to ask), or the tethered dogs shitting their insides out for a hydatids-free New Zealand on roadside dosing strips, the handy hints such as striking a match in the toilet to take away the smell which used to pour out of the *New Zealand Woman's Weekly* – have all gone.

The Tom Wolfe list of the title clearly had to be rewritten. The half-g had died, the quarter acre shrunk and the pavlova was viewed as excessively sweet and fattening. Excluded from the abounding TV food programmes it's now made commercially because no one admits to being able to make it, though 80,000 pavlovas and pavlova equivalents are produced a week. But what was the new list? Chardonnay swilling? Wise winos from Central Otago told me it had to be pinot noir. Smoke-free? The bedraggled groups of smokers in the rain outside public buildings told me that that was some kind of tyranny. Political correctness? That would exclude Mayor Banks and Radio Pacific. Is it now a Paradise *Manqué* (no reasonable offer refused)? Perhaps it's just that yesterday's simple verities are far more complicated, with quiet diffidence replaced by assertiveness, particularly against the Australians. New Zealand has added a mere million people, not many by Chinese standards, but it has grown more complex than a generalisation and offers less scope for the simplistic summing-ups, particularly since change, once the exception, is now the norm. New Zealand is a nation fit for Alvin Toffler to toffle in. At length.

Could the changes be assessed and described? I'd tried to keep myself up to date by regular pilgrimages, by breeding New Zealanders in captivity under lights in Grimsby, as well as by maintaining my membership of the New Zealand Labour Party in case I didn't make it in British politics. Yet I couldn't claim to be as closely in touch with Helen Clark's New Zealand as I had been with the wonderful world of Walter Nash back in the days when dinosaurs ruled the earth. The only way to update *Pavlova* and assess whether it was still paradise was total immersion and rebaptism for me and enlisting the help of those who've lived the changes over the last thirty years.

That New Zealand has changed is beyond doubt. Only rigor mortis could stop that. Once New Zealand had prided itself on leading the world to change with votes for women (1893) and the Seddon system, old age pensions, industrial conciliation and arbitration and the welfare state. Now more Kiwis were jumping ship and fleeing to a world which was changing more rapidly, with New Zealand in the guard's van instead of the vanguard. As Lenin would have asked in a fashion more Kiwi than Communist, who gains, who loses?

Those questions produced this voyage of rediscovery, a Rip

van Winkle's tour round a new world, to talk to my own generation in their zimmer frames, and to those who've taken over the scene and now stride the stage of the new New Zealand. The excitement and the sense of discovery and wonder of my first arrival returned as the journey became a rejuvenation, a chance to be a born-again Kiwi and to discover whether I could be as happy and as much at home in the new New Zealand as I had been in the old.

Contemporaries looked older than I remembered them. At the Otago University Club I wondered who all these geriatrics around me were: until I looked in the mirror and realised that they were all younger than me, some indeed my students. Uncannily I saw many who I thought I remembered, bodies and faces still as young, only to realise before I could embrace them that they were not the same people locked in a time warp, Kiwi Dorian Grays with paintings ageing in some farm attic, but new people the same in physical, facial and character type as my contemporaries, just youngsters whose time is now as ours was then.

The caravan moves on. New faces, new people, new ideas take the stage. They may look the same, do the same things, play the same games, face the same problems and act more stupidly or sensibly than my generation, but it's their world not mine. They'll make their own mistakes and have their own successes, on a stage which is now different. Watching them made me wish I could wind back the years and begin over again to live an apprenticeship to the new New Zealand as I had done to the old. I can't, but at least my Pavlova Pilgrimage and the Pavlovian reflexes it conditioned brought me back in touch with my own Kiwiness as I discovered how much of the old New Zealand remains, and assessed whether Kiwi-land is still the best place in the world. No point in removing the incentive to read on, or damaging sales by giving the answers away. Read on and find out.

Chapter Three

# Kiwis Come From Lilliput

*T*hree influences shaped New Zealand society to make the Kiwi. The stock, in the main British with a Polynesian minority. Isolation, for both populations had come to the end of the world to improve their lot in a unique environment, which they could shape as they wished, though in the event neither had imagination enough to do more than create an improved version of 'home'. Finally, size: 3.8 million is a tiny population compared to great powers.

Some seventy-three of 189 UN members have over four million people. New Zealand is a Gulliver compared to Polynesia's micro world of small islands and big people, but a Lilliput on the world stage.

But smallness is the greatest. Every individual is enlarged in a small society. It is also the only one of the three influences to remain. The stock is more varied, with Asians nearly a fifth of Auckland, the Maori population increasing, the Polynesian strain stronger, making Auckland the biggest Polynesian centre, while the British connection has been forcibly cut and isolation, once the tyranny of distance, has become instant access. Early Pakeha settlers took four months to come, a misery well recorded in letters and diaries with litanies of storms, child deaths, and damp misery. Steam and the Suez and Panama Canals speeded things up to a four-week trip and New Zealand found a role as Britain's overseas farm. Then came air travel by jet. When the first BOAC Comet arrived at Whenuapai in April 1963, to inaugurate regular services to the UK, the world shrank, reducing further with the Jumbos and the 747s. Thus was New Zealand plugged in to the world more tightly than anyone because it was hungrier for it, and distance became opportunity rather than barrier: Europe a day away, America less, the Internet and satellite TV instant. No longer able to hide behind a 13,000 mile protective barrier, New Zealand rode the surf of a fast-changing world where the old certainties of empire, Cold War and American alliance were gone.

Yet smallness remained in a country renowned for sheep (48 million) rather than people (3.8 million) in a thousand-mile land slightly bigger than Britain (59 million). Smallness confers a rarity value on the New Zealander. *L'enfer c'est autre rui*, said Cocteau, and hell really is other people when there are too many of them. Inhabitants of big countries are much subject to that particular hell. But not the Kiwi. For them people come as a pleasure not a nuisance, a pressure, or someone in the way.

As Jonah Lomu *didn't* say, small is beautiful and better. Better to grow in, giving more space to thrive. Better to live in, without the constant pressure of numbers. Better to be an individual in, without the distortions and the crowd mentality of too many people. People *en masse* are unattractive, as individuals delightful. A crowd of Kiwis at a football match isn't an attractive sight, though cleaner than European counterparts, but anyone in a mass society lives their life with such pressures, the Kiwi rarely.

In a mass society people are managed and categorised into boxes. Procedures are lumbering, slow and impersonal. A small society is personalised, about people not abstractions, more democratic, more amiable, and easier to live in, though less comfortable for an élite which is thinner on the ground and more exposed to the multitude. Less than four million people in one of the world's loveliest lands is the Kiwi advantage. It is enormous.

However, in world affairs size is power and big is best. The USA with 284 million people, Russia with 144, China with more than a billion, and Europe with a current 381 million – hoping for 550 million when, and if, East Europe's ragtag and bobtail join – are the big boys who dominate world affairs, world news and the world economy. Big nations talk of destiny and historic missions, usually as excuses for killing other people and repressing their own. Small ones live much closer to reality, and are more manoeuvrable and interesting. Like a rowing boat compared to a cruise liner.

Scale of production confers advantages and size supports military strength. Smallness means opportunity, flexibility, manageability and the potential for fulfilment in other ways. Big scale is remote and impersonal. Small means shorter ladders to climb, less intense competition, more access to top jobs. It's better for people and a better place to bring up children. A nice world if you can get it. The thronging millions can't. New Zealanders can.

A small society produces more rounded people with desirable characteristics which don't flourish in mass societies. It acts like a magnifying glass enlarging every individual in it, whereas a mass society crushes and overwhelms. Large produces sharper, more competitive and streetwise people, tougher climbers and better fiddlers to short-cut the system. Small means nicer. People relate to each other as individuals, and are more likely to know each other, whereas an impersonal and mass society classifies people as categories: élite, plebs, classes or masses, middle or lower.

Which might account for the fact that outside battle and rugby fields New Zealanders are so nice, better known for good and decent behaviour than hooligan Poms, aggressive Americans or raucous Russians. Particularly when sober. People don't lash out or punch people quite as much, or smash cars and heads in petty disputes, for they have to live with anyone they clash with, and face them in the street. The pressures of a mass society breed resentments, hostilities, a thicker protective skin and a greater willingness to trample lest you be trampled. In a mass world aloofness is a strength, indeed a necessity. Wanting a degree of space, people strive to establish distance and avoid eye contact. It might bring importuning, begging, an invitation to buy time-share apartments or twenty minutes of sexual humiliation. New Zealanders look each other in the eye. Usually to assess what's wrong with them and communicate the fact that they know.

Small society is personalised and warm. People draw together, not to embrace – this is New Zealand after all – but to make the contacts avoided in big societies. This is not a touchy-feely country, except when drunk, but people relate to each other and are more generous, helpful and less suspicious. I learned this early on, queuing at what was then the Dunedin post office before it became a combined bookshop, haberdashers, herbalist and *bureau de change*, to buy stamps and one of those pound postal orders which were the only way money was allowed out. I was saving for a Lamborghini, then only a twenty-year investment programme at a pound postal order a day with the car accelerating ahead of me, but found myself a penny short. 'Oh, give it to me next time you're in' said the teller. 'I'm not to a penny.'

In Britain he would have been to a farthing and he'd have given me a free sermon thrown in, denouncing me as a sponger. Kiwis are more inclined to help each other generally. Building bees bring in thousands of skilled workers all with full tool kits, cranes and bulldozers. Break down by the roadside in Britain and you can starve to death. In New Zealand cars crash into each other as people rush to help, to rebuild your engine, or repaint and panelbeat your car. Breaking down is cheaper than a full service and a new engine.

Small is beautiful and better to live in, as a village is better than a huge city; more sustaining, more companionable, more personal, more of a community and a far better place to grow in than one of the huge cities teeming millions flock to all over the world. Cities are exciting and a magnet for the young. The rest of the world lives happier outside.

In New Zealand an optimum population is distributed across the full length and breadth of a beautiful land balanced between provinces and main centres. Once Dunedin, Christchurch, Wellington and Auckland were more or less equal in size, with a series of country towns such as Wanganui, New Plymouth or Invercargill below them in the long roll call down to heartland New Zealand. That balance has been broken by the unchecked growth of Auckland and the decline of the rural population, but New Zealand cities remain easy to get out of, surrounded by beaches and attractive country, and the total population is better distributed than countries dominated by disproportionately huge capital cities such as (extreme case) London, the Great Wen, draining the rest of the country like a cancer, or Paris.

Auckland is the cuckoo in the nest, a moa among the chooks, but as the song goes: 'I've seen your towns. They're all the same and the only difference is the name.' Being the same they make much of their differences, claiming widely different personalities, festooning themselves with flags to tell tourists, and any locals who don't know, where they are, and spending thousands on large models and signs to boast of their uniqueness: a giant bottle in Paeroa, a trout in Gore, in Tirau a big corrugated iron sheep and a huge tin Jesus and an enormous dog (presumably called Rin-Tin-Tin), huge apples in Cromwell (the most fruity town), a sausage in Tuatapere, a mussel in Havelock, an enormous hypodermic needle on Auckland's skyline, and a kilted piper in Waipu.

Smallness can't sustain concentrations of privilege, wealth or perversion. These things congeal together in mass societies where classes, minority and interest groups cluster in their own little worlds. In New Zealand minorities of every kind, from fretworkers to lesbian tap dancers, are nowhere concentrated. Auckland's Pink Power is very pale compared to Sydney's, to which New Zealand gays must flounce for fun and 2002's Big Gay Out was puny by comparison (except for Miss Ribena who was enormous). As for subversives, nowhere has a concentration big enough to support a Communist or al Qaeda cell.

In big societies people crowd on top of each other, which does wonders for the birth rate but is uncomfortable as a lifestyle. In small societies people know each other and know every possible bit of gossip about everyone. They file it in the great Kiwi Collective Subconscious. Maori history and literature were oral. Pakeha folklore is the same, a vast collection of tattletale, floating forever in the collective subconscious like email in space, ever ready to be trotted out. Unlike the police computer at Wanganui nothing is ever deleted, no crime ever expiated. Come back canonised after forty years as a missionary and people will still remember what you did behind the bike sheds. The media folk memory in politics and punditry goes back ten years, so nothing pre-Lange exists. The Kiwi subconscious is forever.

So many people are related to each other, know each other, went to school together, played rugby, hockey, cricket or strip poker with each other, or have friends in common. New Zealand is incest as a nation. When the English meet abroad they try to avoid each other. Kiwis cluster delightedly even with sworn enemies back home. Their conversation is an exploration of common relationships, common education, common sports, common ground and, not uncommonly, lovers in common. When the English meet they covertly assess each other through the class antennae every Pom is born with, to categorise every other so as to know which dustbin to put them in or who to defer to: as natural creeps they need someone to grovel to. The Kiwi just wants another Kiwi to share their common knowledge and the joy of being a New Zealander. Usually they discover sufficient common ground to sustain long conversations, followed by several beers or nights of unbridled lust.

The 'bridesmaid scale' is a measure of Kiwi closeness assessed by the number of bridesmaids any group of New Zealand women discover in common. In every group of ten anything up to a hundred bridesmaids is possible, and one of the key accusations levelled against Christine Rankin at WINZ was not so much the fact that the embarrassed Head of the PM's Department had to ogle her breasts – something no public servant should have to endure for more than a few hours – but that she had appointed her own bridesmaid to run a section of WINZ. Bridesmaids are for enumerating, not forever.

The small society is more intimate and better informed, though mainly about each other. When everyone knows everyone else they also know their faults, foibles, weaknesses and past history, and can dish the dirt endlessly. New Zealand could breed a Tony Blair. The production technique is worldwide. Yet his young Lochinvar image of a man from outer space, unsullied by associations or knowledge, is impossible. In Britain and in America the unknown can be projected as clean and impressive, the man on the white horse, even superwoman. In New Zealand more white horses are available but even the woman in the white gumboots has feet of clay, and everyone knows their smell, size, last airing and verruca score and all are recorded in the Kiwi Folk Memory Bank.

Everyone is known to everyone, and all are prepared to believe the worst about them because everyone is human and has to be kept so. No one is a hero. New Zealand produces zero saints per capita because there is always someone who remembers them picking their nose on the way to school, making immature sexual advances to someone's daughter, or, worse, to someone of the same sex. Hitler got away with having only one ball, a fact loudly proclaimed by Allied soldiers but unknown in Germany. In New Zealand everyone would have known about such unicameralism, even if they couldn't spell it.

If damaging information isn't available it is invented. The tall poppy syndrome is a universal human phenomenon, but only in New Zealand can it access the Kiwi Folk Memory Bank. Immaculate conceptions are impossible. The vicar of St Matthew's In The City in Auckland summed it up at Christmas 2001. 'Imagine,' he said, 'that the Three Wise Men were in fact three wise and politically correct New Zealand women. They'd arrive at the manger with a pre-cooked casserole and, of course, because they were Kiwis, cleaning materials. They'd clean it thoroughly, put an attractive layette trim on the crib, and have a good gossip with Joseph and Mary, possibly discovering a few bridesmaids in common, although possibly not because they might not broach the possibility of the two not being married. On leaving they'd say to each other: "I can't understand how anyone could let their room get into such a mess"; "You'll never get that casserole dish back" and, finally, "Virgin, my arse. I went to school with her." Had Jesus been born in God's Own County instead of His own, less attractive, and less holy land, New Zealanders wouldn't have been particularly impressed by his divinity – they're pretty nice people themselves, but the doubts about his origins, paternity and the cleanliness of his cradle would have lingered for the rest of his life.

Politicians get the same treatment, which humanises, cuts their pretensions down to size, inoculates the people against them and ensures that money can't magnify them. No aerosol gloss lasts for long in New Zealand's fresh air, and Blair-style make-up is detectable in the clear, sharp, light, while the man would be viewed as too clever by half, too preachy, dominated by his wife and almost as prone to collect air points as a New Zealand politician. Everything is known and exaggerated in the telling. So the only national figures with respect are Xena, the Warrior Princess, and anyone sensible enough to go abroad and stay. Even then they get snide cracks. 'I was with that Geoffrey Cox in the Western Desert. He didn't have the foggiest idea how to work his Benghazi Burner. So how could he run ITN?'

The intimacy of smallness gives little need of a security service, or indeed a police force, apart from traffic cops to provide employment for sado-masochists. Every New Zealander is their own police and their own secret service in a society run on gossip and character assassination, where Kiwis know the dirt on each other, carry the full file in their heads and take every opportunity to use it, in such a way that the victim knows that if he gets above himself the full bucket will be tipped. This information is usually doled out retail to improve people, but every New Zealander knows that the threat of putting every weight up against them is always there.

Talk to any New Zealander about any other. They first assess your attitude to the victim, then pour out the appropriate information in a mixture weighted to what you want to hear: 'I've known Snurple forever and he's a wonderful bloke but you may not realise that he used to be a bastard/self-flagellating saint/has a VC/BO/a police record/an unexplained fraud accusation/is a reformed serial killer.' The evidence will include a little favourable but more damaging material to make it clear that they know all, but are too kind to reveal it, about his unreliability with money, children, drink or sheep. I was being driven away after a discussion with Bob Harvey in which geriatric members of the Karekare Surf Senior Citizens Rescue Club had sung his praises to the sky. The driver, one of the praise-singers, said, 'I could tell you a thing or two about Bob. He's cost us a lot of money by launching all sorts of things without asking us.' I didn't ask. I got the information nevertheless. Being English I won't, of course, retail it. Unless for a fee.

In the self-policing society every New Zealander feels a personal responsibility for everyone else and for giving visitors the dirt. They're also ready to correct every other New Zealander for putative follies or any impulse to misbehave, though always for their own good. Even the possibility of folly produces 'Mummy's terribly hurt' looks or 'I don't think your grandfather would have liked that.' The small society is the invigilated society even without the expense of closed-circuit television.

All this is coupled with a generous instinct for helping even those who don't want to be helped. I failed to hear what a bank teller was saying through the glass. The lady behind explained in a loud voice, speaking deliberately slowly, 'You've put the wrong date on the cheque. It's the nineteenth.' She was doing her part-time social worker job in the same way as geriatrics in China are stood on the side of the road to wave traffic on until they become so old they fall in front of it. It's something to do. The lady then went on to explain banking regulations, the penalties for misdating cheques, and the disruption to the whole system it could cause, in some detail.

This social policeman role occasionally requires sterner stuff. Being driven along Lambton Quay in the back seat of a ministerial car, my reverie was interrupted by a frantic tapping on the window from a cyclist. An English reaction would be to wind the window down and tell him to drop dead, before he was able to warn that six-foot flames were shooting from the exhaust, but this was New Zealand and I was torn between Pom and Kiwi personas. We drove on. At the next light he tapped again. 'He's trying to tell you that you've not got your seat belt fastened,' the Minister explained as I smiled murderously at the poor cyclist. What a contrast with the occasion when, travelling first class on our parliamentary warrants with Roy Hattersley, a Young Socialist berated us for not travelling with the workers. 'Fuck Off,' said Roy, shutting the door on his hand.

My wife returned a rental car at Christchurch airport. An enthusiastic passer-by ran up to tell her that it wasn't a public parking place but for rental cars only. 'But this is a rental,' my wife protested. 'What?' said the concerned lady, gripped by shock. 'You mean you're returning a rental car in that filthy state?' Duty done, she went to report my wife to the rental company, like the others who report neighbours for weeds (or weed) in gardens, complain to the SPCA that Mrs Bloggs' moggie hasn't had his evening Go-Cat, or awaken sleeping neighbours to tell them they've left their outside light on and are wasting electricity on a scale which could plunge Auckland into darkness. Again.

There used to be the added bonus of being able to turn in people for fun and profit to the security services, which have their name and number in local telephone directories for just that purpose. With the end of the Cold War the urgency has gone out of this valuable work, though it kept New Zealand largely free of Communist coups. The decline was shown in the *Rainbow Warrior* affair when chambermaids, retail staff and car-hire firms all knew everything about the tidiness, movements and nocturnal habits of the two killers, though not their malign intentions (inconceivable to an honest nation with no concept of *raison d'état* unless it's a coffee bar). The French duo were thoroughly tracked, but with the collapse of Communism the urgency had gone out of reporting. Thank heavens there are still police programmes on telly which make the cops largely redundant, unless to stop kids drinking in public places or to scatter marijuana seeds over Coromandel bush by helicoptering confiscated stacks. Their real work is done by citizens rebuking each other, and uniformed cops are the police of last resort, so the citizenry can turn recalcitrants in because they're unable to take them home and detain them there.

The Universal Surveillance Society still has the potential to be repressive. Though not as powerful as it was it can still inhibit dissent and dislike difference, particularly in times of fear such as war, Cold War, America's Cup frenzies or sporting clashes with Australia. Such fears are amplified by the media and politicians providing grist for the Great Kiwi Clobbering Machine to put down anyone who steps out of line. This GKCM once applied its efforts indiscriminately to Marxists, homosexuals, casual adulterers, any available Chinese or Indians, uppity Maori, and anyone else viewed as a threat to the conservative, white-skinned, and nervous majority, likely to give the kids ideas, or frighten the RSA. Now it rusts in reserve but is still there. Just in case.

People interact more in small societies and are easier to know as individuals so they are less easy to lump into boxes. Big societies, being more impersonal, are prone to categorise. They view each other and interact through the media rather than person to person. Information, news and experiences are propagated over the media rather than the garden fence. Instead of relating to each other at human levels they are viewed through its distorting glass, which colours them and puts their case in its shorthand. They live their lives through soaps and identifying with the characters rather than with real people. Media-speak means less personal contact and less contact with reality. Everything is coloured, hyped and amplified. Newspapers and television need drama, heroes and villains. They stereotype people as 'battling grannies', 'heart-rending losers', 'angelic children' (if raw material allows), 'loony lefties' and all the other stereotypes which real people never really fit into. Media deal in images and oversimplify to hold attention, just as tales in the pub get more colourful the greater the numbers gathered to listen.

New Zealand, in contrast, broadcasts less but everything is known, and all is more personal. Stars are smaller, villains nicer. It's never *tout savoir, tout pardonner* for the Kiwi Folk Memory Bank. Rather *tout savoir, tout maudire*. Yet politicians and leaders speak directly to people not through a media amplifier and what's important to real people is central to the dialogue. Remote, windy concepts of 'nation', 'class', 'grandeur', 'national destiny' and the gallery of concepts mass societies mobilise to con the people, leave a New Zealand audience shaken not stirred. Everything has to be real, personal and as true as politicians can make it.

People know their leaders too well to really respect them. They went to school with them, were taught or legally represented by them or found them wimps on the rugby field, so they well know that politics is the ugly person's show biz. Politicians aren't expected to lead. That's the people's job. The politicians are there to be pugilists and entertainers, fall guys and race runners, punch-bags and hate objects, not men or women of destiny. Which is why Rob's Mob loved rambunctious Rob and his counter punching for so long, even after he went into *The Rocky Horror Show*, why Marian Hobbs took her part in *The Vagina Monologues*; and David Lange went in for stand-up comedy. Fun providers are forgiven everything but their pre-election past. This same reversed binocular effect means entrepreneurs can't be heroes because everyone who's played rugby against them knows the dirty business they got up to behind the ruck or their first propensity to cheat in five hundred at school. People know who's an ugly bastard and no amount of make-up will dissuade them. Academics can't be respected when the many who have met them know they were swots at school. You can't be a moa in Kiwiland.

New Zealand is the real world, not a media world because people need it less, being able to relate to the real world. Small is better, healthier and more boring. It's also more democratic because the nation is small enough to be its own focus group. Not small enough to be an Athenian direct democracy, but enough to give every voice more value. However cracked.

A small society is trial and joy. Joy for those who like closeness and community, difficult for the deviant, the dissenter, the radical, and those who want to mind their own business, such as the quirky English or other perverts. Deviance is easy in the impersonality of a big conurbation where no one cares who's living a life of homosexual troilism, provided they don't frighten the neighbour's dog or fall down drunk in full drag in front of them, in which case they'll stride over the body while mentally composing a letter to the Department of Health. Not so in a small society where poverty is better helped, deviation less welcome, and everyone makes allowances and tries to help because they know each other's business. If the homeless dossed in doorways passers-by would point out a warmer spot while politely hinting that the dosser's downfall was due to not getting qualifications at school, though a few places are still available at Whakapuna High. ACT members might thrust improving tracts into their hands and shout at them, but they're fewer in numbers than rough sleepers.

Deviant groups, atheists, hobby and enthusiast groups can neither cluster together for support nor hide in New Zealand cities. Gays are isolated. So are cake decorators and anyone who doesn't share the majority religion of sport. The intelligentsia aren't concentrated enough even to stimulate each other let alone the nation, so they withdraw into sulky pedantry. The same is true of lesbian groups, transvestites, CNDers, Maoists, Jansenists, photographers, embroiderers and other fetishists who can only connect by the Internet, police allowing. For anything more than that they are compulsory contributors to Air New Zealand, indeed, all that keeps it going. Only in Auckland is there sufficient concentration of some minorities to support festivals or display their culture, as in the Pasifika Festival, or the Hero Festival, or the Auckland Easter Show art exhibition. Auckland minorities miss out on air points.

Ingenuity is born of the small society. The intellectual can repair his own car (indeed on university wages they have to). The gay parader can be a vicious rugby player, the transsexual a good MP, and everyone can do everything. A small society is a jack of all trades society and ingenious with it, making New Zealand a land of simple answers to problems which boggle other systems. The awnings over pavements are an early example which they've still not thought of in Britain. A few years ago in Auckland, flavoured milks could be sold more cheaply than the real thing. So an inventive entrepreneur produced a milk-flavoured milk at a lower price than milk. With a litre of milk costing more than a litre of petrol, and a Fonterra man explaining that this is 'because that's what the consumer will pay', it's clearly time for milk-flavoured petrol. When students got free EFTPOS facilities they brought the system to the verge of regular crashes by using it for everything, from ice-creams to newspapers, preferably always with cash out.

This is the Number-Eight-Fencing-Wire mentality born in the rural areas where farmers use it as the all-purpose tool. That lives on in the cities where everyone, from trained brain surgeons to scouts looking for horses to remove stones from their hooves, use it. It holds sheds together, keeps cars going, and arts, crafts and nuclear physics would grind to a halt without it. Number Eight Wire should be a national symbol to show that New Zealanders are flexible, adaptable and resourceful.

Unspecialised small societies have to be multiskilled because specialisation comes from numbers, which have to be differentiated by diploma, skill, expertise, or from big commercial markets where specialists protect their skills by union rules, professional qualifications, blackmail and physical assault. In a small society more people have to have more skills to survive to higher levels, all practised and learned by doing, not diplomas. Its people are more adaptable and more all-rounders, better able to change careers ad lib. Everyone has done more, and can pass the practicals even if they're regularly defeated by the theory.

A big society puts people in ruts and keeps them there. The camera assistant's assistant or the chicken sexer (male chicks only) can't sing oratorios on the side, lecture on anthropology or run a nuclear reactor in the back garden. They can in New Zealand. Diplomas are becoming a fetish in New Zealand as everywhere, but Kiwi ones are more practical, with combined diplomas in Surfboarding, Sunbathing Skills, Flower Arranging and Hospitality I (Silver Service). These are as good as any in Britain, though less respected there because the British never like to admit any one else's qualifications.

Usually, however, New Zealanders are welcomed overseas, and get on better than the specialists with whom they compete because they can do brain surgery, use a jumper lead, rebuild a house or an engine, and wire a plug. In New Zealand the practical are kings and queens, the plain man the town crier of the kingdom, while the intellectual is irrelevant. This is real democracy and everyone their own intellectual.

Experts and intellectuals count for little against pragmatic common sense of the type deployed in every correspondence column, pub, club or Parliamentary Committee and on every ranting radio. All opinions are equal even if they're total rubbish, but the plain man's are more equal than most. Everyone counts, and even if they're demonstrably nuts they won't be held in the same contempt as experts and intellectuals, the purpose of whose existence is to be discounted and abused, particularly by raving radio ranters. Where else would an apparently sane government consult every citizen by pamphlet on whether parents who don't get their kids to school should lose the benefit, or send every household a copy of the *Mazengarb Report* detailing dirty doings behind Hutt Valley bike sheds. When populism rules anything goes.

How many people does it take to change a light bulb? In New Zealand, a child. In England, up to thirty adults to form a committee to confer about whether it needs an electrician, hire an agency to find one, consult on appropriate qualifications, check the certificates of those applying, devise a business plan, then supervise the job and debrief the doer. New Zealand TV workers have operated cameras, done research, presented programmes, written the story and swept out the studio and cleaned the lavatories, particularly in the small city stations. Accountants have applied their creative skills to the higher reaches of company fraud as well as doing tax returns and cleaning Augean stables. Musicians can make their own recordings, conduct, play solo and build their own Stradivarius. Photographers repair their own cameras, develop their own film and do the body painting for nude models.

Because small means less specialisation New Zealanders develop many skills, though those who want to achieve real success, scale the heights in their field, or really specialise, must go abroad. Yet why bother? People of even moderate abilities, who aren't specialised and have no desire to go abroad, can get further, faster and higher than anywhere else. They can make contributions in any field they choose. This is a nation smaller than many big cities but, unlike them, New Zealand has its own armed forces, diplomats, UN representation, spies and all the paraphernalia of a nation state as well as the local government pertaining to cities, so it has more top jobs to offer, allows more people to develop to a higher level and offers everyone a better chance of reaching the top – any top – which can be more of a threat than a promise. David Lange's rise was so meteoric he didn't have time to learn the skills of politics let alone the job of Prime Minister. So he became brilliant at the theory, poor at the practicals, but much loved because of the fun he brought to the job.

Yet small societies lack confidence. New Zealanders are not as big, bold and brash as they like to pretend, and the obsessive advertising of Viagra and health food potency products tells the real story. Inside every backblocks hero and every rough, tough Speights-fuelled Man of the South is a wimp trying to get out. New Zealand was long characterised by an inferiority complex, diffidence and a colonial cringe – 'a society with a puzzled look on its face' – and always humble in the face of the big, particularly the Brits. That diffidence was demonstrated by the fact that it finds it difficult to believe that anything or anyone it has or produces can really be successful until endorsed by the world outside. Peter Jackson was a beardy weirdy until the world showered him with money and plaudits and recognised New Zealand as best supporting country. Roger Douglas wasn't respected until other nations started hiring him as a consultant on how to wreck their economies and break the unions.

A long succession of visiting experts, Englishmen, academics even, occasionally, people, have been listened to more seriously than they deserve when they come to pontificate, and are deferred to, even when talking tosh in a superior accent as if they had something to offer. They arrive, make themselves experts in a few hours, know more than the locals after a day, then return, putting the Kiwi right as they go. Any confident society would ignore them but New Zealanders are a polite, deferential people, anxious for the approval of visitors and loath to tell them to their face, or anywhere outside the correspondence columns, that they are talking rubbish.

By the same token, every tourist, from drunken backpackers to Bill Gates slipping in secretly to Huka Lodge, is anxiously asked whether they like the country, and in Gates's case, whether he'd consider buying it. No sporting tournament is successful until millions of dollars are chucked away paying Tiger Woods, any woman tennis player who'll show a flicker of knicker, or Bill Clinton, to come and bankrupt the organisation, even the country, by playing mediocre golf, losing the tournament or speaking platitudes they've done to death a thousand times. James Belich could do the first, David Lange the second and Jonah Lomu the third, all much better, but none has the advantage of being foreign.

Small country means small confidence. Kiwis wouldn't dream of going to other countries (outside Tonga or the Cook Islands) to put them right, and much as they'll grumble silently at London's prices, dirt, smells and general mess, they're too polite, in awe of the big and programmed to diffidence, even guilt, to say so to the Poms grovelling for tips. The culture and class of the old and big are considered superior. So the visitors who come from there must be better. Which is why every third-rate failure of British or American show biz has an enthusiastic welcome as they come to New Zealand to die. Where are they now, the flowers of British variety, such as Marie Lloyd or Des O'Connor? Probably appearing in Morrinsville.

But smallness also means openness to change. New moods, new enthusiasms, new fears sweep New Zealand. Fads become fetishes faster and more powerfully than in bigger states where they run up against the breakwaters of inertia, scale and safeguarding institutions. In a tight little, right on, uniform society with a centralised media, moods can sweep all before them. Nonsense is readily believed if it dresses in popular clothes, cranks get a better hearing, and burning conviction carries the day for any amateur St Joan or any nasty nostrum, from banning fireworks or pornography to getting rid of dog dirt on pavements, graffiti, or the TV licence as a reasonable way of supporting public service television and local production. Cranks clamour, the media play them up because news is so dull, mutter becomes shout, nutters prophets and soon the clamour is unstoppable. The Kiwis being reasonable, nice, open-minded, and totally lacking standards of judgement, will consider anything. 'Must be something in it . . .'

Kiwis lack built-in shit sifters and the ability to separate bright ideas from total nonsense, so any lunatic can get a long way down the paddock with his or her total insanity before some small voice says, 'Hang on. What's this all about?' A crazed messianic decides that women should wear burkas for environmental reasons, as Japanese wear masks. A majority, worried dimly about the environment and anxious to protect women suddenly sees it as the way to advance both causes. The idea is taken up by the media and weekend columnists pour out praise at their usual excessive length. Eccentric craze becomes accepted conviction. Petitions pour in. Islamic fundamentalists clamour that any anti-burkaism is discriminatory. Parliament takes urgent action to pass the Burka Bill. Burkas are donned en masse.

Weeks later an Otago medical school researcher proves that burkas induce unhealthy sweating. Transvestites are arrested doing indescribable things in burkas. Several wearers turn out to be Taliban. Muggers and bank robbers go undetected. Avondale schoolgirls start charging fifty cents a look beneath the burka while emancipated women refuse to allow police to look or breathalyse. The mood swings back. Holmes burns his burka live on air. Things return to normal in a burkaless world where it's then found that compulsory sunglasses reduce myopia by reducing eye contact, and stop sexism by making women indistinguishable from men. Off we go again.

In the land of the nice the messianic can be kings and queens. But only *pro tem*, for they have fast burnout rates. Otherwise the country would zigzag insanely through history to exhaust itself pursuing any passing fashion. New Zealand is prone to this syndrome, having no checks, no balances, no shit sifters, no settled standards, no Second Chamber, only the Christchurch *Press* between New Zealand and a populist dictatorship.

'Where lunacy parades as common sense,' as Glover put it, anything can be sold in populist terms. New ideas and fashions usually sweep into New Zealand from overseas. They then spread across the country because a well-educated and pretty uniform society with a uniform media spreads the new in a way impossible in bigger countries with greater inertias, vested interests and counterbalancing powers.

In Britain the birth control pill came in slowly, adopted first by the educated middle class, then gradually filtering down to the great uneducated, but sexually prolific, majority, and opposed by that powerful vested interest, the Catholic Church. So it took decades to become the norm. In New Zealand it arrived and was immediately accepted as a practical answer to an age-old problem, and the key to women's advance. Prescribed almost universally, it became the norm and set women free quickly in ways with incalculable consequences for them, and for males, staggering behind the transformation, duly grateful for its benefits even if some found the resulting demands exhausting.

Women, always the dominant power because their management skills have been crucial to family success or failure, stepped out of the scullery to grasp power, preferring it to back-seat driving. Germaine Greer came in 1972 and was an instant hero. The silent sex demanded the right to orgasms, something men had regarded as their natural monopoly, and the still small voice of the vagina monologue became the clamour of the vagina diatribes. People avidly discussed Germaine's evangel, a message they'd dimly understood for ages but, being Kiwis, never bothered to turn into an ideology. Coming from overseas, she was saying what they'd hardly dared to, and opened up a world more exciting than the Women's Division of Federated Farmers or cake-making skills.

Feminism triumphed, and became a PC norm within half a dozen years. Indeed, by the late seventies it had achieved so many of its goals that the sane majority eased up, leaving things to the fanatics in what became a lesbian-driven campaign against men or their nearest available substitute, the New Zealand male who was judged guilty without trial of all sorts of offences against women, children and animals.

Some women, their overheated imaginations stimulated by reports of child abuse, satanic abuse, porn rings, ritual witchcraft and other exotic practices from Britain, Belgium and the US, were driven into a frenzy. Any mere male responsible in any way for childcare became open to suspicion. The witch-hunt waiting to happen fell around the head and private parts of Peter Ellis, the only male, and a camp one at that, at the Christchurch Civic Crèche. Anxious parents began to question children to discover signs of the abuse they feared. Rumours multiplied, the police investigated. Nothing was found. 'Cover up' claimed the militants, who redoubled their efforts and, in the words of Lynley Hood in *A City Possessed*: 'After three months of parental questioning about Peter Ellis, nudity, sex, breasts, vaginas, penises, ejaculation, bottoms, scariness, naughtiness, soreness, secrets, yukky touching, toileting, poos, wees and the crèche, the kids started talking dirty.'

They coughed up not only what their parents wanted but a lot more – about secret tunnels, murdered babies, a dug-up Jesus. All this should have discredited the whole shamboodle. It wasn't allowed to be quoted in court lest it harm Ellis, who was imprisoned: another triumph for the Vigilante Society and the Kiwi panic propensity, though that was now being exhibited by parents and devotees of Political Correctness, whereas similar witch-hunts in Cold War days had been triumphs for right wing populism.

The hold of conservative orthodoxy had been broken by another imported phenomenon, the politics of protest.

Vietnam War protests shaped a widespread new radicalism which paved the way for an explosion against South Africa and racist tours in the early eighties. This was a highly organised mass movement with power, passion, numbers and protesters who, with Kiwi pragmatism, developed a body armour of rolled-up copies of the *Listener* and crash helmets to combat the less well protected but better armed forces of law and disorder who were defending a Muldoon line no one quite understood. The old, small town conservative New Zealand and the new were at war. The fight was officially a draw but, effectively, the new radicals won, having demonstrated both the power of protest and the inability of the forces of conservatism to hold the old line. The old New Zealand had died when the traditional exchange of bleats became confrontation on the streets.

The craze cycle works the same way whether the change comes in from overseas or is domestically generated. The South Sea Bubble would have been bigger here had New Zealand been settled in time. Since then everything from miniskirts to Play Station, or the rush into kiwifruit production, and out of it, into deer, goats, ostriches, mussels and wine, shows the same gold rush mentality which a small society is prone to. Indeed, it's surprising they've not gone big on frogs for France, cocaine for China, or dinosaurs for Disney, assembled in disused farm sheds all over the country.

This Kiwi lemming syndrome is manipulable. An egalitarian country has become surprisingly obsessed with the multimillionaire's sport of yachting because the 'fever of excitement' over the America's Cup was largely media stimulated, to the great benefit of Auckland, its rich, and the wealth which owned the media. The reaction to Peter Jackson's *Lord of the Rings* was highly hyped by a government anxious to attract film jobs, and television boosting one of its own, whilst Matamata strove to change its name to

Hobbittown. The press renamed Wellington 'Middle Earth', an eccentric Oxford don, Tolkien, became a Kiwi, almost as big as Crump, and the nation was asked to rejoice in the huge killing made by a few Kiwis, big American investors and a greedy film company, though the nation got no cash return on its own investment in tax allowances and promotion for the film.

New Zealanders become new zealots because messianic madmen have a disproportionate influence. Being concerned citizens, Kiwis are easily convinced that 'something must be done' and are persuadable to seemingly easy answers. Apart from Ruth and Jenny, monetarism was a masculine ideology designed to allow men to get their own back by punishing women, the poor, the public service and anyone else who'd inconvenienced the rich over the years. By cutting wages, increasing unemployment, breaking unions and attacking social security as 'dependence', the élite got its own back for decades of paying taxes for the ungrateful poor and having to negotiate on a near equal basis with unions. It was a programme such as Sir Otto Niemeyer had recommended to New Zealand on his 1931 visit – 'The heart is gold, the name is Otto. Women and children first, the motto' – but its time came because the economy turned sour.

'Madmen gain credence when times are hard', as Hitler once told me over a quiet müller thurgau. The triumph of such an un-Kiwi creed as economic liberalisation in the eighties and nineties confirms this. The élite rammed its medicine down the throats of the people, helped by the receptiveness of a small democracy where fashions catch on like infectious diseases. Even those who suffered most were soon talking about 'the rigour of the market', 'world-class competitiveness', 'contestability' 'corporatisation' and other gobbledy-gook.

They were predisposed to believe it because programmed

to guilt, and half inclined to think that they'd had it too good, weren't working hard enough, and that enterprise should be better rewarded. They thought they were doing what the world wanted and, being New Zealanders, did it bigger. The world took little interest, but the triumph of economic sado-masochism was more total and more damaging in New Zealand than in any of the bigger Anglo-Saxon countries which flirted with the same malevolent mysticism.

Fashions come in from overseas. New Zealand is a fashion taker, not a fashion maker, a trend follower, not a trend maker, except perhaps for buzzy bees which never caught on much elsewhere, despite Princess Diana's enthusiasm. Other things generated in New Zealand, from hakas to downtrous, remain obstinately unexportable. In every other area, from cover versions of pop to academic plagiarism, New Zealand lives by imitation. It likes to feel that it's up with the world. Look at any area of endeavour, be it cooking and home improvement programmes on TV, styles in art from impressionism to neo-realism, or in photography from pictorialism to candid, through hot pants and flares to Californian casual in clothes, New Zealand is a Copy Country.

The small nation is incomplete, and dependent, because its critical mass is insufficient. The big have strength, inertia, mass markets and self-sufficiency. Small is more vulnerable. So New Zealand, ever since it emerged as a settler society, was a province of a larger entity, dependent on others for defence, culture, ideology and attitudes, the pinnacles of career ladders and the wider stages of opportunity and challenge. Britain was New Zealand's finishing and polishing school though the world is now taking that job on. Mass societies are sufficient unto themselves. Small ones are limpets and need rocks. New Zealand's recent history is the search for other rocks as the first, Britain, crumbled.

Bigger limpets like Canada, Australia, and South Africa

weaned themselves gradually. New Zealand, the smallest, was more dependent, being Britain's overseas farm importing British manufactured goods and sending back food. The relationship flourished when Britain was strong and happy to be fed by the cheapest producers, to keep wages down so Pax Britannica kept the world safe for New Zealand butter to spread in and British cars to break down in. Then when the comparative failure of the British economy compared with the faster growing German, French, Japanese or indeed almost any other economy, dragged New Zealand down the scale of living standards, Britain scrambled with indecent haste into the Common Market. New Zealand was left as the world's first rockless limpet.

Its culture, lifestyle and institutions were imported from Britain, but always to be improved on in New Zealand as they were adjusted to the Pacific Basin lifestyle. Housing was built better than Britain's overcrowded, drab, living conditions. Westminster-style democracy worked better, the education and the university systems were improved upon. Yet the culture remained dependent. This yielded benefits in being able to grow and develop as part of a wider whole. It combated the insularity small societies are prone to and plugged the small into a wider world, and provided a bigger stage for its talent to perform on. Witness the contrast between the vigour of the enlightenment in eighteenth-century Scotland opened up by the wider union, and the debilitating introspection of Irish politics and economics from the 1920s to the 1970s. Pom paternalism enriched both countries through interchange, and still does to a more limited extent, though the British are foolishly depriving themselves of many of the benefits of the New Zealand input under pressure from the EU. Katherine Mansfield, Ernest Rutherford, Liz Calder, Dan Davin, Kiri Te Kanawa, Nyree Dawn Porter and all the others would all have had to go home after two years to give work to Germans. Peripheral societies make a disproportionate contribution to the suns around which they revolve and New Zealand has certainly given Britain more than its due.

Britain remained the higher reaches of New Zealand culture and society, its finishing school the upper rungs of so many New Zealand ladders, though New Zealanders now also look elsewhere, to America and also to Australia and Canada, rather than exclusively to Britain, because a small society must enter other orbits, and the United States has far more to offer.

Australia too, has become an increasing influence, though less benign. Two societies so alike find it difficult to get on, and the relationship is really a non-love affair. New Zealand doesn't want to go waltzing with Matilda and is happy competing with her but Australia is New Zealand's safety valve. Kiwis go there when the New Zealand economy is doing less well than the Australian, as it has for most of the eighties and nineties. With the flow largely one way, benefit fatigue has resulted in Australia, with the restriction of automatic Kiwi access to benefits. Australia is now a New Zealand suburb. It used to be three expensive seasick days away on the legendary *Wanganella*, but is now three hours, and cheaper than a flight to Dunedin. Auckland to Dunedin return is over a thousand dollars because of Air New Zealand's policy of cutting the South Island off. The cheap fare to Australia is $600 or less, so many younger New Zealanders have their introduction to the excitements of metropolitan big city life in Sydney, not the Auckland substitute.

The interchange means a growing Australianisation of New Zealand life. The Commonwealth emerges as the land from whence all blessings flow, from possums to painted apple moths, Ansett to poisonous snakes and spiders. Assertive aggression and boastful attitudes which don't come naturally to New Zealanders, unless they're nervous, have become the language of sporting and other conflicts. Asking

Kiwis which team they support when they're not playing produces the answer 'anyone who can beat Australia'.

Journalists whose careers cross the Tasman have imported an Aussie vocabulary such as 'rorts', leadership 'rolls', failures who become 'dog tucker', budget 'blow outs' and lavatories translated as 'dunnies'. None of this would have been heard in any self-respecting pub thirty years ago but it's now the lingua franca of politics.

New Zealand has a dependency problem. A small society is incomplete, its career ladders short, its specialisation less, its challenges smaller, its competition less intense. Air New Zealand, like an ever-running stream, bears Kiwi sons and daughters away, following A.R.D. Fairburn's advice to the young:

> *If you're enterprising and able*
> *Smuggle your talents away*
> *Hawk them in livelier markets*
> *Where people are willing to pay*

For him this was an issue of finding livelier lands than egalitarian New Zealand, a clean but dead society:

> *This land is a lump without leaven*
> *A body that has no nerves*
> *Don't be content to live in*
> *A sort of second rate heaven*
> *With first-grade butter, fresh air*
> *And paper in every toilet*

And probably softer paper than the *Otago Daily Times* at that. Yet the real problem was not Kiwi culture but critical mass. Small size offers a better quality of life but not the challenge of competition, of climbing higher pinnacles or winning in the wider world. Anyone can do anything in New Zealand but not necessarily well. The city as nation offers more people the opportunity to rise further but does not ensure that the able stay. The loss of the best and the brightest is, therefore, in inverse ratio to size, resulting in the Mansfield syndrome. From Rutherford to Fred Dagg, Phar Lap to Kiri Te Kanawa, the greats have gone. The Kiwi problem is: at what stage and at what population size is New Zealand less dependent; its own society rather than a province of another? It wasn't with two and three quarter million people. Is it now, with nearly four? If it isn't, will it ever be?

New Zealand's loss has always been the world's gain. Small countries do contribute well beyond their weight. The classic examples are Ireland and New Zealand. Both stand out for their contributions to the arts, literature, film, entertainment and international governance, with medicine and science added in New Zealand's case, music in Ireland's. The world is a stage for talent nurtured in the sustaining smallness of both countries. Each provides a great environment to develop, grow and advance talent, even if neither has the critical mass to keep it. Both impose the choice of go or stay for the able, with the inevitable follow-on, come back or not. So life is full of might-have-beens for the young and able, even if it keeps the airlines busy. These tensions are greater for New Zealanders than the Irish because New Zealand is further away from the world it needs as finishing school by twenty-three hours and several thousand dollars.

Chapter Four

# Dunedin

*I*n the beginning was Dunedin. For New Zealand, because the gold rush made it the new colony's biggest and richest city as well as its commercial, financial and industrial capital, Dunedin retained a leading position until well into the twentieth century when less worthy cities roared ahead and the Edinburgh of the South began its long, elegant decline, losing population, businesses and head offices. A beginning, too, for me, providing my first job, first home and first experience of New Zealand: a solid, staid, older version, perhaps even a purer distillation, but New Zealand nonetheless, whatever Dunedin's sentimental attachments to Scotland, its imported haggises, its third-degree Burns.

I arrived on 8 August 1959 after a two-day trek down from Auckland by train, inter-island ferry, then another train, to arrive at what was then a working railway station, its platform littered with luggage and suitcases, much of it mine, plus the staff of the History Department paraded to meet their new colleague. In commemoration I came back by train, 'the Southerner', sadly truncated to three carriages with a microwave equipped, chardonnay-serving, buffet car. My fellow passengers were the old, the poor and students, mostly on their way from one airportless place to another. There were three or four tourists where there could have been lots, for properly marketed and promoted the journey down the Otago coastline is a great train ride. Building business was beyond the capability of Tranz Rail, which shortly afterwards closed down the whole service, leaving the magnificent station trainless apart from the Taieri Gorge railway. Dunedin has long been a little paranoid, but that and the fact that it's four hundred dollars more to fly to Dunedin from Auckland than to Australia could be seen as real persecution.

I loved Dunedin. Small for a city and getting smaller, it was the perfect size for a university town, the only real one in New Zealand; and small enough to know everyone who mattered and to walk everywhere. I never had a car, but Dunedin had a superb taxi service. You could ring them to ask where the best student parties were that day and be transported there. A wonderful service. Unless the party happened to be mine.

The only barrier to happiness is the climate, which never lived up to Dunedin, so swimming at St Clair was a brass-monkey experience. Life was good for young lecturers in first jobs and all newly married, but we weren't so good to the students. I was always one lecture ahead of them so the library books they needed were out being read by me.

Now Dunedin's railway station is a foretaste of the town. Tarted and painted up, it symbolises a town transformed. George Street is thronging with cafés, restaurants and wine bars. The pubs – once the staple of social life, particularly after six o'clock – have contracted except for the Captain Cook, which has a huge beer garden. The Robbie Burns (which Erich Geiringer called the Rabbi Burns) was raided one night in 1960, and police discovered one member of the university staff under the piano claiming to be tuning it, and another in a cupboard upstairs claiming to be looking for the toilet. Now it has tables on the pavement and a bottle store bigger than the pub. Even the Settlers Museum dropped 'early' because it now incorporates Maori who arrived long before the stern-faced Presbyterians gazing down in their crowded box room, unable to express their disapproval of a Dunedin changed from Presbyterianism to Hedonism.

The industrial heart is now mainly closed or converted into failing restaurants and gymnasia. Even the ANZ Bank, where I struggled to get ten pounds out of the Reserve Bank to join the Fabian Society, something which shocked the teller (who later became Labour MP for Dunedin Central) when he saw that it was 'a socialist society', is now decaying and the magnificent Exchange Building, described as the architectural gem of the southern hemisphere, has been pulled down.

So Dunedin is really the University. With just over 2000 students when I came, Otago is now a production line for 17,000. The university has grown as the town has shrunk, collapsing in on what is now its major industry, bringing in millions of dollars from thousands of students because it's so much cheaper than the real world. Whereas Dunedin once ignored the university, now it is so dependent it will do anything for it, from closing Castle Street so the university could build over it, to giving planning permission for some of the world's ugliest buildings and turning the campus into a vast tow-away zone surrounded by cheap housing.

The baronial gothic main building was home to the History Department and the library, where we'd go for hours to gawp at Fleur Adcock. Now it houses the Vice Chancellor and his large staff and has been expensively renovated to levels appropriate to the CEO of Dunedin's biggest company. That change symbolises the transformation of Otago and every other academic institution, from university to poly, to a business run by its Vice Chancellor. Once a remote and largely irrelevant academic figure, today's VC is Chief Executive, backed up by a large management team running an educational business churning out graduates at a lower cost per head than keeping people in jail.

I came to meet old colleagues who'd taught with me, been students under me, or worked there at the same time: collectively, those who'd stayed to do their duty, educate students and make their contribution to knowledge and to a better New Zealand, while I'd been gadding. Gathered in what used to be the Registry, but is now the staff club, were Professors Jim Flynn, Keith Jackson, Tony Wood, Eric Olssen (my student and son of my colleague in that department, Ted Olssen), Mary Ronnie, former City Librarian, Bunty Herd, wife of Eric Herd, former Professor of Modern Languages, and Stan Rodger, former MP, Chair of the University Club, former Minister and Registrar of the Dental School.

How did they feel the university had changed? Was it a better place to be or worse? And parenthetically the one pathetic question I didn't dare to ask: How had they managed without me?

## Keith Jackson

*We've done better over the years. I liked the early years because you knew the students and it wasn't the mass education we've had since. There is certainly pressure on universities now but the work that the students do is actually better in many cases.*

*Standards are being pressed down by pressures from the students themselves. They want to pass. I'm not sure that it's necessarily all that bad because many of the students work much harder now than they ever did before and some of them are doing much better. Others perform in an even more mediocre fashion than we were accustomed to, although when we were here, the number of people to whom you said 'If you work hard you can get an A' and they said 'I'm not interested. If I get through that's all I'm interested in' was very discouraging.*

## Jim Flynn

*The standards have dropped in the sense that we have so much broadened the intake, that the requirement for a pass has gradually gone down and down. That doesn't mean that top students aren't as good as ever, but where previously you would give an A minus, now you give an A plus. Where previously you gave a forty percent and failed, now it would be a fifty percent and pass.*

## Bunty Herd

*But everybody can go to university now, can't they? There are such a lot of people who are going to university who are really more suitable for training. They really want a job.*

## Jim Flynn

*There are whole departments in this university now who only teach bad courses on a kindergarten level that weren't there in the old days. I've walked by a tutorial and seen a lecturer sitting there. I thought maybe he was meditating, so I said to him 'Why are you always sitting in this classroom?' He said, 'I'm conducting a tutorial but no one comes.' So he could fill out his sheet he would sit there for an hour. So let's not romanticise what we've got today.*

## Mary Ronnie

*In Dunedin the university has become more important and more appreciated than ever before. The three tertiary institutions have never been better appreciated in New Zealand. The biggest industry in this city is now tertiary education and the university is the biggest of the three. It's twice as vital as it was twenty years ago, and having gone back to university myself and done a course for the first time in thirty years, I found that the teaching was more vital, that the students around me were more vital, I was more challenged. I was very impressed.*

## Eric Olssen

*We don't feel cut off from the corpus of knowledge and expertise. In the new library building we've a vast bank of computers on the World Wide Web. Our students can do research on American history, all sorts of things that were inconceivable. There is a virtual world being constructed around us. That wasn't the case in our day. That's the beginning of another revolution.*

## Jim Flynn

*The place is run by the worst managerial thinking. The Vice Chancellor deserves credit for keeping us in the black, so I am not attacking him, but this managerial ethos that there are principles you can apply whether you're running a bowling alley, a university or a convent, given that sort of idiot psychology, we are really in the hands of people who are bad administrators, bad psychologists and who suck up too much resources for themselves. The administration now has all the power, and academics and students are effectively powerless.*

*Now that the administration has no political restraints it can do worthy things that take over the university budget.*

*The administration now sucks up far more than its fair share of resources. There was one time when they let the cat out of the bag. They had a five-year trend and during that period university research staff was up seven percent, teaching staff up seven percent, female administrative staff up seven percent, and male administrative staff up twenty-five percent. There is an enormous growth in administrative staff, and a similar reduction in the number of full-time academic equivalents.*

## Eric Olssen

*It is true we now spend a lot of time on budgets that we didn't, but it's partly driven out of Treasury insisting that the money is given to teach. They want to make sure it's being used to teach so you can't lock up more and more as some universities used to. In an institution this size the amount of money locked up by departments secreting it is actually very considerable.*

## Jim Flynn

*There is much less money available per student. You don't have the complete duffs that you used to have but I know that just to protect my staff's time, to do any research, we cut courses from thirty-nine lectures to twenty-six, we started having more tutors doing marking of essays, we had fewer tutorials and essays assigned.*

*When you justify a new course now you have to do a cost benefit analysis which includes predicting how many students are going to take it, how many of them are likely to be foreign students. Of course, you're tempted when faced with such an insane task to say I have heard a rumour that the Methodist University in Anchorage, Alaska, is closing down and three thousand of them are going to come down here and take my course.*

*It's a good thing to admit far more as long as they are flunked at stage one if they can't hack it. Until the last ten years I didn't have people who would write 'Aquinas thought God was a perfect Knower' and write 'Noer'. I didn't have people who wrote that old English word, 'Inotherwords', which means they heard you say 'in other words'. These people now pass. They don't necessarily pass my course, but they get passes, and certainly a first is a very different thing today. But that doesn't mean the kids are going downhill. I think they are pretty much as they used to be. It's probably true that they work a bit harder and ninety percent of the kids in the old days wanted nothing more than to repeat what the lecturer said, and that's, of course, what ninety percent of them want to do today.*

Everyone is worked harder – staff and students alike. A staff recruited in the old, easygoing days now feels more pressured than ever before. They have always felt underpaid. Now that feeling is well justified. Students, too, are underfinanced, as is the whole university system.

# Eric Olssen

*Students used to go off in the summer and get jobs and work. That was a valuable part of their education and it also meant that they were much more self-sufficient. Now these poor students who can't get jobs during the summer are just piling up this huge debt which means that they want results. So they are demanding why isn't this an A mark instead of a B-plus. We've paid you to teach us well. So get the results.*

*Numbers are the key for finance. If you get the numbers you get the finance for the department. Before, you had departments that were considered necessary because they were part of the university, like the Classics Department. It never attracted numbers at all.*

*Nobody knew on what basis the government funded*

*universities when we were students. There were negotiations between the Vice Chancellor or the University Grants Committee and the government, and somehow some money came and it got distributed and you had notions like a staff establishment. Now everybody is much more conscious that it's bums on seats.*

## Tony Wood

*Government funding has declined substantially over the last twenty years, so staff/student ratios have declined substantially from about one to fourteen when I came in 1959, back to one to twenty. So we're working harder and more is expected of you, but I wouldn't say the students are getting a worse deal. When I was a student, the History Department was a very good department, but across the entire university that wasn't true. A lot of people never did a day's research in their lives. They were on sinecures basically. Now it's much harder for people like that to survive in this place. Everybody is forced to work harder.*

## Jim Flynn

*The middle class now expects all of its kids to get degrees in the job market. This has meant a far larger percentage of the population going in, which goes beyond what the taxpayer is willing to tolerate. So you can do one of three things. You can have a pecking order of universities, where only the ones at the top are real universities in the old sense, like you do in America. Or you can have a pecking order of departments as you do in Britain. Or you can do the insane thing of having a pecking order of individuals.*

In my day Neville Philips, Vice Chancellor at Canterbury would point out that Charlemagne was part of New Zealand history so, he inferred, more important than Michael Joseph

Savage. I disagreed, seeing it as the responsibility of New Zealand universities to study and stimulate New Zealand. They now do.

## Eric Olssen

*New Zealand is the core of the curriculum, whereas when I was a student there would be a number of strands in the curriculum. You did medieval Europe, that was two papers the first year, you did three papers in stage two, on the expansion of Europe, the sixteenth and seventeenth centuries and one seventeenth and eighteenth. The third year you got a little bit of choice. I did French Revolution. It was an entirely Euro-centric curriculum. There was no New Zealand at all. The Pacific didn't get a mention except probably for Cook coming in at the end of the expansion of Europe. That would have been it.*

Paradoxically, with this new emphasis on the society around them, New Zealand has to recruit more students overseas because they bring in more money than the locals. So Vice Chancellors spend much of their time flying round the world raising money, offering courses, coming to partnership deals and recruiting students. Some have nose bursts if they come down below 30,000 feet.

## Eric Olssen

*My department's income depends upon recruiting a certain number of international students each year, largely American, but not entirely. All of that involves paperwork, especially if they're incorporating studying at Otago into an American degree. I don't think this was a major issue when I was a student, but nowadays it is very complicated. Yet we do have a more international student body and that's all to the good.*

Yet debt is now sending New Zealand students the other way, preparing New Zealand's sons and daughters for export almost as surely as its lambs.

## Stan Rodger

*It's sometimes as if we're training people to export them. You sometimes feel maybe we're all going to end up showing visitors around national parks, but as far as I can see this society will continue to be an exporter of people. It's a highly skilled society. It's a highly literate society, and it's a very resourceful and capable society.*

## Eric Olssen

*A lot of our best students now head overseas to earn the money to pay back the loans. Some of them will come back, but a lot of them will end up marrying in Japan or wherever it is they go. They are the right age to be finding somebody to marry, so it's inevitable a high proportion are going to stay away. There is no national sort of system of accounts for determining how many of the young you can lose and remain viable, but I suspect many won't come back as I did for family, country, and quality of life.*

## Ian Church

*I was from a working-class town, Port Chalmers, and I was a working-class boy, and we got paid to come to university. I was on a Post Primary Teachers' bursary. It's so different now. The kids from Port Chalmers that I still know are up to their ears in loans. But we were paid to come, and if we hadn't been paid we probably wouldn't have.*

Leaving my fellow oldies hiding in case the VC had bugged the room, I went to talk to today's students on the lawn in front of the old building. They weren't the public servants, insurance salesmen, trade unionists and housewives who'd come in part-time to get the education they'd missed out on. These were sons and daughters of the middle class but more serious and dedicated than I remember students ever being.

## Hannah Craig
*I came to Otago because it's more of an all-round education. It's not just academic, it's the whole way of life, and having such a campus environment. They really encourage you as a student.*

## Eddie Gray
*It's cheap here, the whole economy of the town is geared for students. Student accommodation is amazingly cheap compared to Auckland where I come from, though maybe I'd have got a better education there. Dunedin's a university town. Sure, you have trolleys thrown into the lake and broken beer bottles down the streets and things, but anyone who is involved in small business in Dunedin is forced to open up to the student dollar and they have to mould their business around the spare money of the students.*

## Craig Rodger
*I grew up in this town and it's changed a lot. Further south, down Princes Street, there used to be shops, there used to be restaurants, there used to be stuff down there. Now no student bothers going there and most of the Dunedinites don't bother going there because everything has moved down here, the bookshops, the restaurants.*

## Charlotte Hill
*I think the first three years are a lot easier in regards to debt, but this is my fifth year. The first three years you still have things like clothes left over from school, shoes left over from school. Five*

*years on they've all worn out and it's difficult to live. I've got another three years and I've got sixty thousand dollars debt now, and it will be a hundred thousand, between ninety and a hundred thousand dollars, when I finish. As long as the fees don't go up. I'm going to leave the country. I'll come back, but there's no way that I can pay that off here.*

## Tommy Robinson

*I'm in my final year so I should finish under twenty grand, but that's not a big problem because I know I'm guaranteed a job at the end of it, so I may as well spend the money now.*

## Charlotte Hill

*I don't get any help from my parents. They didn't go to university but they always brought me up to value education and thought that if I got educated I'd do better than they had done, and it was something that no one could take away from me. That's how I was brought up. But I didn't expect that it would cost too much and I don't know whether they imagined it would either. Allowances are based on your parents' income until you're twenty-five, and I'm twenty-four, so it's still being based on my parents' income and they haven't given me any money at university.*

## Jeremy Burgess

*You learn a lot about what interests you. That's the thing about university, everyone is learning about what interests them, so you don't get people like you do in school who are sitting there because they are forced to. People who go to university shouldn't be looking for jobs. A university is somewhere you go to become educated, not to get a job. Which is why there are some people who believe that professional courses, like medicine, pharmacy and accountancy should be taught at a polytechnic, not at a university.*

## Nicola van Leeuwen

*You are here for an education but you're here for an education to get the job you want to get, because you can't get any job without qualifications. I'm doing Physics, so I want to be a Physicist and I can't do that without going to university. It's a bit of both. I love Physics. It's fun, it's hard, it's challenging, it's incredibly satisfying because it is such a challenge and you are pushing the barriers of what we know and that's amazing. But you've also come for a job.*

## Charlotte Clifton

*I want to go overseas. I'm not saying I don't want to work here as well, but I want to eventually be involved in film and television production and I don't want to end up working for Shortland Street. There are so many more opportunities. New Zealand has got a pretty small film production and television market and although I would be interested in trying to work to expand that, as far as experience goes I think it would be really good to be able to work overseas.*

## Eddie Gray

*I want to be a journalist and New Zealand really only imports journalism from overseas. There is just no way you can do political, international political journalism or anything of that sort in New Zealand. You have to go overseas.*

## Stacey Chadwick

*It's a choice. If you go overseas, you get experience and come back and be more valuable or you choose your job here and get to live in New Zealand. There's a risk that I might not come back. If I find that my ties are stronger somewhere else then I might stay. But I might not.*

## James Adams

*It's important to see new places but the main thing behind it is because New Zealand is so small and we are such a small part of the world and we're not really involved in big things, like America is. We don't have huge industries like America or Britain or places like that. But New Zealand has a hold. It's just really special. I've been overseas a couple of times but New Zealand is a lot of very different things and very variable, many beautiful things in a really small space. The beautiful thing about New Zealand is everything is accessible.*

## Stacey Chadwick

*I don't think that if you don't come back that you're not still adding something to New Zealand. I don't think that we should think that people overseas are a lost cause. Just because they've left the country doesn't mean that they're not part of New Zealand and can't make a contribution, particularly when they're only a few computer strokes away. We could just use the world as a network of New Zealanders and stop saying, 'Oh, look, we're so isolated' and say, 'Well, actually we spread ourselves around so that we can make the most of it.'*

## James Adams

*You're a big fish in a small pond so even though you can't go right up to the top, at least when you're getting up there you're in a small enough environment – there's not so much competition that you just get squashed.*

## Charlotte Hill

*My number one reason for wanting to go overseas is just to pay off my debt so that I can come home. I don't want to live overseas long term at all. I really want to live in New Zealand, but I'll go overseas to make the money to pay off my loan.*

I couldn't hack it as a student at today's University of Otago in these more specialised, harder-driven, more demanding times. Nor could I live up as a teacher to the quality or the idealism of the students I met. The cream of the crop perhaps, for the lunkheads, the sporties, the alcoholically obsessed, might have been less forthcoming. Yet they must be a joy to teach rather than the hard work that we had to put in to excite the part-timers, the professional students and the dictation-takers of old. 'Could you slow down, please, Dr Mitchell?'

The University of Otago, followed as always by the other New Zealand universities, was founded out of a proper concern for education and a practical desire to provide the professional workforce, the teachers, doctors, public servants, lawyers and accountants the new nation needed. They performed that job better than their grudging resource allocation deserved but always with the consciousness that their finishing school, further research higher degrees, greater contributions to knowledge, lay overseas. They were incomplete, outposts of a wider system.

In the years since I left they have extended their role, reaching up to the higher levels of graduate education and down to educate a wider range of students in a softer range of subjects and diplomas when the traditional basics of Biology and Chemistry, History and English are supplemented by space-filling courses in Sociology, Women's Studies (violating the edict that the proper study of mankind is man), Surfboarding and Hospitality Studies, Business Studies and Media Studies. The universities are degree and diploma factories where both staff and machinery are overworked and underfinanced. Nevertheless they have also reached out to New Zealand and to the world, bringing increasing earnings from growing numbers of overseas students who pay higher fees to make up for inadequate government financing of domestic students.

This role will be of increasing importance. Universities are a big earner for New Zealand, building on the benefits of English language teaching and high standards to make educational provision for the young tigers of South-East Asia, China, the underdeveloped Pacific and Oceania, Africa and even the UK, Europe and the USA. Education Inc is a major New Zealand Industry, and universities work at overseas earnings in partnership with overseas universities to develop and expand knowledge, training, and skills in ways mutually beneficial to all.

The future lies in reaching out to the wider world for students, relevance and money, serving the wider world community rather than just New Zealand. The prospects are exciting but the process will make major demands. It is counterproductive to hand-polish overseas students while driving Kiwi graduates overseas because of the burden of debt they graduate with. Students will go overseas, but New Zealand needs them to come back and can't afford to either boost the numbers going or inhibit return by hanging a huge burden of debt round student necks. If University education can't be provided free, as it should be, then loans should be on a zero interest basis, not paying higher than the mortgage rate. They should also be written off for those who take jobs, particularly teaching jobs, in New Zealand, and reduced for older students prepared to take on the mentoring role so many overseas students need to help them adjust to a new language, a new country, a new system.

As a competitive export industry the universities now need to be properly funded to maintain and improve on the excellence which alone can make them successful in the increasingly competitive international market for overseas students. The odds favour the old established and prestigious universities and systems, but New Zealand can offer more personal treatment and support for overseas students. They must however improve quality by attracting better staff and allowing slack in the system, which will permit individual attention for more students in language and induction courses to ensure that they benefit fully from the courses they are taking.

New Zealand has a higher destiny than to become a bargain basement degree and diploma factory competing at the downmarket end, while giving its own students a less adequate education than they deserve and imposing a crippling burden of debt. Being world-class holds out the prospect of a massive return for a nation, which needs to develop its competitiveness in every market, provided the universities are viewed not as a grudgingly funded nuisance but as a competitive industry adding more value than any other as it produces skilled and trained Kiwis and overseas students, at least some of whom will want to stay and should be allowed to. New Zealand universities have always been better than the nation deserves, but only if their competitiveness is boosted can they come into their own as national earners and educators to the new New Zealand, upgrading its skills and people and boosting its prospects.

Chapter Five

# Southland

'Invercargill,' quoth Mick Jagger on his only visit in 1965, 'is the arsehole of the world', 'and Gore is thirty miles up it' added wits. One councillor even suggested that Invercargill should join the long list of places with symbols by building a huge polystyrene arse so that visitors could enter Invercargill via the sphincter. The arse was never built and, almost alone in New Zealand, Invercargill has neither entry symbol nor billboard of attractions. It should have both because Southland is booming, pointed out to me by everyone I talked to as an outstanding example of the new New Zealand. Invercargill, once the little town that Santa Claus forgot, is now go ahead and pleased with itself. Southland produces nearly a fifth of New Zealand's GDP with three percent of the population. Now it's getting its share of the action.

Invercargill was planned as an imperial city. Broad streets, impressive buildings, glowing prospects, and keen to replace Dunedin as New Zealand's commercial capital. It didn't. Instead it's declined to the point that when I used to go there to give adult education lectures I found it a conservative, stodgy, fading Southland dream, surrounded by rich sheep-farming areas where farmers, as wealthy as they were rough, prospered by watching sheep eat grass, then sending them to meet their meat destiny at Makarewa. Sophisticated Dunedinites talked of Southland farmers as if they were New Zealand's Newfies and told stories of farmers putting sugar in the wine because it was too dry.

It was downhill from there on in. Maureen and Hunter Howe, whose farm at Wyndham we'd visited, regularly told me the sad story.

## Maureen Howe

*I'd never been on a farm as remote as ours and I knew nothing about sheep. I didn't know that when sheep died, after a few days, you had to go out plucking the wool off. Sometimes there were maggots and all sorts of horrible things. I learned unpleasant things like that.*

*I remember the first time that you came to see us. We were just turning the corner into Wyndham and you said, 'My goodness, this is a one-horse town.' I was quite put out and thought, 'I've never seen a horse in Wyndham.' There wasn't a vehicle in sight. But there was one horse tied by the side of a street. Wyndham was small but it was still badly hit by the economic reforms of the eighties. Farmers couldn't afford to employ staff. They had to cut back so the rural communities, the small districts, lost people. The schools lost children and there were schools closing. The store closed because of the depopulation.*

## Hunter Howe

*Rural life became less enjoyable. Three mercantile firms had stores in Wyndham. That cut down to one because the subsidies were cut back. Now I don't know if there is even one in Wyndham. Now the farmers are diversifying. Deer is a very profitable diversification. There's a lot of deer farming done now. Ostriches, I don't know really, that's just a starting runner. I've tasted the meat and I'm not that keen on it. But oil is one of the other things they're talking about. Some of them are going into tulips, into market gardening and the cut flower business in a big way. My brother's son is growing ginseng on part of our old farm after Topo Climate told him it would grow there. Then you get into the grapes up here as well, which has changed things completely. The New Zealand farmer will adapt to anything. I think we're very much do-it-yourself. If you have to repair something, you can. We don't have to get somebody else to do it for us.*

*We carried on in the farm you used to come to until about 1980, then we leased it. That did hurt a wee bit. But none of the boys wanted to go farming. So I decided, why should I do this when I could find something else that would make me a long way more relaxed? It was a strain and I suffered badly from migraine. So I pulled out of running the farm and I haven't suffered from migraine since.*

*There was a downturn in farming from about the early 1970s on. Then we started to get assistance on fertiliser and so much a head per lamb, but farming was always a struggle because our farm was more than a one-man unit. So I relied on*

ABOVE: *One what? Though it was near Clinton . . .*

RIGHT: *Branch of People's Sperm Bank. Hamilton*

*Have a pint on me. Taumarunui*

ABOVE: *He can't take your call at the moment. Please leave a message after the thunder. Taumarunui*

RIGHT: *We're organising a piss-up in my brewery, want to come? The Edge, Auckland*

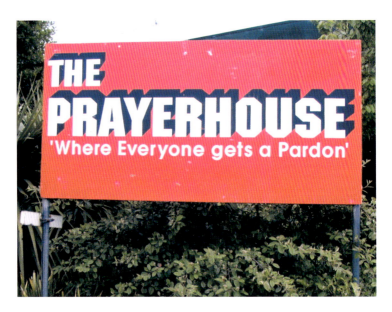

ABOVE: *Reductions on eternal life – Southland only. Invercargill*

LEFT: *Hello, pork pie. Taumarunui*

ABOVE: *I also have a day job. Sam Neill, Alexandra*
BELOW: *Just keep smiling and look united, dammit.*

ABOVE: *A toilet called Rin-Tin-Tin. Tirau*

BELOW: *Ladies shall be deemed to be men after dark. Hunterville*

ABOVE: *Exports: A lot of balls. Southland*

RIGHT: *. . . but Australian waiters. Queenstown*

ABOVE: *Complete with flying saucers. Mangaweka*

BELOW: *Overdrafts for afters. Clyde*

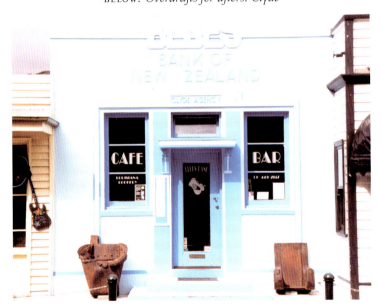

*my two brothers who'd had farms next door to us to help. Too big for one man, not big enough to employ someone else as well. I pulled out of that, rented out the farm on a three-year basis, and went and helped a friend to do the lambing. I ended up spending about eight years there, but it was much more relaxed because I didn't have the responsibility.*

*We've missed out on the bonanza Southland is now going through but it's eleven years on since we got out and it's only this last couple of years that they've had that rapid growth. Hindsight's wonderful but we have no regrets having sold when we did. When I go back now I think they're doing the right thing. In 1958 there were all these small dairy factories dotted round Southland. Eventually there were only about two big dairy factories in the area. Now it's a complete cycle, back to one dairy factory, Eden Vale, which is doing it all. Dairy farming wasn't profitable at that stage and the sheep were profitable, and it was very easy for dairy farmers to convert to sheep. Much cheaper than converting from sheep to dairy. The expense of converting a sheep farm into a dairy unit now is enormous but in those days they were small dairy units. A farmer milked twenty cows or thirty, but there was nothing like the big units of today.*

As farming declined, Invercargill exhibited every symptom of mild rigor mortis. The streets filled with charity and bric-a-brac (called antiques) shops, the population fall accelerated making Invercargill the fastest declining city in the Southern Hemisphere.

Two things saved Southland. Cows and Tim Shadbolt. The cows coming back to sheep country and quietly munching. Tim coming down from Auckland and loudly mouthing. Even more by his enthusiasm and pizzazz. The former agitator, hippie radical and author of *Bullshit and Jellybeans* brought all these talents, except the jellybeans, to promoting his new cause: Invercargill.

Originally invited down to take the mayoralty by mates he had worked with on the Manapouri tunnels, his efforts to make Invercargill an international airport in conjunction with Korean Airlines and an Australian entrepreneur ended in bankruptcy and a fraud trial for the Australian, but no international flights for Invercargill. He was then thrown out as mayor, returning when his successor failed, to be re-elected in 1997. The second coming of New Zealand's first self-made mayor.

By then Southland's land prices were beginning to rise, as cattle replaced sheep. Queenstown was booming, drawing in workers; tourism was building in Stewart Island and the vineyards were developing – indeed one Tim suggested on Bluff Hill in Central Otago drew supplies, workers, and wine tanks from the south. All this began to revive Invercargill. Its growth was then boosted by a development programme. That required money. Southland had it. The city's investments had been carefully conserved and protected from the degradations of central government. Like other places it had a community trust, but also the profits of the licensing trust set up when Invercargill renounced its dry status, and now ploughed these back into community development. These two primed the pump and paid for the key local developments: civic attractions, stadia, sports grounds and facilities, civic architecture and conference facilities, all aimed at making Invercargill a good place to live for citizens, visitors, conference delegates and the incoming executives and workers the town needed to attract.

Ten years of promoting causes, ten more of promoting himself, made him a super booster:

## Tim Shadbolt

*When I came down here, I discovered that Invercargill was the fastest declining city anywhere in Australia or New Zealand. I thought, right, we've got to do something about it. Let's get stuck in, bring our ideas together, and get people working together and just go for it on a grand scale. We had some spectacular failures. Like the international airport. We put a million dollars into it. We beat Queenstown. We beat Dunedin. We beat the lot of them. But no planes have landed yet. We see it as a brilliant success waiting to happen. We're the closest city in the world to Australia so we save on fuel costs and there are difficulties with landing in Queenstown. It's high, it's surrounded by mountains, and has every sort of fog or weather problems. They can't land at night because there's houses too close to the runway. So we're the natural airport for the Southern Lakes.*

*Our renaissance isn't just because we've got more dairy cows. We've got the same amount of cows now that we had in 1910. But this time instead of it being a little farmer with twenty cows and his wife helping with the milking, you've got conglomerates forming dairy farms with two thousand cows on them. Instead of lots of tiny little dairy companies all over the province, you've got one big new progressive dairy company. So it's all part of a renaissance, a new beginning for Invercargill and Southland.*

*This renaissance has a very strong flavour of celebration. It's heritage buildings, writers, the film-making industry, having a local television company so the locals can see themselves and their kids playing footie on the weekends. All that lifts the area. We are starting to explore all sorts of other areas that aren't associated generally with provincial towns, like artistic development – Shakespeare in the Park and all sorts of cultural events. We've just bought the house where Invercargill's famous son, Dan Davin, grew up. The front two rooms are going to be a little museum. The back two rooms we'll have as a writers' residence. They'll give lectures, attend schools and teach writing.*

*We built an Olympic-sized swimming pool. The Olympic Games happened in Sydney but the Italian team couldn't find* a swimming pool anywhere in Sydney. So they came to Invercargill, and that gave us a great international boost. Our netball team won the national championships three times in a row but the consultants told us the biggest stadium we could build here would be for two courts for a city of 50,000 people. We built nine courts under one roof and it turned into a brilliant stadium, where we've had events that we never imagined could happen in Invercargill.

Government grants are on a population basis. That worked against us with a declining population. There was an enormous pressure to centralise into the big urban centres. All the big government departments we had, like the railways and the post office, literally thousands of civil servants and middle-class Southlanders, left our city overnight when restructuring took place. Where there's a disadvantage there must be an advantage. Let's start looking at potential benefits from the fact that we are being penalised and we discovered that every student in New Zealand gets a $10,000 fee from the government. Our overheads down here are so low compared with the major cities, so we could provide education at a far better price than the more expensive cities in the north. So we got the licensing trust to agree to pay the fees, attracted 700 more students by abolishing fees and got the extra government grants on each student, which more than covered the cost.

Then there was transport. To try and unblock Auckland and the gridlock in the big cities, they introduced a seventy cent subsidy for everybody who climbs on to a bus. The cost of running buses is so low down here that we could make our buses free. Then we could get the government subsidy and make a profit as well. The people benefited, the city benefited and we deserve it. As far as I'm concerned we are entitled to everything we can get.

Tourism is a growing industry. So a whole building got turned into a backpackers hotel and it's been doing very well.

*The motels and the hotels and the bed and breakfasts have all been doing well as a result of all the events going on around the city. We have become very good at attracting conferences. They will come if you've got facilities, good sporting facilities, things they can see. We've attracted the New Zealand National Headmasters Conference, the New Zealand School Trustees Conference, all sorts of things. In a town of 50,000 people when we get a conference of eight or nine hundred people, it has a big impact on the local economy.*

*In tourism we tend to attract the free independent travellers. We don't get a lot of the coach tours coming to Invercargill. They tend to head towards Queenstown which is a couple of hours up the road. But we still get a lot of benefits from the tremendous tourism potential of Queenstown. They get a million visitors a year, and there are only 20,000 people out there to look after them. So a lot of our young people go up in the holidays and work in the hotels in the tourism industry. We do the wine tanks for all the vineyards that are growing up in the area. The boats that take tourists around Milford Sound are all built in Invercargill. So we get a lot of the downstream benefits of tourism. The tourists that come here tend to be those who are on their own. We're the gateway to Stewart Island and that's in the process of becoming New Zealand's newest national park. Which immediately puts it into the international arena.*

*We have to maintain the momentum. I think we can expand this pool of wealth that we've got down here. Then we can introduce ideas that will wow the socks off this country.*

Matt Hodson is the Carnot, the Organiser of Victory, Tim Shadbolt the inspiration. Tim supplies the impetus, Matt the organisation financed by local authorities and businesses through Project Southland. He came to New Zealand from Britain to play rugby and stayed to develop it.

# Matt Hodson

*I'm encouraging businesses to come. If you are going to set up a business in areas such as engineering, fishing or agriculture, Invercargill or Southland is the place to do it. We've got access to all the international markets through the airport. We've got a lot of skilled people, and a lot of people here prepared to take semi-skilled type jobs as well. We've got a really supportive community which is one of the most important things.*

*We have just undertaken a big promotion throughout New Zealand to get people to come down and fill the five hundred or so job vacancies we have. That's been a community initiative, with the public body and promotion people, the business community, the media, the newspaper, all together, a whole community effort. That's what I think Southland and Invercargill has to offer. A strong community, strong support systems, and the infrastructure of a city much, much larger than what we're in. Plus it's a great place to live.*

*The Southern Institute of Technology has been very successful in marketing itself, and it's starting to develop a reputation and planning for the future, offering a mixture of information technology and entrepreneurial science. We've got a very strong engineering cluster here, through businesses created by Southland growing and developing with the aluminium smelter, which is the eighth-largest in the world, just down the road.*

*We've got to diversify because for too long Southland has been reliant on commodity prices. That's great recently because the dollar has been weak, commodity prices have been high and we've really benefited. But we do need to diversify. That means strength in education which is absolutely crucial. It means increasing the impact of information technology throughout the business community.*

*Southland's time is now. It's a convergence of some really lucky factors that have all happened at once. Mayor Tim's enthusiasm rubs off on everybody. We've got a really proactive and innovative CEO at the Southern Institute of Technology with a zero fee scheme that caught everybody in New Zealand completely unawares. We've got clever real estate agents. We've got good marketing people. We've got excellent engineers. We've got a wonderful community and we've also got a time where a lot of people are thinking throughout New Zealand and throughout the world about downshifting, about the fact that quality of life is just as important as the money that they earn. We don't have the nightlife that Wellington or Auckland or Sydney or London or Paris does, but what we do have is a great place to grow up, a great place to do lots of different things.*

Land sales are promoted by Southland agencies. Farmers get advice on what will grow most profitably from Topo Climate, a pioneering free service backed by the Crop Advisory Service, which advises on crops and market prospects.

## Craig Howard

*Topo Climate was designed to map the soils and climates throughout Southland. That's the data. Once they've got that, the crop centre here tells farmers and land users how they can use that information. It's difficult to tell someone what to do. We give them recommendations. We give them advice and give them as much information as they need so that they are comfortable making their own decisions.*

*There's a lot of flower blocks going in around the place though some farmers think flowers are effeminate. It has been more difficult over the last two years because dairy farming has gone nuts in this district, and sheep and beef farming is making a lot more money than it was.*

*A lot of people come in here and say I can grow this or I can grow that. I say, well, I don't really care. It's what does the market want. We have to be market driven which is a change in thinking for a lot of people. It can be quite difficult for people to get their head around that. They want to grow something but if the market doesn't want it there is no point in them doing it.*

*Our organisation is unique, we are community funded, community based, the advice I give is free. We're about a community service and that's what we exist for. If we get these little units up and running all over Southland I will do myself out of a job in another three or four years. I won't be very happy but it will be a success for the organisation.*

The result is exotic crops all over Southland, such as Japanese plums (umeboshi) grown for the first time in New Zealand, by Ian Stewart near Alexandra, a farm entrepreneur of the new Kiwi kind.

## Ian Stewart

*I'm not an expert in farming. I'm a businessman. So I thought I could apply some of those principles to working on the land. We purchased this forty-acre block six years ago, and started off with a concept of having a large olive grove because all the olive oil is being imported. So there is a market to produce oil for the New Zealand market. Then to avoid having to put too many eggs in one basket we diversified into cut flowers for the export market. They are all sent to exporters in Auckland, and distributed through agents to different parts of the world. Some go to Japan, some go to Korea, some go to America. It depends where their marketplace is on the day.*

*It's all a question of what to do with this very dry arid Central Otago land. We got the idea of growing umeboshi. We were looking for something that we could do with this type of land, and we knew that Central Otago is renowned for stone fruit as well as pip fruit, with the cherries, the apricots and the peaches. Someone had just come back from Japan and said umeboshi (pickled plums) are very popular over there. They fetch a good price.*

*So we had to go for Japanese plums, and it was a very difficult procedure to get the trees here. By the time we got them through quarantine and were informed by the bureaucrats that we could now have them I had to pay an enormous charge for getting them down fast freight to our site. Ten days later they ended up dried, withered sticks, looking as though they were all going to die. We broke the land in and planted them. All but four grew. We were really delighted with that.*

*We're concentrating on them to build that market up now we are quite confident that we can grow a good product. It's quite large when it starts off on the tree, but from there we pickle it and dry it out in the sun and then soak it back in its own brine for the marketplace. It's a delicacy, almost unique to the Japanese people. It's very salty and also very tart. Once it's put through that pickling process, with our secret ingredient, it becomes very palatable. We would need enormous volumes to work into the Japanese market – fifty, a hundred tonnes a month for the supermarket type of sale – so we concentrate on supplying the delicacy to the Japanese residents of New Zealand and Australia. There are a lot of them and they are quite happy to pay a good price for a good product, and we are told by many Japanese that it's a superior product to the home-grown ones in Japan. We're in negotiations now with the Japanese to sell it in Japan, putting the product on their marketplace out of the season.*

Development in Southland isn't all agricultural, though that is currently the most profitable area. New industrial projects flourish and one of the most successful is Stabicraft, making aluminium boats for a world market from an idea generated by Bluff fishermen. Its founder and MD is Paul Adams.

# Paul Adams

*I didn't start out building boats. I had had an apprenticeship as a coach-builder, a similar activity. The boat-building side came from some Bluff fishermen who were looking at the stability of little rubber inflatables but without the problem of the inflatables deflating and wearing out. They wanted a boat that was stable, that was safe, that was durable, and rubber is not that durable in their sort of conditions. So they came up with the idea of aluminium tubes. We took the idea and ran with it.*

*I started out with two people, working out of a small shed; a couple of welders, an overdraft of $500 and feeling pretty nervous about breaking into the world. The initial sales came from word of mouth from commercial fishermen, eelers, and some serious recreationalists. Then it moved on to more recreationalists, and our customer base has grown to all ranges of people. Stabicraft are not the most beautiful-looking boats. But they're very stable and very safe. The pontoons are sealed off and full of air and you can fill the boat full of water and it won't sink. That's quite a big part of the decision when you've got mum and the kids to consider.*

*You'd have to pay me a lot of money to move to Auckland. Two years ago when we had some consultants coming in to ask us questions about our business, they said would you consider moving to Auckland or one of the bigger cities. We said no. The reason was lifestyle. We've lived here all our life, family, friends, all those sorts of things. In hindsight it may have been easier if we were not in Invercargill. Production skills, managing people, financial people and some of the people with expert skills are not plentiful in Invercargill. But it's more fun here.*

Invercargill is also the home of one of New Zealand's most successful car plants – something rare since local assembly stopped – but Barry Leitch builds and rebuilds racing cars, Rolls-Royces, Bentleys, anything that comes to him from anywhere in the world.

# Barry Leitch

*I started racing go-carts when I was about fourteen, and raced carts for about ten years. I met my wife, she raced as well. When we got married and bought a house I couldn't afford to go racing. So we pulled out of it and after a couple of years I wanted a car that was a little bit different. So I bought a Mark II Jaguar and restored it. I'm a registered electrician not a motor mechanic, though my father's a motor mechanic, and I learned an awful lot from him.*

*I restored the Mark II Jaguar and I suppose I was lucky. I won a lot of awards in shows with it. A few years later I wanted a sports car and I couldn't afford one, so I built one. I was lucky enough to be able to copy a Lotus 7. Some of the people here decided they wanted them as well, so I suppose my little backyard business started then, building cars. I used to build under the bedroom. We had a two-storey house with a garage. I was still working as an electrician at that stage and I built my first six or seven cars in my spare time.*

*Then we looked around for somewhere that we could shift to with a workshop and we bought this place, just out of town. It used to be a blackcurrant farm, and this was the sorting shed. We turned it into a workshop and started building cars when I started working for myself in 1988. It was a struggle for a long time. I was working by myself but we wanted to keep a cap on our quality. Everything that goes out the door has got to be good enough to be our own.*

*So we have slowly built up from working by myself until we got to having five people. Now I'm looking at taking on somebody else and there will be six of us, but I don't want to get too big. I'd rather do a good job than a big job. We advertise in the* New Zealand Classic Car *magazine and I've got an agent in Australia that sells our cars and he advertises as well. A few years ago we had a Japanese guy come and ask if he could sell our cars in Japan, so he started buying our cars and sold them quite successfully in Japan until the Japanese downturn. We don't sell our cars to America but we do a lot of restoration work out of the States so it's expanded from being just a local business into working for people all over the world.*

Gore is the home of another pioneering venture. New Zealand's first and biggest Internet chemist. It works out of Mark La Hood's pharmacy.

## Mark La Hood

*Fifty years ago, when my grandfather wanted to reach a broad audience, he got on a horse and cart and moved round the area. Then the Internet came along, we decided that maybe this would be worth a show. We started from a back office at home, and then grew to offices upstairs and a staff of five people.*

*Initially we had a lot of problems with sourcing enough stock. A lot of our suppliers were dubious. Some of them just wouldn't supply us, but now some of them are very happy. We spend a lot of money advertising and we have found all sorts of advertising avenues – search engines, adverts and American Airlines magazines.*

*We've made a lot of mistakes, but we're a little bit wiser for it now. About eighty percent of our sales go offshore and twenty percent of it is in New Zealand. It's amazing, the emails we get from people round the world who thank us. Our Internet business is almost as big as this pharmacy here, but it's growing much faster. Probably by the end of this year we'll be much bigger than the pharmacy. We're selling a lot of pharmaceuticals, vitamin supplements, cosmetics, haircare, camera equipment, binoculars, virtually anything that you would tend to find in a pharmacy or cosmetics store. What's one New Zealand dollar will often be approximately one US dollar. So the customer can save considerable sums. One of our big advantages is the New Zealand dollar at the moment.*

> *It's needed a lot of Kiwi ingenuity. We have spent hours burning the midnight oil but Gore has been a good place to run it. The cost structures are very cheap. It's a handy place to live. We can walk home for lunch and come back to work after we've had time at home. New Zealand Post have been tremendous. They send vans each day to pick up our parcels. Gore hasn't been a hindrance at all.*

Invercargill is now an exporter of chocolate from the Seriously Good Chocolate Company, formed by Jane Stanton and expanding rapidly.

## Jane Stanton

*I've always liked cooking but I turned diabetic and couldn't eat the produce any more. So I started making for friends. I had a friend that was a bit down in the dumps and I thought, how can I cheer her up? So I took along some chocolate truffles. She was a hairdresser and unbeknown to me she started handing them out to friends. The phone started going at home and people wanted to know if they could buy some.*

*I was teaching at the time and I worked out I was $90 down the tubes and I couldn't afford to keep working to give people chocolate. Keith and I talked and we realised we might be onto something. So I started trialling the different flavours. As I was teaching, one of the tricks was if they did their homework they got a treat. A chocolate. So I started trialling the different flavours on the students. Then I got this idea of blending in the wine. I just matched the wine to the flavour. Being diabetic gives me a very high sense of taste, so I know if something is going to work or not straight away.*

*I tootled off to Gibston Valley in the school holidays and said 'I could make you wine chocolates, and just to show you, here are some' because I had swiped a bottle of the Gibston Valley pinot noir out of Keith's cellar. Ross McKay met me and said 'we would really love to do this'. So we started talking colours and boxes. We were quite thrilled about Gibston. So we took the Gibston Valley and other wine chocolates to Melbourne. They were received extremely well.*

*We opened next door in October and now the factory here is six times as large and the showroom seven times as large as the original. We have a good product and the thing that's been great for us is Southland. Southland people are very proud and we knew if a flavour took off in Southland, because they're very conservative, it would go anywhere. For New Zealand we do a hokey-pokey chocolate truffle, for the Japanese they love the wine chocolates. We do the kiwifruit because that's the thing to do out of New Zealand. We trial everything out of the shop here. It's flying out, and basically export is our biggest market.*

Local raw materials are a competitive advantage for many local industries, from textiles to sheepskin rugs. Nowhere more so than in Graham Maxwell's fur business built on dead possums. The conservation argument has destroyed fur coat making but doesn't apply to that New Zealand pest. At least Graham hoped so when he set up New Zealand's first new furriers in Winton after years of decline.

## Graham Maxwell

*I'm now the only trained furrier left in New Zealand. I was looking for an out of school job when I was living in Christchurch and applied for a job as an after-school delivery boy for a furrier, and the owner of the business asked me if I would like to take it on seriously and complete an apprenticeship.*

*He had a very good reputation for high-quality products and what I learnt was to produce the very top end of the market. I started my apprenticeship and because it had been so long prior to that that anyone had done one in New Zealand, there was a lot of rigmarole to go through to become firstly a bespoke tailor and then a furrier.*

*It took me seven years to do my apprenticeship. When I first started in the fur trade it was very buoyant and we had a wonderful market throughout New Zealand. Then the environmental issue came and people felt less comfortable wearing fur. So it became less popular and quite rightly so.*

*There's been a twenty-five-year gap in the industry and no one has really had any interest or enthusiasm to take on the trade. I've been involved in a variety of things but I never forgot the trade. It's something like riding a bike. Once you learn to do it you do it and remember it. I was really nervous coming back into the trade to see if I could remember how to do all the things that needed to be done. But we've got there.*

*My partner, Rosemary, and myself decided that we would set up and produce a range of fur products and see if we could create a business from it. We use two kinds of fur. Technically one is not a fur, it's a wool, it's a by-product from a lamb called Broadtail, and the other one is the possum. New Zealand is suffering a huge plague of possums. We have around seventy million and they breed at the rate of around twenty million a year. They have a gestation period of sixteen or seventeen days and because of that they fluctuate between seventy and ninety million. The ones that you see dead on the side of the road constitute around twenty million a year, so our best efforts are keeping the population pretty static.*

*The Department of Conservation statistics say that they estimate they're eating 22,000 tonnes of foliage a day. So as possum fur becomes acceptable, the skin values will go up. That means it's economically viable for the trappers to go out and trap them because the good skins are predominantly in the most rugged areas of the country, but with more skins coming in, more product being made, then it benefits New Zealand.*

*We've been absolutely ecstatic with the response from the*

*marketplace. We were fortunate enough to win an award judged by some major designers in New Zealand and the acceptance has been really strong from a lot of the public. We are working with people in the States and also in Milan in Italy. We want to revive this industry and we are not producing grandma's old coat. The things we are making are very modern, up-to-date and fashionable on the world stage.*

Everywhere in Southland is on the move, even the remotest parts like Tuatapere, forty twisting kilometres from Invercargill. It had been harder hit than most by the decline of timber. Today it exemplifies the Southland spirit and is fighting back. The first round is the establishment of a new tourist walk to bring the tourists – the Tuatapere Hump Ridge Track – opened by the Prime Minister in November 2001. Anne McCracken, a local, and professor Harold Marshall, who retired to Tuatapere to fish, are joint chairs of the development committee.

## Anne McCracken

*We've been planning this grand opening since April to bring people to Tuatapere to celebrate with us eleven years of planning and hard work, finding some money and getting our dream to fruition. It's taken us years of work, meeting legislative requirements, and working through the issues. We even had a little hiccup with the name, which we had to go back and consult on – $3400 extra to put that little word 'Ridge' in. Then we had to apply for a resource consent which was granted in December 2000. So we only started building the track in January last year. Now here we are, up and running. On 1 November last year we put the first walkers on the track. They're back and just fizzing.*

## Harold Marshall

*Development follows ideas. The people here are an extraordinary community of doers. Everybody buckles in and they are prepared to do things. The ideas just simply flow from that. We're looking at organic farming, at a farmers' market, into putting on music and cultural events to bring people in from Invercargill and the whole of Southland. I've started growing four acres of hydrangeas for export.*

*People are doers here, they get stuck in. We want Tuatapere to develop and to be flourishing, to have the infrastructure like its school and its hospital. This is the spirit of Southland here in Tuatapere and we don't want to lose that. A slow build-up of people will be great. We don't want lots. We'll share our secret. Come in and have a look, stay a little while, that would be great. We've got some land to sell I have to say, be quick, because it's going up in price.*

So is the rest of Southland, once the most boring part of New Zealand, now a classic example of the new dynamics of a nation on the move, driven by the ingenuity of extraordinary Kiwis. The Number-Eight-Fencing-Wire mentality has turned into a whole system of economics.

## Chapter Six

# Central Otago

If Wordsworth hadn't suffered from the crippling disadvantage of being a Pom he could have lived in Central Otago among lakes lovelier than Cumbria's. He might have had to write about lupins rather than daffodils, and Dove Cottage would have had a corrugated iron roof and been situated by Hawea because Queenstown is outside the price range of poet or peasant. He'd have had to mend fences and drive a four-wheel-drive rather than wandering lonely as a cloud. The locals would have gossiped and joked to his face about his ambivalent relationship with his sister, Mary. Yet isolation makes everything or anything acceptable to neighbours, and allows funny folk to follow their interests, even William's High Tory politics. Here people have a rarity value.

Yet a Kiwi Wordsworth would have been sterile. No dramatic events to inspire his *Prelude*. A cold, austere landscape in which man is alien, not a part. Central Otago inspires painters and photographers, and boosts the profits of Kodak and Fuji, but does nothing for poets or writers. So New Zealand has no Lake Poets, no Otago School of Writing, not even an Otago farm soap, the everyday story of Otago folk. Only an occasional *Country Calendar*.

Which is paradoxical. Otago, as well as being the most beautiful part of New Zealand, is also its fastest growing: a dynamic, changing economy thrusting up in a heritage museum of old New Zealand where even the gold rush remains are now part of the tourist plant. Otago is fertile with its spreading vineyards but barren in its empty hillsides. It is rural but also industrial with Manapouri, Roxburgh and the Clyde Dam, New Zealand's powerhouses. It is rugged but sophisticated, for the wine industry is the heights of sophistication; barren, but also New Zealand's fruit basket. A land for tourist thrills and spills and roaring jet boats, but also quiet waters, lonely walks, and the contemplative glow of retirement. Otago is whatever you want it to be: heartland for Dunedinites; adventureland for tourists; safe playground for serious money, all in one of the most beautiful places on earth.

Those from Otago, and the Dunedinites who kept it their secret garden for years to keep other people out, have a more romantic view. Otago is their version of heaven. Grahame Sydney, who has immortalised its stark landscapes, sees Otago as his promised land.

## Grahame Sydney

*The older I get, the worse I become in this territory, I don't want to be anywhere else. I'm trying to find ways now, and I have since 1974, of making my art, making my life out of what I love most. What I found I love most, and what I literally dreamed about, and what preoccupies me when it comes is thinking of images, thinking of paintings that I want to leave behind when I go, the things that matter, the things I care about most. This connection, this anchoring in Dunedin, in this province and Central Otago in particular, it just seems to be getting stronger in me all the time. I can't help it. You don't work for other people, it's an utterly selfish occupation, a terribly egocentric business. I work for me alone. It's a gift to realise that you are doing things that other people might value. I'm trying to find out ways of saying about where I belong, and why it matters to me. You never think about that at the time. That's the life of paintings after they leave this room. The rest of New Zealand could be cut loose from Otago. I wouldn't mind if it floated away. Whenever I come home, and I'm flying south, I love it when I cross the Waitaki. I can't explain it. It's just a mad parochial connection which has become more and more powerful with time, and that's now what fuels me.*

Sam Neill feels the same, coming back whenever his international acting career allows him.

## Sam Neill

*If I had to give up the day job I could happily do a number of things in Central Otago. This is the place where I would feel most planted. I am decidedly an Otago man. My family has been here since 1860 and this is the landscape that I relate to most of all in the world. Although there are many places I like, this is the place that I love. I do live here and I commute to whatever work it is that I'm doing. Down the road there I'm growing a number of herbs, including lavender. Now I'm distilling lavender oil, a beautiful thing to do. I'm now growing cherries, by accident really. An old codger I came across many years ago said, 'if you want to grow grapes look for where the apricots are' and in this particular valley they grow some of the best apricots in the world, and it necessarily follows that some of the best wine in the world comes from here as well.*

A revival of gold dredging is planned, but at the moment the gold rush is in wine and particularly the new fashion, pinot noir. The first vines in Central Otago were planted by a Frenchman who'd come up with the gold rushes. He planted vines in Clyde and made some wine for a few years but drifted away. Nothing then happened for decades, though the prospect was always there. Sam Neill's father, who'd served in Greece in the war, would remark as he drove the family up to Otago that it was wine-growing country like Greece: 'Someone should grow grapes.'

Eventually someone did. Alan Bradey, Ed Gibston and Rolf Mills dispute the title of Otago's first wine-growers but Verdon Burgess, who started his Black Ridge vineyard in 1982, has the strongest claim.

## Verdon Burgess

*I originally came up from Invercargill to build two houses as a carpenter. Then someone else spotted that I was working really well and said, 'Do you think you could come and build my house?' And someone else put their hand up. So all of a sudden I had a full-time job up here.*

*I loved the rocks of Central Otago. They were fascinating. Every weekend I would be away up into the hills shooting rabbits and going for bike rides. Another carpenter introduced me to this block of land here. In Invercargill there were never any rocks, so when I got into this block, ah, wow, did I have some fun. I had the block. So what was I going to do with it? Other than grapes, the most economic thing was cherries, but it was uncertain how much frost they could take, they would only use fourteen acres. Grapes would push it up the hill further to give me twenty-one acres.*

*I didn't know much about wine. Up to 1980 I had drunk six bottles of wine and six ton of beer. So I was definitely from Southland. Six months later I had turned round and drank six dozen of wine and very little beer. It was a risk. No one had grown much wine in Central Otago but there was enough research already done. All I did was pick up on that information and one night someone said in the pub that I should grow nothing but classics. I hadn't heard of what a classic was so I had to do research and there's only about six of them in New Zealand. We picked all of those six and selected the areas to put them in the vineyard. We found out quite a few of the clones were really old clones that actually did really well.*

*The first harvest was lovely. In 1985 we had our first lot of grapes. So I said, I'll see if I can actually make wine. The next year we did the same thing. For three years running I actually made the best vinegar in New Zealand. Those three bottles are still sitting up in the winery there to remind me why we employ a winemaker. By talking to the winemaker about the problems he's having, I can take that back out onto the vineyard and do better for the following season by providing what is best for the plants.*

*It's actually growing in rock. We've got four inches or a hundred millimetres of topsoil. From there down it's harder and harder rock. So it's actually sucking all the goodness out of the rock. Because we get so little rain we're actually irrigating our plants through the whole of the growing season. But we're only giving them two litres of water per plant per day.*

*Sales sort of happened all by itself. The word got out about this crazy idiot and the most southern vineyard in the world planted amongst rock. I didn't set out to set that up. I set out to make a commercial enterprise out of growing grapes on the information that was available. That told me it was going to be all right. It was going to be commercial. I had the idea that there was only going to be one vineyard in the whole of Central Otago. Now there are ninety vineyards and thirty-two wineries. The competition helps because now there are more names out there and more advertising dollars going out to promote the area.*

*When they come into Central Otago they say 'you've got to go to Black Ridge. You've got to see what he's done there. It's unbelievable'. It's top of the range wine. We are definitely a boutique winery and that is what we are aiming for. Our total production off this block when we're in full production, which will be about another six or seven years, is going to be four and a half thousand cases all told. So you're looking at sixty thousand bottles at maximum. It will be nice to make a profit but it's been good. I've enjoyed every minute of it.*

Odd to call a vineyard by such a hard, unattractive name as Black Ridge, particularly when Verdon is so green and attractive, but *chacun à son goût*, and with earlier vintages like Carpenter's Groin, Verdon has already put humour onto labels. Now he takes it more seriously, using a graceful, tall bottle unique to Otago. Profitability is a long time coming (the current estimate is next year) but Verdon Burgess has proved that Otago is wine country and set an example many began to follow.

Big money moved in. So did wine enthusiasts like Sam Neill who, like Verdon Burgess, has a day job to support him while he pursues his interest.

## Sam Neill

*I lived in England for quite a few years and I was lucky enough to live round the corner from an excellent wine merchant who got me interested in burgundy, and you could buy at his shop a really good premier burgundy for anything between ten and thirty quid. I was earning a bit of dough by that point for the first time in my life. So I spent quite a lot of it in his little shop and developed a taste for wine. I don't regret it at all.*

*When I started growing out here I was jumping on the bandwagon. One of the most important mentors in my life was Rolf Mills. He died last year and he was a lovely, lovely man. He planted probably the most beautiful vineyards in the world at Rippon and I thought, well, if old Rolf can do it, why can't I? So I bought some land and the rest is history really.*

*These vineyards are on the edge of viability. They have to be to grow that grape successfully. It's a very risky business. The Central Otago pinot is always going to be extremely difficult because there is so much labour involved and it is always going to be an expensive product. There's not a lot we can do about it. What we all need to be mindful of, and I certainly am, is that it exports. It's very important to develop your markets overseas because the domestic market is clearly saturated already.*

*It doesn't worry me so much, but if I was, for instance, a middle-aged couple that was going to sink my life savings and pension in a little vineyard, then I would think again because one of the things we tend to do in New Zealand is jump on bandwagons, and everyone does the same thing at the same time, so we have all these classic blowouts like goats and kiwifruit. Wine may easily be one of those. That is an anxiety, but nevertheless it is a quality product. If you get a good brand on your product I don't think there is that much concern. But people will go broke, there is no question about that.*

If winegrowers do go broke they can't afford to seek refuge in Queenstown, now one of the most expensive housing areas in New Zealand. It takes serious money to live in Queenstown. When I first went there in 1960 it was a tatty little town straggling out into a collection of sheds along the lake-front, hired out by their owners to holiday-makers in the summer and skiers in the winter. The population was perhaps 2500, its visitors mainly walkers and skiers. A holiday escape, but with far more limited opportunities than now. Trips went to the head of the lake on the *Earnslaw*, then a working steamer carrying more livestock than passengers, which ferried people there to chew inedible venison. There was climbing for the suicidal, and skiing at Coronet Peak: a pound a day for hire and instruction – I splashed out on one full day (no halves, no reductions for university staff) and hated it.

Yet I loved Queenstown and Otago, where so many of the university staff spent weekends and holidays, nominally to think, in fact to get away. At that time some university staff could afford 'cribs', their name for sheds, in Otago. Dunedin's rich owned sizeable properties. Maurice Joel, descendant of Vogel, Dunedin solicitor and member of the University Council invited people to his 'bach' in Queenstown; we described it as a palace, but it was small and poverty-stricken compared with the luxurious premises going up now as people build ever more lavish houses to sell on to rich Americans, Japanese, or anyone.

Tourism has transformed Queenstown, bringing casinos, the cupola and the cable car, Japanese hotels, sushi bars and a hundred ways to die, including poisoning. The *Earnslaw*, now re-engineered but belching diesel, provides dinner and dance, running only as far as Walter Peak Station and back. Retirement villages multiply. Arrowtown is a boutique town and Queenstown placarded with ads for white-water rafting, jet-boating, bungee jumping, parapunting. This is the New Zealand thrill industry. Each year a million visitors pass through Queenstown, usually quickly, for few can afford to stay more than a few days at peak periods. They buy expensive mountaineering gear from the outdoor clothing, boot and equipment boutiques, then parade up and down the shopping mall slung with ropes, clasps and crampons. Some even carry ice-picks as walking sticks, as if on their way to meet Trotsky rather than looking for a sushi bar.

The first run-holder sold it to the government in 1862 and was paid £10,000. At today's prices that would allow him to stay for just over a month in Eichardt's, once a rowdy pub, now an élite hotel where sheikhs and drug dealers can afford to stay, but ordinary mortals do better getting an estimate before buying a drink.

No man has done more to shape this booming tourist metropolis – which would be a Kiwi St Tropez if only Lake Wakatipu weren't so cold and the country around so stark – than Queenstown's four-times mayor, Warren Cooper, 'One-Coat Warren' to his Labour opponents.

Warren Cooper came to Queenstown with his parents to run a pub in 1955. His first job was as assistant janitor at the borough camping ground. Being naturally bolshy, he quit because they wouldn't pay him time and a half at Easter. He stayed in the town, worked and saw the future.

## Warren Cooper

*You could see development was going to come. It was a beautiful place but it suffered from distance. It was just at the start of the wide-bodied jets. I went on the early tourist missions so I knew that within the first three or four years it was going to be a high-class resort area. You had to keep promoting, you had to get out there and sell. We had to go to Christchurch, Auckland and then Sydney.*

Whether as mayor, minister or MP he has always promoted Queenstown. When the fall of Muldoon checked a never-very-successful career he came back as mayor.

## Warren Cooper

*We had farmers farming around here trying to provide green paddocks and clean sheep for overseas business, but not making any profit. They needed to subdivide to survive, so their kids could get a go. I've always believed in opportunity so I set out to develop it and let people subdivide.*

Warren's planning is free market, like his economics. The market will regulate itself because if development makes a mess people won't come. Minimal restraints but maximum market with no attempt to impose a common style requires buildings to blend in, or requires a return in investment in public facilities from developers keen to get into Queenstown. The council could coerce them. It doesn't, it gives in because with a million visitors and only a few thousand ratepayers, it needs the rates.

## Warren Cooper

*There were certain places you could allow development, and others that were absolutely sacrosanct. Subsequent to that, of course, some people got the impression that I said yes to everything, that I was the one that gave all the resource consents. Absolutely not. I was always wanting to be a facilitator. When I was a kid it was always the case of giving your next-door neighbour an opportunity. But it's absolutely untrue that it was easy to get planning permission. In fact, it has not been as easy here as in many other places. This idea that we wouldn't notify everything so that everybody had a say about it – we did more notifying than most local authorities in New Zealand. There wasn't a lot of opposition. There will always be development. It won't take place overnight, but there will be a point in time when those people that want to come to Queenstown could be turned off if it becomes garish, noisy, has the wrong sort of environmental quality altogether. The market finally will say, not a judge in the Environment Court, not Warren Cooper, not Sam Neill; the market will finally say, as it does in all the resort areas on this planet, that's enough.*

Exactly the wrong approach, says Sam Neill. Unique landscapes should be preserved, not become the playground of market forces.

## Sam Neill

*Central Otago is very important to me and this is a very unique part of the world. You only have to look around to see that. The Wakatipu Basin where I live is a landscape of national, if not international, importance. The previous council started to lose all control over what was a desirable development and what was not. They gave permission to all sorts of things that are now being built. Suburbs around Queenstown are creeping into the Wakatipu Basin.*

*I believe that to be wrong. It would not be permitted in any other sensible part of the world. If you go to England to the Lake District, you can't build suburbs there. You can't build suburbs in the Cotswolds and you shouldn't be able to build suburbs in the Wakatipu Basin for exactly the same reason. If you start building a suburb outside of a place like Queenstown it takes a lot of people to build a suburb. Those people have got to live somewhere so you build a suburb for them, and now everyone has got houses, but now you need jobs for those people so you have to build another suburb, and so it goes on until eventually you just have a place that's covered in one big suburb. The place is knackered and you've lost sight of what was there originally – that's a particular landscape that is absolutely special.*

*The same thing happens with tourism. Tourism is a very important part of the economy up here and has been for many years, but how many tourists are desirable? For years they've said, 'Look, there's a shortage of beds for tourists, let's build a big hotel.' They build a big hotel and suddenly there is not enough tourists to fill those beds and there are spare beds around town. So they say, well, we've got to get more tourists in because we've got empty beds. So they spend a lot of money getting more tourists in and suddenly there is not enough beds, so they build another big hotel and so it goes on.*

*Ultimately you have to make a decision. Enough is enough. This is as much as the place can absorb. There are as many tourists as we can handle. Now has anyone asked the question how many tourists are desirable in a place like Queenstown? They haven't. The idea is that progress is getting more and more people in, making more and more money, this will be good for everybody, let's build more and more houses because that's good for the economy, and ultimately the place will end up – and it's in danger of already being so – absolutely rogered by that sort of short-sightedness and greed.*

Pure NIMBYism retorts Cooper. The objectors have got their stake. Now they want to exclude everyone else.

## Warren Cooper

*There was a small coterie of people who came here and actually got what they wanted through subdivision but then decided that it had gone too far because their view was being affected, the typical NIMBY group. We've got Sam Neill leading them. They've put up this straw man to do that and I think he did an effective job, but he's complained mainly about it where he sees it. But he doesn't complain about it in other places. I've got this feeling that we have to share and there has to be opportunity for others. They believe that the opportunity shouldn't exist in their back yard. We're not growing in an unlimited fashion, we're growing according to the principles of the Resource Management Act. In the last few months it's been the Environment Court in New Zealand that has been more flexible on five occasions than the council were. The council decision was taken to appeal and a more liberal approach was given by the Environment Court. You never hear that from the NIMBYers.*

*There are areas here, including these beautiful ranges, this park, that park down there, that are totally sacrosanct and will never be touched. But there is a liability to understand quite clearly that where development has been put into the district scheme it will take place, those areas will change. This is a magnet and a mecca for people who love beautiful places. I live here. I came back here because I love beautiful things. We ask the developers to respect the aesthetics and the environment quality of this superb area. It's got more expensive but if you want to move it further upmarket and make it more élite then stop the development. Then Sam Neill's plot will be worth twice as much next year. The message is you have got to have balance.*

## Sam Neill

*Some of my opponents would say, Sam Neill, he's an élitist, he's made enough money and it's all right for him, but what about the other people? But actually it's not germane to the argument. The debate is about whether it's good for the landscape or not. I really want to save that place in Central Otago, not because I live there, obviously I have a stake in the place and it's close to my heart, but I think all the people that live there haven't gone to live there as a suburb, they've gone to live there because it is a special place with unique qualities. If you build over those qualities those things have gone. It's also for our children, for New Zealanders in general, who like to go there.*

Otago is changing for the worse in the eyes of Grahame Sydney, though he's prepared to exempt the wine industry, even Sam Neill's shed.

## Grahame Sydney

*We shouldn't be yearning for Mediterranean here, we should be yearning for Central Otago. I love the fact that the wine industry is here and doing so well. I hate the fact that Central Otago is greening, with irrigation and forestry. That's taking away a terrible amount from what its true beauties are and turning it into nothing more than economy. I am sickened by the cancerous growth of some of the tourist towns in areas where I think development could have been much more widely controlled to make a much better legacy for the future.*

In Cooper's eyes there is protection enough and nothing will undermine the splendour. But demand must be coped with.

## Warren Cooper

*I think you probably will have houses all along the hillside. I think you'll have elegant homes and apartments but it will be a replacement of one dwelling with three or four on the same site. You will have a higher density and you'll have right across the park these vast mountain areas that are totally sacrosanct and, in my opinion, should be no-go areas for development. It's true that they are going to build round Lake Hayes but not ring it with houses. They are going to make certain there is high-quality water, high-quality development. A cap goes on it when you can't get any more sewage treatment or water supply.*

New Zealand's adventure capital is a land of thrills and spills. Parascending and jet-skiing are both inadequately regulated in a free market dicing with death in which, amazingly, nearly everyone survives. Jet boats are now big business. So are A. J. Hackett's bungee jumps from Kawarau Bridge, and from the cable car platform. Most adventure firms are small, one-man businesses, often run by German alpinists or French skiers. Lydia Bradley is a native, just starting her own company to turn the experience she's gained as New Zealand's foremost woman mountaineer and the first woman to climb Everest without oxygen, into an adventure business.

## Lydia Bradley

*Mountaineering was largely a male thing but it is changing hugely in New Zealand. In the guiding scene, for example, there are a lot of women participants, a few who are fully qualified and a lot climbing up through the qualification ladder. I was quite ambitious and got into mountaineering from tramping. Tramping opened up a whole lot of doors because I met all these really interesting people. People who I thought were extremely old because I was only fourteen or fifteen, a whole myriad of people, a cross-section from different work backgrounds. I found it really fascinating. I like people and mountains. Going into the mountains for me was a huge journey of discovery.*

*So I tramped and climbed for the view, for the companionship, and then being quite ambitious I went into mountaineering. I wasn't particularly good at it. I'm just strong and quite determined. I was hopeless at sports at school but as long as I could put one foot in front of the other I could do basic mountaineering. That was a huge door opening for me. I had just turned eighteen the weekend before I first climbed Mount Cook. It was so beautiful.*

*Mount Cook is a stunning mountain. It's beautiful to climb and it's exciting. I got taken up there the first time by a much better climber but we did a good route, and then in December we did the Grand Traverse which is something like a mile and a half long, along some of the ridges of Mount Cook. So I had a fantastic first summer when I was eighteen. I was scared all the time. I'm always scared on the mountains and I think that keeps you alive. Some of the people I know who have perished in the mountains were not scared and I think it's really important to be humble. You don't conquer mountains. If the weather is good enough and the conditions are good enough and you're good enough, you get up.*

*I've climbed Mount Cook ten, eleven times, something like that. It's just stunning. You can see the water on the east side of New Zealand, the water on the west side, mountains forever, and it's taken a lot of hard work – getting up at midnight and leaving at one o'clock in the morning. I hate that, but if you're high on the mountain and the sun rises and everything is pink and you've only got another couple of hours to go to the summit, it's divine, and it's scary and it's exciting and it's tiring, and then you get back, and you feel fantastic.*

I first met Lydia when she took me to the summit of the Ball Pass along with Helen Clark. Helen, fitter, younger and much more determined than I, made it over and down the other side. I was judged too clumsy and old and too much of a liability, so I came back down the way I'd gone up, guided by Lydia. The first to tell me how to do it, how to use the sticks for balance, how to distribute my load, all things our German *übergruppen-führer* should have told me on the way up but was too busy looking after Helen to do so. Poms were expendable. Now Lydia plans her own adventure company.

## Lydia Bradley

*You're selling an experience of wilderness. I call most sports 'car sports', sports that you drive to, you do and you're never that far away from your car. The experience of being away from your car, away from the road and away from other people is wonderful. We've built up this adventure industry just because we can. We have a lot of different geographical situations. We have canyons, rivers, deserts and mountains. New Zealanders are quite small-business oriented and we have lots of people who participate in those sports in a small area, so some key Queenstown-based businesses triggered it all off. Plus, of course, the famous Outward Bound business and things like that. So people come to New Zealand expecting to do what we call lightweight adventure things on their holidays. So there is bungee jumping, rafting, jet-boating, canyoning, which are one-day events, and then there is the mountaineering. Guiding in New Zealand is just taking off. People are realising that the mountains here are beautiful, they're accessible and we're quite cheap. And we've got great guides. So I'm beginning to make a living out of it. My selling point is the spirituality of the outdoors, of the wilderness. I'd like to call my company after the Maori name for the South Island, which is Te Wai Pounamu – greenstone waters. I think it is a stunning name.*

I'm up for it if she'll take zimmer frames. If she won't I can always admire Central Otago in the paintings of Grahame Sydney.

Chapter Seven

# Christchurch:
# A Godley Land

Christchurch, the city of the plain, the downright ugly, and the elegantly English, is sometimes described as Auckland for those who can't make the real thing. What it's for is a mystery, though more to me than to those who so contentedly live there: the once and would-be English denizens of a cathedral city so impressive, that Japanese visitors think it's Salisbury with a self-appointed Wizard in place of monks. It's a city of wannabe public schools like St Margaret's and Rangi Ruru, potting sheds of the New Zealand rose, which ensure that none get potted, even by alumni of that other custodial centre, Christ's College.

Christchurch is a would-be England, English snobbery and hypocrisy were imported on the First Four Ships and live on in the staid *Press* which imitates the dullest aspects of *The Times*, in the swamps of Fendalton, and the heights of Cashmere, and in backblocks inhabited by such historic names as Deans, Murchison, Elworthy and other families who interbreed with aristocracies in Hawke's Bay or the Wairarapa.

Christchurch shouldn't be taken seriously. I didn't when I was there. Nor does my old friend, Jim Hopkins, Christchurch's resident wit and raconteur, knackered chef, and philosopher of the new Kiwi monasticism: the shed. I found him personally thanking uncomprehending Japanese tourists for coming to Christchurch.

## Jim Hopkins

*Christchurch has changed for the worse, if you ask me. Look at that great monstrosity towering over the old Post Office. It was supposed to be further back, where the relationship between the two buildings might have actually worked. But, as it is, oh dear me. Look at the Chalice, that public sculpture that's just gone up. I don't think anyone quite knew where to put it. So they put it there. It's very good. If you've got a fag packet you can just chuck it in.*

*They've pedestrianised the square. They used to park up here and I can remember as a student wandering along the footpath in front of the Post Office in a duffle coat of a Saturday evening, and the bodgies and the widgies would be leaning over the bonnets of their cars sneering and jeering and taunting you, and mocking your virility and making you feel paranoid. It was wonderful. Full of life.*

*People say New Zealand is great on technology uptake. I think we're also tragically good at ideology uptake. Somebody comes up with a new theory of how to do things, and we leap at it. Like planning. Oh, we must plan. So after allowing the country to grow in a chaotic, shambolic and shed-like fashion for many years, suddenly there's this vast armada of people who know better how to organise space. This grey, sterile, lifeless void is the result. This is an artificial heart of the city. It's stopped beating. All roads lead into the square but you can't go down them any more. The buses don't come here. The end result is a wilderness in which no activity is allowed to occur.*

*The heart of the city has to pull people in to it for the heart to beat. Now why would you come here? I grew up in Church Square in Addington, which was a really magical place. We had a big, old, ramshackle, Harry Potteresque two-storey vicarage. There was a lovely Mountford church, great green lawns, and a belfry, and it was a wonderful little island in the middle of all those little factories that belch out smoke. It was great. I loved it. There are little islands of it that are still nice and wonderful and magical and mysterious.*

*The great tragedy of Christchurch when you were a lecturer and I was your student, learning nothing from you, but enjoying the experience enormously, is that the university has gone. It was a two-minute walk down there, and at about four o'clock, at the end of the day, this vast, hairy, Beatle obsessed, slightly Bohemian horde disgorged from the university and came in and offended and shocked and outraged the genteel who were trying to get their appropriately wrapped items from Ballantynes. The students added to a miserably lifeless city. They gave it vitality, a kind of life, and an edge that's gone now. You never see students. They're all moaning about the loans and all the rest of it. They're tragic creatures. Why don't they just go and become gunrunners in Marrakesh? Stop moaning. Get a life.*

> *The tourists are no replacement. You do feel sorry for the poor dears. They've come all the way from Tokyo to stand and be photographed in front of the cathedral. New Zealanders, in that oddly puritanical way we have, we sort of think that the tourists should arrive at Auckland Airport, make a donation, say they love the place and leave straight away. We feel a bit cheapened by the fact that we actually have them here. But if you accept my proposition that the square desperately needs life, the tourists who come here paradoxically provide it. Anything that brings the world in is good.*

The real love of Jim's life is not Christchurch but Lyttelton. There he lives on a steep building site, which will some day become a house.

## Jim Hopkins

*I've always liked this place. If you take this idea of something sewn into the genes from generations before, there is something in me that is drawn to water and hills, I can't explain it any better than that. I can remember taking trains through to Lyttelton as a kid, going up to school trips and sports tournaments in the North Island and seeing this little settlement nestled in an inner room of a long-dead volcano and being astounded, coming back in on the inter-island ferry in the morning with all the chimneys trailing smoke. It just captured me.*

*I loved the idea that the streets were too narrow for two cars to pass. I loved the fact that all of the kind of boring stereotypical, stultifying, dull, prosaic monotony of planning was absent. You didn't have to have all your houses sit back a regulation number of feet or metres from the road, and you didn't have to have all of that standard, hideous, mind-numbing, stupefying tedium that passes for a well-ordered residential life. Houses cluttered up, nestled against each other right on the pathway, little modest buildings.*

> *They weren't wannabe Southforks screaming bad taste and too much money. It was just lovely. I mean, I wanted to live here. The town served the port and there was a bit of ancillary industry, and the people were shaped by that and had attitudes and assumptions that arose out of that in a hard-working town.*
>
> *Then you put a tunnel through it and it's like when they first put the Suez Canal from the Red Sea to the Mediterranean. All these species whizzed up from the Red Sea, up the Canal, and hurtled into the Mediterranean at a rapid rate and gobbled everything. To some extent the same thing happened here. So it's a community, and in a sense it's also a suburb. Talk to people here and they'll say, you come out of the tunnel and it's as if you are in a different world. Whatever was on your mind when you went into the tunnel, you come out, see the hills, see the water and it's just like going on holiday. I believe that.*

Auckland is a more logical place to pursue a media career. Been there, done that and successfully. Wearied of competing with 'clones', Jim chose freedom and Lyttelton to live a far more satisfying life as a jack of all trades and a panjandrum Kiwi philosopher concentrating on the New Zealand metaphysics of blokes, mates, mateship, and the sheds into which men withdraw from a woman-dominated Kiwi world to plot their rearguard action against it in the blokes' last bastion. The Hopkins' shed, like the Hopkins' house, is unfinished.

## Jim Hopkins

*This is a shed in transition. It will be the centre of my various dynamic enterprises and leisure activities. I'm thinking of building a full-size replica of the* Titanic *in here. I'll probably restore antique clocks and generally go quietly mad. The rubble will be cleared away to create a display area for the antique vehicles that I'll restore, like a 1905 Silver Ghost. I'll hand hew the pistons with my own chisel.*

*When New Zealand got settled massively in the nineteenth century the world was in the middle of a technological explosion, probably more fundamental than the one that's happening now. Suddenly traction engines and all those things were whacking around the planet. For the first time in human history there were things that went faster than the foot or the horse. Anyone who wanted to use any of those things here shipped them out and then if a bit broke you had to wait a year for a spare part. So ingenuity and the ability to repair and restore and renovate and keep operating were essential. Everyone who has come to New Zealand has a number of things in common. They have got to be adventurous. They've got to be experimenters and adaptors and innovators. Everyone who lives here came here from somewhere else. But once you are here you're in a space capsule and you have to do what you can do yourself. If you can't do it yourself, your whole enterprise may collapse. So the shed was a workshop, it was a factory, it was a laboratory.*

*Women are from shops and men are from garages. Men define themselves by what they do, and women by what they feel. In a shed a guy can be worried about something. He will go there and he'll wait, and he'll chisel, and he'll say nothing. Another bloke will turn up, 'G'day.' 'G'day.' 'What are you doing?' 'Well, I'm fixing it.' 'Oh, yeah . . .' And they'll stand there for about half an hour and the conversation will be monosyllabic. It will have nothing to do with the problem at hand. At the end of that time the guy will feel 'problem solved, I can return to the world'.*

*I'm worried about what's happening to good old mateship. The image that a boy growing up would get now of masculinity is universally and distortingly negative. What you would see would be the drunks, the wife-beaters, the child-batterers and so forth. Those men exist. That is part of a legacy of testosterone that is black and bleak and unacceptable in a world that we want to be safe and open. But it's not what all men are, and the thing that bugs me at the moment is, other than sports heroes, where are the role models, where can a boy look at qualities of loyalty, qualities of support, of trust, of honesty? A process of political transformation has stripped half the human race of far too much of its self-esteem by defining it negatively, representing it negatively and by failing to assert what are good and worthwhile and fundamentally decent and worthy qualities. Mateship is the essence of male bonding. It's a thing to be proud of.*

*It's possible for two women to be mates. I'm not suggesting that that's not the case. I was simply exploring in mates an idea that I thought needed reiterating simply to redress the balance. If you look at the accounts of the last ten years, that men are emotionally numb and ungiving and can't express their emotions, that's bollocks. That's psychobabble. That's therapy talk. Professional caring. It's an oxymoron.*

*Many of the characteristics that shape New Zealand are masculine in essence. That is in no way to demean, disparage or dismiss the role of pioneer woman, but in terms of the external impact the country had on the world it was masculine qualities of resilience, self-reliance, a strong focus on the team. Tribe and team are actually two sides of the same coin, and we are attracted to those things. Team New Zealand. Those are things that we should trust and we shouldn't trust this nonsense that men can't express their emotions. What it's actually saying is men are allegedly not behaving emotionally in a way that the other half of the human race thinks they should. Well, tough. The other half of the human race behaves emotionally in a way that men actually think is a bit dodgy and daft. In the end we get over it, you get used to it. Men are not emotionally cold, withdrawn, unable to make commitment. They just do it a different way.*

*There's still a whole army of unsung bloke heroes out there and they are doing extraordinary things. They are inventing things, they are rebuilding things. There are guys in this country who, when the wealthy of the world want their 1905 Rolls-Royce rebuilt, they send them to men who fix them in cow sheds just out of Hamilton. When Arab sheikhs want their Lagondas restored, they go out to Wanganui and get fixed there.*

*All over this country there are men who are maintaining that tradition that goes right back to farms and factories. Ernest Rutherford, the first experiments he did that gave the world atomic power were in a building at Canterbury University called the tin shed. Pearce did all of his stuff in a shed. The first car engine was built by a little man in Timaru who made his own engine in his own foundry and built his own car, and the Post Office bought about three of them and they delivered mail in South Canterbury before the beginning of the twentieth century. That's a tradition that we should be proud of and we should stop actually apologising for.*

Confession time. When I lived there I never particularly liked Christchurch. I kept quiet because it would have shocked the natives, who regarded the city as God's personal gift to New Zealand (She being English and an Anglican, of course). Too flat, except for the Cashmere hills, whose residents look down on the huddled masses below. Too English, with Captain Scott's statue proclaiming the courage of the poor Poms he led to their deaths and the Avon (actually named after a Scottish river) flowing through it, the parks, the punting and Christ's College, where Biggles became a system of education – churning out chaps.

Most of all I disliked the council's efforts to prise the university out of the city centre. Universities should be convenient for the bars and brothels, not relegated to the isolation ward of Ilam, hidden away like a leper colony in case they shock or infect the citizenry, which, as far as I was concerned, was their purpose. The council won. The university went, leaving its buildings as an under-used art centre. The brain-box of the city is empty. Just like its heart in Cathedral Square.

Christchurch is a city without a purpose. Not a university city like Dunedin, with 12,000 students diluted among 310,000 citizens. Not a government and power centre like Wellington. Not a bustling commercial city like Auckland. Christchurch just is. It sits and spreads like blancmange across the plains, consuming more and more land to less and less purpose. Once it was an industrial town. Rogernomics closed the manufacturing, the textiles, clothing and footwear factories, the foundries, the railway workshops, the Islington Freezing works, the timber and building yards, even Griffin's Biscuits.

The Council has made a valiant effort to fight back by intervention and support so active that Douglas Myers attacked it as the People's Republic of Christchurch. In fact, it was effective municipal enterprise which led to the City Development Corporation and the encouragement of clusters of development stimulating growth in electronics, where Tate is a world frontrunner, computer software and IT with Jade, PDL, Trimble, Global positioning systems and the section of the DSIR sold off as Allied Tellysyn to a Japanese entrepreneur. The result is a healthier economy, though the firms are smaller and scattered rather than concentrated in the industrial heartland, which once kept the city going. But visitors no longer come in through the railway station – moved to Addington and then closed altogether – but down the leafy roads and prosperous suburbs from the airport into Cathedral Square, with its sushi bars and tourist shops, mainly Japanese-managed and staffed.

What is Christchurch for? The original purpose is still central as a service and support centre for the rich, rural areas of the North and South Canterbury plains across to the tourist wonderland of the Southern Alps. Butler's 'Erewhon' lay in the Alps, though nowhere is really Christchurch, which serves the farmers-dressing Harris-tweeded squatters, and provides the Canterbury Club, for their dull and deep potations, and supplies them with all they need. Canterbury farmers have always been more quietly prosperous but far less rough and ready than the Southland farmers I knew. Not quite a gentry but living in bigger and older houses and 'stations' watching grass grow while their animals ate it. They grumbled, as all farmers did, and do, between overseas holidays, but more genteelly than the chorus of complaint from other, rougher areas. The burden of their complaint was that while they earned the country's money, inconsiderate townies spent it, sponged on them, protected manufacturers, overcharged them, whilst government squandered the money they earned overseas, and suppliers and workers gouged them. In the dim and distant days when all New Zealanders did well together, the paranoia and grumbling endemic among farmers because bred by the isolation of rural life, where there's not much else to do, was a dull ache. It became a deep pain when things went badly, as they did in the eighties.

Canterbury's main crop, like New Zealand's, was sheep; closely followed by grumbles, for farmers have always been the most effectively unionised section of New Zealand through Federated Farmers, a pressure group so powerful it permeated the National Party at the grass roots and largely dictated its policy. It was in Canterbury that grumbling first turned into revolution, making farmer grievances a counter-ideology of economic liberalisation, propagated by Canterbury farmer Ruth Richardson at Federated Farmers, extended by her neighbour Jenny Shipley, and by Peter Elworthy, squatter president of Federated Farmers at the time, who toured the farmlands defending Rogernomics to his doubting members. The missionary effort was so successful that the farmers in

Canterbury, as elsewhere, now feel that they were the shock troops of the revolution. Today they tell the tale as if they were the victors of a great battle over the evils of subsidy, government intervention, insulation and welfare, all deliberately designed to crush the farmers.

In fact, they had colluded with the processes, particularly when their party, National, was in power. Which was for most of the time. The deal was that farmers would generate the wealth, their government, National, would give them what they wanted, then distribute the remainder to the rest of New Zealand. That was transformed when farm exports suffered. Farmers then became dependent on the government for help but even then National still did the farmers well. The subsidies farmers now condemn were poured out at their request, to keep them going so as to inherit the better times, which all assumed must lie ahead for farmers as good as they in a world where people would eventually need the protein New Zealand produced.

The real force for change was neither free-market ideology nor any desire among farmers to kick away the crutches. It was Britain's betrayal of its overseas farm by entering an agricultural protection club, which excluded New Zealand's produce as too competitive and cheap. New Zealand's basic products – lamb, wool and dairy – were a glut on protected world markets. The comfortable assumption that a world undergoing a population explosion would eventually want to eat what the British once had, remained strong. So government and farmers colluded behind a strategy of survival by subsidy and encouraging farmers to increase a production which couldn't be sold. Producing more of what people wouldn't eat kept farm profits high but was producing for subsidies not markets, a short-term survival strategy that became more and more expensive, requiring massive overseas borrowing to bankroll it.

Markets declined but production increased. By 1984 nearly two-fifths of the gross income of the average sheep and beef farmers came from subsidy, and the whole structure of support prices, fertiliser subsidies, finance from the boards and tax transfers cost up to $772,000,000 or thirty-five percent of the average farm income. That boosted land prices and increased input prices and the whole cost structure rather than cutting costs and preparing for the worst. New Zealand was waiting for the world to guzzle what it had once sold to Britain. The world wasn't hungry.

Something had to give. Labour came in, in July 1984, and swept away thirty different production subsidies and export incentives in its first budget. In New Zealand politics each party can hit those most opposed to it hardest. National bashes the unions. Labour bashed the farmers. Today they like to think they rejoiced and danced in the streets. In fact, the cries of pain were loud. There were reports of farmer suicides, forecasts of 8000 farm closures and bankruptcies, ritual slaughters of sheep and dumping of bloody sheep's heads on ministers' doorsteps. Some fronted up to it, particularly Roger Douglas and Richard Prebble, who told the farmers they were liberating them from scrounging and announced their home addresses, asking for a few dead sheep to be dumped there for Sunday meals.

The National Party in opposition was all over the place, providing neither consistent backing nor an alternative. Farmers were divided between those who wanted the pain stopped and those demanding that it be applied to other sectors by deregulating labour to reduce their costs and industry to reduce the cost of inputs, and by floating the exchange rate to make exports competitive. They did get a twenty percent devaluation, but that was soon reversed when the dollar perversely went back up because international finance had so much confidence in New Zealand. That process went on even after the dollar floated in February 1985.

Today the survivors like to believe that they not only wanted the cold turkey treatment but inspired the whole thing in the first place. That particular rewriting of history goes so far that one Canterbury farmer told me that the reports of suicide were much exaggerated. Farmers, he pointed out, are more inclined to commit suicide, and if some did it was no more than those who would have killed themselves anyway. Perhaps even the same people. Cold comfort for those underground, but for a time things looked so bad that a government which had initially hoped that free markets would work their assumed magic without pain was forced to introduce small measures of relief to cushion the blow. A grant scheme allowed those going out of farming to do so with a house and a car. Only a handful took it up. A subsidy was provided to rip out müller-thurgau and replant with more up-market vines, which became the stimulus to a surge in the wine industry.

When the land price fell the government brought the financial institutions together to avert a panic collapse. The Rural Bank, which had provided long-term low interest loans took the lead, calling lender-borrower conferences under a neutral chair to repackage the debt by raising the interest rate and reducing loan terms, provided all creditors held off. In most cases they did. In the end only 800 went out of farming, many of them older farmers taking early retirement, and some of those who'd inherited the family farm but not a real interest or skill at the job. This was survival of the fittest. And in financial terms, the fattest.

New Zealand farmers survived better than basic industries back in Britain survived Margaret Thatcher's shock treatment in the same decade. They did so because the family farm is the base of New Zealand agriculture. Families can make sacrifices, cut costs, and endure a low or even negative rate of return when big firms can't. So farmers hunkered down, closed cheque books, ceased to renovate, paint or even maintain properties, took the kids out of private school, used less fertiliser, cut back on inputs, kept cars longer, sent wives out to work, and laid off labour. Farming areas and towns imploded as jobs were lost, services contracted, and people drifted to the cities. The old, easygoing rural myth on which so many New Zealanders had been reared was demolished. The countryside became a colder, meaner place, an outdoor factory run without sentiment but developing a whole range of new products.

The benefits were slow to come through. Labour enjoyed a bubble boom and an asset and share price bonanza in the cities, Canterbury and the farming areas endured real pain. Sheep numbers reduced from over seventy million, many of which must have been subsidy sheep, to forty-eight million. Reclamation of new land stopped and much reverted to bush. Huge freezing works closed, putting hundreds out of work and some, like Vestey's Weddel Meat Company, went bust. The big British stock and station agents, who had done so well out of New Zealand agriculture, pulled back to the elephants' graveyard of the British economy, whence they had come.

Yet hunkered down in a sinking world, the farmers came through. Eventually they did so by adaptability, ingenuity and inventiveness. Farmers in other countries prefer to do what they've done for generations. New Zealanders pursue profit. Others are so attached to the land they hang on bitterly. New Zealanders are unsentimental. They swap, lose or sell land as profit dictates. 'I'm not attached to the land but I do get to miss the cows', one told me. Big farmers like to own their equipment. New Zealanders co-operate, swapping and trading services, land, sheds and equipment as efficiency dictates. Corporate farmers need a return of ten percent or more. Family farmers can manage on half that. Small businesses are quick to adapt and change. With family providing the labour, and the ability of incumbents to sit out falls in the land price, the turnaround was fast. Sheep farming shrank as farmers went into deer, more profitable than its British counterpart because antler cutting is illegal there. Because the animal welfare lobby is weaker and the legislation was passed earlier, antlers can be cut four times a year under veterinary supervision, yielding a profitable crop of velvet to be sold as aphrodisiac in South-East Asia, and finding new medical uses in treating arthritis and athletic injuries in New Zealand.

Ostriches and emus walked where the moa once trod. Kiwifruit and timber grew. Dairy conversions, usually on a fifty-fifty share-milking arrangement between the owner of the cows and the farmer, multiplied. One ambitious young farmer told me he began with a hundred cows on a mortgage, paid it off in three years, moved up to 350 cows, paid that mortgage off in another three, then up to 800 which, when he'd paid this off, provided the finance to buy a 200-acre farm with 275 cows. Sadly, his aim of never milking another cow after forty was not realised.

New Zealand's climate allows it to be more efficient in both dairy and sheep, than areas where cows and sheep are wintered indoors. New Zealand uses cow power by year-round grazing, not horse power by harvesting grass. Even sheep farming eventually returned to profitability. Soon New Zealand was getting more meat out of fewer but fatter sheep than it had out of double their number. New freezing works like Fortex started preparing cut meat and soon employed more workers by introducing shift-work, preparing cut and packaged meat rather than shipping carcasses to England to be cut up there by traditional butchers. Fortex was billed by Ruth Richardson as the pioneer of better labour relations but it went bust with two executives sent to jail, but others prospered with the same formula for success: bigger sheep giving better cuts, individually packaged to meet the requirements of supermarkets and consumers.

'Look, we have come through', is the farming mood today. They take credit for changes of which they originally felt themselves to be the victims. Farms are bigger. Small sixty- or a hundred-cow farms merged to 200-cow farms, survivors bought land from neighbours, while some moved to the South Island where land was cheaper. Corporate farmers sold out and split up, except Landcorp, still the biggest farmer in New Zealand and state-owned, surviving as a bank of land for Maori claims, as a bank of genes to upgrade the stock and by innovation and efficiency. Investment has been low, the lifestyle meaner and the farms shabbier. Yet everything picks up with profitability and the basic pattern of the family farm remains intact, with wives now replacing outside services as co-managers, accountants, book-keepers, part-time labourers, hostesses for farm holidays, even as milk maidens for up-market ranch holidays and, in some cases, as farmers, by taking over small patches of five acres or so to produce flowers and other immediately marketable crops.

Units are now bigger but farming remains an open industry. Entry is harder but still possible for those coming in through share-milking, by working after graduating from agricultural college, or by buying small properties and building up. The real problem is to persuade a more citified population to live in the country in the first place – something more difficult than breaking into farming for the young and ambitious. By the mid-nineties this diversified, competitive and efficient industry stood ready to benefit from any upturn in markets, and in the late nineties that was forthcoming from the fall in the dollar and the improvement in markets for dairy, beef and sheep. Farm incomes rose, land prices with them. Farm profits were actually lower than in the subsidy days but productivity was much higher and rising fast.

Enough to allow the industry to cover the higher charges and transaction costs of sending smaller quantities to more diverse markets.

By 2002, a decade and a half after the revolution, a revived, even over-confident farming industry was generating more revenue abroad and a greater proportion of GDP than before the revolution. The energy of the entrepreneurial, hard-working, mean-living New Zealand farmer had been liberated. A change, which began by making everyone worse off, had ended up enabling farmers to make everyone better off. New Zealand, trying to diversify out of farming ever since the turn of the century, had learned another lesson. Better to diversify farming than to diversify out of it. In Canterbury, as in the rest of New Zealand, a tougher, younger, more entrepreneurial breed of small businessman farmer has taken over from the more genteel, gentlemanly, squatterocracy. It has done so to more purpose and with greater success.

That reverses the old image of gentle decline for the South Island. The agricultural revolution has accelerated change and boosted an island where land is cheaper, the potential for transformation greater and the tourist industry growing faster, which strengthens its long-standing feeling of being different but better. As I went about the island this seemed far stronger. Indeed, most of the people I spoke to were tinged with South Island patriotism. For them the Mainland is now the real New Zealand, insulated from the evils of Auckland, from racial tensions, pluralism and from globalisation, and moving ahead again. Jim Hopkins speaks for many:

## Jim Hopkins

*I love the west coast, I love the smell of it and I love the wildness of it. I love the idea of looking at these hills, so serene and green and calm, and thinking of the violence that created them. You can walk around the waterfront and there's still molten rock that was frozen at a moment when it was incandescent, and it's still there. I love Oamaru for the buildings. It's one of the few towns in New Zealand where the buildings are built of one material and to one style, and you have something that's common in Europe where a whole town speaks of a time in human history. The South Island is magic, you'd have to be mad not to be here, wouldn't you?*

*I don't know what defines me as a New Zealander. I was born here. I know this place. I know how it works and how it thinks. This is where I became who I am. The South Island is where planned settlements took place in Dunedin and Christchurch. There was an astonishing, and you have to say in terms of the time, an amazingly courageous idea of taking a culture in microcosm and transporting it. It's done something fascinating by importing a two-thousand-year culture and imposing it in a totally new place where it's mutated and changed and adapted, but where resonances back to another time and place are still quite strong and feed out through the generations.*

*I think that's a wonderful legacy to have and one that should not be resiled from, nor apologised for, nor abandoned lightly because it is truly a way of having the best of both worlds. If you wanted in simplistic terms to describe New Zealand, you would say in essence that the South Island is old and white and the North Island is young and brown. In very crude terms, sociologically, that's what it is. I think it's going to create some fascinating and interesting tensions and opportunities later on.*

Chapter Eight

# Absolutely, Positively, Wellington Dunnit

*W*ellington isn't just another New Zealand city with worse weather. It has the most beautiful situation, and a harbour which makes Auckland and Sydney look like paddling pools. Its kids have higher than average IQs. It's the capital of this city-state posing as a nation. It's the élite with real people segregated out of the way into the hills, the flat sprawling suburbs down the

Hutt Valley, and the distant delights of Wainuiomata and Porirua, to leave the city free for power to prowl the streets.

Wellington has all the appurtenances of a capital: embassies, international organisations, and national organisations such as Federated Farmers, the Knights of the Business Round Table, burnished knights (now a vanishing breed with no more knighthoods available) all burning to burn regulations. There's the Federation of Labour, the political parties, the lobbyists and – still powerful despite all the free market assaults – the government, its departments and Parliament from whence all blessings flow, plus master of all it surveys – the Reserve Bank smiling malignly down on mere mortals. Wellington is the home of government, politics and power and their servants and hangers-on, all growing in number as government's role has been cut back and the great beast of power tamed by the market.

It was in Wellington that New Zealand's welfare state and the machinery of economic insulation and management were built in the thirties and forties. Here, too, that it was all pulled down or daubed with monetarist graffiti as the grand design of a government-free government emerged in the eighties and was carried further in the nineties. Power, particularly in matters economic, was transferred from politicians and administrators to the market. Governments of both parties proclaimed their dearest wish as to do themselves out of jobs, give up power, make the world fit for the Round Table to rule in and get down to the essential job of government: abusing the other party.

Economic problems were the lever of political change. By the 1980s the economy was stagnant, none of Robert Muldoon's continuous reorganisations, new regulations and controls, initiatives and plans for Thinking Big, Small or Petty had been able to kick-start an economy living on debt. The Reserve Bank and the Treasury, already taken over by monetarism imported from Chicago via Christchurch through the recruitment of Canterbury University's dimmer graduates, was beginning to despair of Muldoon's ability to deny what they saw as the laws of economics. Horrified at the growth of debt, and deficit, unheeded and unwanted, they set out to undermine the last Great Socialist.

Behind the scenes they plotted a counter-revolution and began to develop an alternative programme which some believe was shared as the election approached, with Labour's Finance Spokesman Roger Douglas, a businessman with an accountant's view of government, who had already set out his own nostrums in *There's Got to Be a Better Way* in 1981. There had but that wasn't it. Until the Treasury put backbone into it, helped by a business leadership which had long felt that its natural genius enterprise, initiative and drive were being frustrated by New Zealand's incomprehensible reluctance to reward it on an American scale. This chorus of grumbles was brought to a crescendo and turned into an ideology by the Round Table of top leaders, a kind of All Knight Party whose Director, Roger Kerr, became New Zealand's mini-Milton Friedman.

In the beginning was R.D. Muldoon, the pygmy giant against whom this whole plot was being organised. Larger than life and twice as ugly, Rob Muldoon bestrode the New Zealand scene like a crumbling colossus and one viewed more affectionately in hindsight than he was at the time.

# Tom Scott

*We hated Muldoon for the wrong reasons. It turned out he was the last Socialist Prime Minister. He had more dark energy trapped inside that small, pear-shaped body than he knew what to do with. He frightened us. He was aggressive and he was a bully on television. And we didn't like his table manners any more than his politics. Yet for a while Muldoon was hugely loved in this country. Because Muldoon's instincts and prejudices appeared to be the nation's: Rob's Mob. After a while, as he got older and obviously the demographic of the country changed, his views seemed to be less and less relevant. But he was a huge fan of the kind of Mickey Savage welfare state, which Treasury hated, and in the 1975 Superannuation Campaign lifelong Labour Party people went and voted for National. Then you got on a plane in 1976 and there were drips hanging along every seat. 'Coffee, tea or saline?' There were thousands of old people flying overseas spending their superannuation.*

*He had a conspicuous intelligence. He had this great big head, ferocious memory, and he was very quick and very acute, so we were intimidated by his intelligence. But he lost contact with the electorate. He was running a one-man show. He just assumed because he was so smart it was OK. He developed a certain amount of contempt for his Cabinet colleagues, which was relatively justified, and he did assume, like Napoleon, that 'I am the nation'. The end was terribly sad. There was a combination of alcohol and diabetes medicine, and he was exhausted. He didn't know how he could keep going. He was just weary, absolutely weary.*

*I think he suspected he was going to go anyway, and in the end he just called a snap – or schnapps – election and lost. The night of defeat there was a party in the Intercontinental Hotel in Auckland and Fred Dobbs, one of Muldoon's closest friends, sat with Muldoon for four to six hours. No one else arrived. Fred Dobbs said to me, that night he realised he was sitting with the loneliest man in the world.*

The economy was up a well-known creek; Rob had lost the paddle. The subsidies and spending doled out to keep a rickety machine going put the deficit up to eight percent of GDP. Controls, particularly on wages and prices, distorted the economy, and a dollar way too high was undermining production. Debt was accumulating, the reserves running out, exports faltering and politics turning sour. The reign of King Rob was coming to an end not with a whimper but a bang.

## Brian Gaynor

*I remember the huge enthusiasm for him. He was going to be the reforming messiah. The business community was really enamoured with him. As time went on they became very disillusioned and looking for change. Muldoon had become very interventionist. He was regulating everything. You'd wake up in the morning and interest rates were regulated. The currency had changed. The banks could only lend money to certain people. They had to lend to agriculture. They had to lend to housing. Almost every day you had a new regulation around your neck. Business endorsed the National government but Muldoon went far too far. Bob Jones helped the transformation. His New Zealand Party helped the election of Labour in 1984.*

## Sir Bob Jones

*We got thirteen percent of the vote and that put National out. We had a very good manifesto, which was about rolling back the estate, floating the exchange rate and letting the market work. Labour's policies were duplicates. They copied us. They'd put out an economic policy that was just a series of platitudes on cyclostyled sheets. They virtually implemented my policy as set out in our manifesto for the New Zealand Party.*

*If I'd been in power I would have been a natural compromiser and softened the brutalism with which the farmers were dealt. In hindsight that would have been wrong. You really had to go cold turkey to do it but my inclination would have been to say, 'Hang on, let's do it in stages.' It was very sharp and sudden. But the outcome has been outstanding. We have probably the best, soundest farming base in the world.*

Labour came in unencumbered by a manifesto. There had been no time to sort out a policy, so this was effectively a new party untainted by the past, with a new economic approach from Roger Douglas and a new leader, David Lange, a big man in every respect except the physical, where he was enormous. Lange was the most brilliant, charismatic leader New Zealand has had, and the first frontbencher to stand up to Muldoon.

## Tom Scott

*The first time I saw David Lange on TV there should have been a sign that came under his face, 'Do not adjust your set, this man really looks like this.' You'd go, God, who is he, he's so grotesque, he's hugely fat. But Lange had this wonderful, physical presence, and this fantastic voice, and this extraordinary wit. This strange South Auckland lawyer, it turned out, had done all this amazing pro bono work in the courts for all these deadbeats and dropouts. He was a wonderful man, wonderfully intelligent, a gifted raconteur, with a great deep voice.*

*Within a matter of weeks in the House it was clear that Lange was going to be Muldoon's nemesis. There was a silly exchange in the House, it might be a year and a half after Lange had arrived. Lange wandered into the House and Muldoon yells out across the benches, 'Ha. Your belly's even larger than mine.' Lange goes, 'My belly may be larger but it's higher off the ground.' This is hardly Oscar Wilde but right there you could see there's been a change here, Muldoon is losing, Lange is winning.*

Lange was helped into the leadership by the Auckland clique who viewed him almost as their front man. Their leader was Remorseless Roger Douglas, Minister of Finance, the Man with the Plan. This may have been given to him by the Treasury. Certainly when Labour came in, without benefit of a manifesto because of the snap election, the Treasury plan given them in a bulky document plunged some into deep gloom.

## Richard Prebble

*The group of ministers elected by the caucus to be the Finance ministers were in favour of deregulating Muldoon's programme, which had taken the programme of the loony left, things that we had fought against, and implemented them, and proved they didn't work. He had full price control, he had gone in for this huge programme of Think Big, which we had said was a bad investment. He was subsidising sheep, everything. Having gone through the election campaign, attacking the Muldoon government and thinking that I was perhaps exaggerating a little bit, I discovered when I came to office that things were worse than my worst nightmare. We didn't know that every one of these Think Big projects had a letter from Sir Robert Muldoon, saying if things go wrong the government will bail you out. In the case of New Zealand Steel, that cost over $2 billion, a letter of comfort that he'd never told Parliament about, or probably hadn't even told his Cabinet.*

*Treasury did much better briefing documents than they had normally done. Sir Robert had stopped using them. So they had a lot of time. They sat down and wrote these papers. It was a thick wad, I read them all in one night, it took me until about four in the morning. They showed problem after problem. The first came and I thought, 'Oh, this is how we can handle that, then this,' but as I worked my way through I realised there was no way to handle them. So at three in the morning I put them down thinking, 'We're going to be a one-term government. We've had it. There's no political way of fixing this problem.' I brooded some more and thought, 'There's no political answer to this. We've just got to do it so we might as well go for it because we've had it.'*

*That was the consensus of the Cabinet. That we were*

*completely had. There was no way we could get re-elected. It was an appalling situation, and it was going to be touch and go whether we had to call in the IMF. We discussed that for a while and said, 'No, no, if it's got to be done it's miles better that we do it.' We were absolutely stunned when we started doing well in the polls, because we were doing things that everybody knew weren't popular. We were getting fruit thrown at us, and things like that. I went to a farmers' meeting, the Cabinet only sent me once, and I went in and said, 'I really enjoy talking to meetings of welfare beneficiaries.' They roared. They were very angry anyway, and they shouted and things.*

Labour followed Treasury's plan almost to the letter. The first step was to devalue by twenty percent. Then came floating the dollar. Soon Labour was headlong down the path of deregulation, corporatisation, privatisation and marketisation, all preached as a new evangel: Rogernomics.

## Brian Easton

*Rogernomics is a reference to Reaganomics and Thatchernomics. It's the ideology of the new right that says monetary control is all you need worry about. Don't worry about the export sector or whatever.*

*It was a very extreme policy, and probably New Zealand's gift to the world in the eighties and nineties was to show how disastrous those policies were. One has to say that at one stage people used to come along to New Zealand to admire our policies. When it became increasingly clear they were a disaster they didn't bother. Now they look elsewhere.*

## Sir Bob Jones

*In February 1985 Roger suddenly announced on Sunday morning that from now on all exchange controls were lifted. You could invest anywhere you want. The concern was that a great flow of money would pour out of the country. Well, it did. But they stuck to their guns and after a few months people realised they actually meant it. Then there was a huge flow back in.*

It all felt very un-Labour but it was exciting. It gave the government an impetus, and caucus and country were carried along with it. Nothing could stop Roger, remorseless as rust. Lange, never an economist, went along hoping to use the confidently predicted benefits to improve social security. He could do no other, having no alternative of his own, disliking confrontation and having too much fun to do the nitty-gritty of building up his own support.

## Tom Scott

*Roger had the best and the brightest in the Labour Party Cabinet on his side. Prebble was a devotee, de Cleene, even people like Palmer and Helen Clark appeared to have a certain sympathy for what Roger Douglas was doing. It all seemed so refreshing after the grim controls of Muldoon. It seemed refreshing, modern, long overdue and necessary.*

*If you've got nineteen people in the cabinet who equivocate, nineteen Hamlets and one Hitler, Hitler will win. Someone who has absolute faith says, 'This is exactly what we've got to do. This is the magic bullet.' The equivocators and the Hamlets will go, 'Alright, okay, we'll go along with this.' And they do. Ruth Richardson has a very simple world-view. So does Roger Douglas. His pig farm collapsed and went broke but that doesn't matter. Give him the whole country. The pig farm's an unfair test. Nothing could stand in Roger's way as he wrong-footed all his opponents.*

## Brian Easton

*New Zealand has a very thin constitution. We don't even have a House of Lords. And, of course, Britain has a whole series of informal constitutional arrangements, which hardly exist in New Zealand. Our caucuses were remarkably quiet. We didn't even have those sorts of protections. So it was possible for extremists to take over the country. You can think of New Zealand as a fort, which was designed to protect New Zealanders against the rest of the world. When the terrorists actually get inside the fort they could just mow everybody down and that's what happened. The fort worked on the basis that it was our side that was running it.*

## Brian Gaynor

*They were a young team. The Cabinet members were so refreshing compared to the outgoing Cabinet members who were old-timers, World War II veterans whose era had come to an end. It was a baby-boom Cabinet. They were in their thirties. This was new for New Zealand. They spoke the language of the baby-boomers and it was quite appealing. New Zealand had gone through a very restrictive era. So it was very refreshing. Unfortunately, it was built on clay. When the share market collapsed in October 1987 it was really devastating. The wealth that was being created through the stock market at the time was huge. Auckland, for example, was on a complete and utter roll. Share prices were going up daily and people were becoming very wealthy. But it was masking the problems that were going on underneath.*

The Royal Commission on Welfare on which Lange had placed all his hopes as an alternative, which would redistribute the growth generated by the reforms, turned into a damp squib. His opponents in Cabinet ensured it would be.

## Richard Prebble

*I think David Lange discovered it had become a Roger Douglas and not a David Lange government. What Labour parties have traditionally done when we couldn't agree, is to have a Royal Commission. I was the caucus representative on the policy committee and argued against one. I said that would be three years wasted. We told Lange that it wouldn't work, and we knew long before the Royal Commission reported that it was going to be a joke. I was stunned when Lange said at the opening of the Christchurch campaign that we would implement the Royal Commission's recommendations. The Cabinet never agreed to that. The Labour Party Policy Committee had never agreed to that. You never hand over policy to an unelected group. We were petrified by that. Then they turned up with an unworkable document. Biggest doorstop in history.*

Lange was badly let down when the Commission dumped six enormous volumes of undigested research on him. Normally Royal Commissions take minutes and waste years. This one just packed up. Lange was becoming an exile in his government.

## Tom Scott

*The two most exciting politicians New Zealand's ever had since the war, both extraordinary men in their own ways, both fabulously gifted people, Muldoon and Lange, have both ended up being tragic figures. They've both been the architect of their own misfortune.*

*David was the stalking-horse for Rogernomics. He didn't realise it at the time, but he was. It was seen as necessary to remain in power, to have people like Sir Doug Myers and Fay Richwhite, all those rich people in Auckland, on your side. I remember going to a meeting in a yacht club in Auckland where they were introducing Roger Douglas for the first time to the Auckland business community, and Roger gave a speech and all the businessmen clapped and said, 'We can work with this man.'*

Getting religion broke Labour. It won the 1987 election, then fell apart. The share market collapsed, more damagingly in New Zealand than anywhere else. Lange tried to call a halt for 'a cup of tea'. Roger upped the ante, demanding a flat tax rate, which would have tied government spending down. Lange belatedly commissioned research, which showed that it didn't add up, and replaced it with a two-rate structure, the top rate thirty-three percent, supplemented by a regressive VAT, christened GST.

Roger went. Along with Prebble and De Cleene, calling themselves the Backbone Group because they thought Lange had none. Caucus re-elected Roger to cabinet. Lange had to go. And went. Caretakers carried on with a quick-change leader strategy, moving the target by changing the PM: Palmer resigned after a year, Moore came in a few weeks before the 1990 election. But Labour had busted its own flush and was heavily defeated, bringing National to power, in theory to get back to normal, in fact to finish what Labour had started by carrying forward the revolution into the fields of welfare and social security which Labour had scrupulously protected.

## Brian Easton

*The National Party is, fundamentally, a party of conservatism, but it also got seized by ideologues and, for a while, those ideologues drove the party, particularly in 1990 and 1991/92. You had the National Party doing all the measures that Labour couldn't quite get its heart round, like totally liberalising the labour market, virtually reducing all protections, driving down work, pay conditions, and pay rates for low-paid workers – incidentally with no benefit, of course. Eventually, the National Party began to drift back to its more conservative level but it always had these wild ideologues who would sell off anything.*

Ruth Richardson, author of the Mother of All Budgets, then, after a decent interval, Jenny Shipley, vigorously attacked the welfare state. Social security was cut, the Employment Contracts Act removed protection for workers and deprived unions of their role. Health investment and public spending fell, state house rents rose and 'user pays' became a mantra. The results were so disastrous for workers and the unions it looked as though the National Party had decided to drive Labour's core support back into the fold. Darien Fenton, Vice-President of the NZCTU and National Secretary of the Service and Food Workers Union, saw it from the trade union viewpoint.

## Darien Fenton

*In the union that I worked for we had low-paid workers, mainly women workers. We did a survey in 1993, and fifty percent of the women had had a pay cut in the first two years of the Employment Contracts Act because employers came after things like weekend rates, overtime rates, sick pay and so on, and tried to strip it out wherever they could. Lots of people said we don't have to belong to a union, and then the employers went on a terror campaign to make sure that people didn't belong to unions. In my union, membership went from 70,000 in 1991 down to 30,000 in the first two years of the Employment Contracts Act.*

*What was worse was the impact on working people. We saw it time and time again, workers were not allowed to have access to the union organisers because they weren't allowed in the workplace. Employers were using consultants and lawyers to help them with the new Act, so there was this terrible sort of imbalance of power that, overnight, took away years and years of conditions that had been won through the union movement. I saw workers locked out, I saw workers dragged into the boss's office late at night. We took a case to the Employment Court about a hotel, and the manager described unions as 'interfering mother-in-laws'.*

It was a Liberal *auto-da-fé*. Until the electorate, by now thoroughly fed up with both parties, threw the National Party out in 1999. Liberal economics had comprehensively failed to deliver. Promised benefits were always just around the corner but never materialised. Electorates can't live on promises when everything is getting worse. It was. Unemployment rose. Exports suffered. The productive economy languished.

Why did it all fail? The politicians had no idea what they were doing, but basked in the approval of business. Treasury was implementing its dogma and the practical consequences hardly mattered so long as the theory was implemented. The needs of production and exporters were not taken into account. Nor were the special problems of a small economy, though the enthusiastic argued that it was because New Zealand was so small that it had to lay out the welcome mat for capitalism by sweeping away anything which might deter it. As 'the last bus-stop on the planet', New Zealand had to give capitalism everything it wanted.

## Richard Prebble

*When you look at New Zealand, what can we do? There are really only two things that we can do. We can have a lower tax regime, and the second thing is to have less regulation. To have a more business-friendly environment. That's what the Labour Cabinet had worked out we had to do. That's what we were doing. And we stopped.*

Monetarism was a system of economics appropriate to a huge economy like the United States – as if sauce for the elephant would not drown the mouse. But such practicalities hardly mattered. Industry had to be exposed to the cold shower of competition as if it were a recalcitrant child at Christ's College being made virtuous. Phoenixes rise from ashes. So the more ashes the better. Rogernomics was very good at ashes.

## Brian Easton

*Monetarist theory just didn't include an export sector. The model was of a closed economy which didn't have an export sector. Ideologues were thinking of America, and America's such a big economy that, on the whole, it can largely ignore its export sector. Whereas if, for instance, you look at Britain you know that it's very important that the export sector is functioning well, otherwise the economy screws up. That's what happened in New Zealand, too.*

*That situation, with various modifications, continued right through the 1990s. So look at the New Zealand export record and we have one of the poorest in the OECD. They were promising us better economic performance but not in exports. We were superb importers, though. Outstanding import performance.*

National assets were first run like companies for profit then sold off at knockdown prices to pay off government debt overseas. It was more important to be run as a business than to serve the public.

## Brian Gaynor

*I support privatisation but through the sale of shares to the public, like British Telecom. Australia adopted a very different approach. Most of their companies, like Telstra, like the Commonwealth Bank, like Qantas, were sold to the Australian public. What that did was it fostered ownership amongst the public. There was an improvement in the performance of those companies when they moved to the private sector. The benefits stayed with Australia because the shares were owned by Australians.*

*There's no question that there has been some improvement with some of our companies, like Telecom, but most of the benefits have gone offshore to the overseas owners, rather than to New Zealanders. We sold them too quickly at a time when not many New Zealand investors were in a position to buy them and we sold too many of them to overseas interests. They went at knockdown prices because the ideology was that you sold them as quickly as possible and almost regardless of whether there were buyers around.*

## Brian Easton

*Telecom was a major mistake over the actual regulatory environment. So we've had ten years of litigation in which competing companies have tried to get involved in the Telecom market and have been blocked off because we have such inadequate laws in the industry. At one stage the courts decided that if a competitor against Telecom was successful then they had to pay the profit loss that Telecom would have received from the superior service. That actually went to the British Privy Council in London and the decision was that that was the law. If I out-competed you then I had to compensate you for your loss of profit. It's Mickey Mouse stuff.*

*They sold off the electricity system and what we are now doing is trying to untangle the shambles that's been caused. Even this year we had a lack of capacity to produce electricity, simply because we didn't have any planning behind it, and because people were playing market games and wasting water and not having the amount of generation. A couple of years ago we actually closed down the central city of Auckland by having no power because the cables overheated. There'd been no planning and no thinking through of those sorts of issues. So this ideology went on right to the end. Some of the National politicians tried to control it but the extremism existed right through to 1999.*

Roger Douglas extolled the virtues of competition, but in a small country his reforms didn't produce much. Air New Zealand soon had a quasi-monopoly on internal air services where it overcharged. Tranz Rail milked its monopoly market. Local bus and airport monopolies went largely unchallenged by competition and the Reserve Bank used its monopoly of money to keep interest rates too high. As for the 'wisdom' of business, New Zealand's private sector was much better at self-enrichment and siphoning cash out. The presumption that businessmen could succeed where politicians were bound to fail wasn't true even in their own backyard.

## Brian Easton

*It was a curious view that businessmen could run politics better than politicians. They said politicians couldn't do business, but business could do politics. The record is that in area after area businessmen had a lot of trouble even running their own businesses. Lots of big New Zealand companies have fallen over. We have a single airline, Air New Zealand. It was sold off at a relatively low price to Brierleys. Then later that was taken over by a Singapore company and they virtually ran it into the ground. Earlier this year the New Zealand government had to re-nationalise it and made a big profit on the re-nationalisation because the company had been so badly run. There's a joke going round, 'How does a New Zealand businessman get into small business? He starts with a big business.'*

## Brian Gaynor

*One of the disappointing things about our reforms is that New Zealand business hasn't performed as well as it should have. The old boys' network is still fairly prominent here. We talk about corporate governance, which is a key issue, but there's still a tendency to appoint people from the right golf clubs, from the business clubs, rather than to pick outsiders who are good and innovative, and who are different. We're not very good at including outsiders who don't come from the rugby-playing/ cricket-playing nations, who don't come from the same type of schools, and don't speak the same kind of language.*

Instead of investing for success at Telecom, Air New Zealand, BNZ, Tranz Rail and the other privatised assets, people like Alan Gibbs, Michael Fay and David Richwhite grabbed the money and ran.

All these failures were compounded by a disastrous monetary policy. Having floated the dollar, instead of allowing it to fall to the level where exports became price-competitive, the Reserve Bank kept interest rates and the dollar too high. Overseas money flowed in to buy up privatised assets, pushing the dollar up further. As government debt was being reduced private debt soared.

## Sir Bob Jones

*We went through very bad times in the nineties compounded by an outrageously stupid monetary policy. It was not as bad as Argentina's, but it was similar in principle. It was just so dumb and so doctrinaire and so short-sighted. The monetary policy was targeting, through one instrument, a non-existent entity, namely inflation. They were chasing ghosts.*

*It was a total misunderstanding of all the reforms that had happened in the eighties. The monetary policy was a denial of the market economy. We should have flourished in the nineties and we didn't. We wallowed. The country went downhill and people left in vast numbers.*

New Zealand wasted ten years in stagnation and low growth, higher unemployment and lower productivity. The promised benefits were perpetually postponed. Similar economies, like Ireland, grew far more rapidly. Australia too did better. New

Zealand grew more slowly, endured more unemployment and lower productivity growth, poorer export performance, and higher foreign debt than the OECD average. Only inflation was lower.

No matter how many widows and orphans are sacrificed on the altar of economic liberalism the ideologues always demand more. So having held up New Zealand as an example they lost interest when the supply of sacrifices dried up. The nation which had provided the example of social reform in the 1890s and the 1930s had turned itself not into a brave success for the opposite ideologies but a ghastly warning. Brian Easton sums up.

## Brian Easton

*Since 1985 we have one of the worst economic records in the OECD, excluding, of course, the Communist countries. On any measure of economic welfare, like jobs or the standard of living, we've done very badly. The Australians did much better than us. That was a bit surprising because they actually faced a worse external environment. Their prices for their exports fell more than ours. Nevertheless, Australia's done roughly as well as the OECD average, and it's grown a lot better.*

*Whereas once we used to think of ourselves as having roughly the same standard of living as the Australians, we're now about twenty percent lower. What was interesting was that the Australians actually had the same mad ideologues and they regularly came over to New Zealand and said, 'Look at all these clever things New Zealand are doing. We should do them.'*

*Their political processes were such that they couldn't actually implement extremist policies because there were mechanisms to stop the extremism. It was said at one stage that New Zealand had a cunning plan to catch up with the Australians. We were going to get them to adopt our policies and then really slow them down.*

*What I'd like to say to the rest of the world is that it's been a disaster for New Zealand. But you can learn. We've run an experiment. We can show you how not to do it. I guess that's not a very great achievement, but at least it is a contribution.*

Revenge was left to the people. They took it by voting in an electoral system calculated to prevent the politicians ever imposing their will again. They hadn't wanted liberalisation. It had been forced down their throats. They preferred the old basics: equality, public spending, a fair society and an effective health service; the world they had known and still loved. They felt betrayed by both parties, who had combined to destroy a postwar settlement they quite liked.

## Tom Scott

*MMP grew out of the ashes of Nazi Germany. Let's devise an electoral system that will stop a person with a simple stainless steel and titanium-coated policy system. The electorate said, 'We want equivocation.' Basically it's the Hamlet system. To be or not to be is a perfect MMP system of government. It was in a response to the extremism of Roger Douglas, pursued even more zealously by Ruth Richardson, that MMP was born.*

In 1993 they took their revenge by voting in proportional representation to keep the politicians on a short leash. Politicians were forced to work in coalitions to fulfil the wishes of the people. After the war Germany had adopted proportional representation to prevent another Hitler. New Zealand now did the same, to roger Roger, and Ruth, by abolishing the elective dictatorship. Jonathan Hunt explains:

## Jonathan Hunt

*In the old first-past-the-post system, after election night, you got a result. One party won, one party lost, and the majority party had control of the agenda for three years. There was never any suggestion that the majority party would win every vote. The minority party could delay and could frustrate but in the end, the majority party could take urgency, sit all night, and get what they wanted through. That can't operate now. The present Government is a minority government, with fifty-nine out of 120 seats. In order to get its programme through it has to deal with one or other of the minor parties, usually the Greens, but also New Zealand First, and on occasion, even National. That means that there's a great deal more in negotiation between the parties.*

MMP also allowed New Zealand to manage the multiplicity of parties, which had broken away from Labour and National under the stresses and strains of liberalisation. Margaret Wilson watched this fragmentation process go on as President of the Labour Party. She struggled to hold the centre together and failed.

## Margaret Wilson

*During the three years I was President, trying to keep the various factions together, I came to the conclusion that sometimes the centre can't hold because the parts really have to be allowed to go their own way. Unlike the Australian Labour Party we didn't formally factionalise though that was one suggestion that was put to me, that we just say you've got a right, a left and a centre. I resisted that because I felt that we are a small country and once you put people into those sorts of camps it's very difficult then to be able to cross over and to get an essential unity back. I wasn't at all surprised when Jim left because I think the way in which he wished his politics to be played out was inconsistent with where the centre of the Labour Party was going and the same of course with Roger Douglas and Richard Prebble. So the extremes split off, and then they had to find a political home, and under a first-past-the-post system there was no political home. That seemed to me to be undemocratic and counter-productive for government.*

However, MMP was nearly discredited immediately. In the first PR election in 1996 Labour emerged as the largest single party; Winston Peters and New Zealand First, which had campaigned against National, held the balance of power, and after weeks of complicated negotiations National outbid Labour by offering Winston a specially invented post as Treasurer. Jim Bolger, the National Party Leader, was forced to accept Winston Peters, a man he loathed, as second-in-command.

This damaged the credibility of MMP, and Jim Bolger's even more. As New Zealand First broke up in a frenzy waka-hopping Jenny Shipley took over and National's waka sank. Only Labour's 1999 election victory, built on a coalition with the Alliance, began to restore faith. Labour would neither have won nor formed a government without MMP. Power soon reconciles politicians to the unacceptable.

## Jonathan Hunt

*I think MMP is here to stay, certainly in the short term. If you ask anybody if they want the size of Parliament reduced to ten they'd say yes. But you've got a realisation that MMP is still only five years old. It isn't a perfect system and there are other systems that are worth looking at. But we've adopted this as our system and I'm convinced that it will be here for at least the next four years. After that there may be a review, there may be a suggested change. But I suspect that in the longer term we're going to always have some form of proportional representation.*

Helen Clark is less willing to commit herself to permanent MMP, but feels the system is more democratic. Prime-Ministerial life may be more difficult but government has a firmer base because everything has to be agreed rather than imposed as an exercise of will.

## Helen Clark

*The truth is that over quite a long period of time, first-past-the-post governments in New Zealand abused their power and authority. You would have to go back to the period of Norman Kirk to find a government that at least really tried to keep faith with the electorate that put it there. And after that the departures from election programmes, the sense of betrayal the electorate felt, built up a lot of cynicism around New Zealand politics, and we saw our participation rates starting to drop off at elections. Nothing like as low as Great Britain, but bad enough for New Zealand to have barely eighty-four percent of people turning up to vote.*

*So we've had a mission to try and restore trust and faith in the political process. The vote for MMP was a very deliberate vote by the electorate to kneecap governments and to say that you will not have power as a single party on your own, except in quite extraordinary circumstances. It's not impossible but it's difficult. You're going to have to work with other people. It is a more difficult job, but I think the solutions you come up with are more durable, because you have to build a majority around them.*

The people's revenge had transformed politics. It brought sado-economics to an end, installed a Labour government ready to return things to normal, gave New Zealand a new system of politics, and a younger more lively set of politicians, with more women, more minorities and more Maori. It imposed a check on governments by requiring them to stay close to the people. The nightmare was over. Once again New Zealand was leading the world, this time to a better democracy. And it was the people wot done it.

Chapter Nine

# Wellington: Women Rule – OK?

*T*he most striking change in New Zealand over the last decades has been the rise of women, not to dominance, but to a present situation where the Prime Minister is a woman, the Leader of the Opposition up to the end of 2001 was a woman, as is the Chief Justice, the Governor General and the Cabinet Secretary and a third of

## Wellington: Women Rule – OK?

MPs. Women have made their biggest advances in politics, including councils and mayoralties, though they have been less successful in business, the law and the universities, except the positive discrimination zone of Women's Studies. They've got nowhere much in rugby coaching, but women's sports – including rugby and soccer – are really taking off. Antipodeans like an aggressive chauvinist image and New Zealand is becoming a woman's world, though one without frills or simpering.

Old New Zealand was a paternalistic, male-dominated society. Men earned the bread but couldn't make much difference to the family's standard of living. In an equalitarian society pay differentials were narrow, kept down by the low universal ceiling. It was the financial cleverness, the management skills and the efficiency of the women which was the key to success or failure, to a higher standard of family living or a lower one. That long experience made women the stronger characters compared to weaker, sport and booze-obsessed males, hiding out in sheds, gardens, pubs and clubs while the women ran the homes like a small business, generating a dividend for men to waste.

All that was changed by the pill and abortion. Women took control of their bodies and their own reproduction. Reduced childbearing responsibilities and home mechanisation meant more women had more time. More went to work, more were dissatisfied by their subordinate role and many weren't prepared to put up with the unequal society in which the 'better half' was relegated to a simpery lesser role where they were neither doers nor movers. So women advanced and improved their lot, by careful management and by working together to help each other. Man Alone is the Kiwi archetype. Women Together replaced it. Helen Clark has been both agent and beneficiary of the change.

## Helen Clark

*I think there's a couple of things that have advanced the importance of women. Firstly, we're the baby-boomer generation which got the opportunity to go to university, succeed, and come through as a critical mass to positions in the professions, commercial life and politics, both at central and local government level. Secondly, we're a small society so when trends catch on they can move fairly quickly through a national media with a limited number of local television channels and a national radio system.*

*We are a small national culture so ideas move fairly fast. But I don't think it should be assumed that it was easy. Becoming established as a potential candidate for Prime Minister was the hardest job I ever did. It was very difficult because there was no image of a woman leader, and there weren't too many models overseas either, which you could draw from. There were women leaders in the Indian subcontinent but they were there because of family and dynastic ties. They didn't have to make it on their own in the sort of political system that we do.*

*So it was hard. But once having achieved it, many others can come up through the broken glass ceiling where one almost broke one's own head. We got to twenty percent of the Parliament being female, even without proportional representation. With proportional representation it immediately jumped up to a third. Still a way to go, but the reality is that women are very well accepted in politics at all levels now, as they are accepted in the professions, the union movement, and increasingly in the corporate world.*

How it was achieved was explained by three leading women politicians, Jenny Shipley, the first woman Prime Minister, much to Helen Clark's annoyance, Sandra Lee of the Alliance, and Labour's Marian Hobbs. They came together in a surprisingly non-partisan fashion, to analyse how women had risen to political power. No jokes about not daring to interrupt. I was superfluous to a discussion they ran as efficiently as they run the country.

## Sandra Lee

*In every war men disappeared and women played quite a strong role in all the things that keeps society together. They ran things. Then they always stepped back. There was no third war. There was no major exodus of men again. But by the early 1970s we were stirring to go. In the seventies and eighties we started to go on our own account. The whole society was moving forward. I am a child of that age – well, I'm not a child now, but it was stirring times, we went for it.*

*It's nonsense to say that New Zealand women weren't controlling massive chunks of New Zealand society and New Zealand economies. Maori women were driving the system behind the front for many years. I think there's an emergence and a realisation that the role of government within our lives and within the economy as a whole became larger and larger, that just being absent was no longer acceptable. Government does more today so because of its effect on people it became part of the agenda of women in the early seventies, firstly in local government but eventually in central government. Women were very active in the economy and very active in the lives of their society. Some were treated poorly but a lot were very assertive and very influential without necessarily being in politics. The fact that Maori women have always been politically active is in no small part because they had no choice. A lot of our male population was wiped out in two world wars.*

*New Zealand is quite good at being the first at stuff, we were the first to introduce votes for women, but the track record after that was appalling for a very long period of time. Even now, if you look at the number of women that have been in the House of Representatives compared to the blokes it is pretty appalling for a country that fancies itself as being embracing and egalitarian. The reason why women were grossly under-represented was because New Zealand was a very staid place. Parliament in the sixties, fifties and forties was incredibly polite, incredibly boring, incredibly rural, and incredibly conservative, and also incredibly male.*

*It was seen as having always been like that and probably always would be. It took a long time for women to get their head around the fact that they have a place as of right in the House of Representatives. It took a generation and a movement and a worldwide mood of young people to want to start knocking on some of these political doors. It's harder in a colony like New Zealand. I can remember people like Sir Keith Holyoake and Jack Marshall, and it just seemed like they were there, they would always be there, they were the kind of people that were meant to be there. That's how it was.*

*Feminism was getting another lurch forward and there was massive social change. I came out of secondary school in 1968/69. Our generation could choose our occupation. That changed massively in the seventies and it created controversy and an environment where you had to have a view. Suddenly it meant something to be able to make a difference centrally. That was one of the changes that eventually led women to say, 'I'm going to be there and share the responsibility of those decisions because we have a view.'*

## Jenny Shipley

*In the seventies there was a really dynamic movement amongst women. It was partly driven off the feminist movement but it was also a movement to put women in decision-making. It first came through local government. A number of us in Parliament today went through local government before central government. I can remember on one of the boards I was on as part of my first county council term, their biggest problem was: would I be able to use the bloke's loo, or would they have to build a new one? It was important that that change happened. There was an awakening amongst, certainly my generation, that we should be here too. Women supported women and set ambitious goals for themselves. So we got here.*

## Sandra Lee

*My father was a trade union activist. He went through the 1951 lockout here in Wellington so politics was around the home I grew up in. But, like Jenny, we both got elected to county councils, which had been a bastion of males, in the early eighties. When I campaigned for my county council they thought that having maybe one woman on the council might be okay. But any more than that would upset the balance of the other eleven blokes. Things have changed a lot in the last few years.*

## Marian Hobbs

*My father was always interested in politics. He was a journalist. So politics were in the air. But it was always a politics of observation rather than being involved. I made a deliberate choice when I was about twenty to get involved because I've always seen that life is all about political choices by representative politics. I went out and joined the St Albans branch. I lasted one and a half years, because I was a woman, and relegated to making the tea.*

*While I was in local government I realised that someone else was writing the law and allocating the taxes. When you're at the table where those things go on, you can make a difference to your country, for women, and for your goals. I set my sights on that. To be fair, I was provoked. Ruth Richardson, Sue Wood, other women from centre and centre-right parties were looking for people who had talent, ability and commitment. So there was a conducive environment. Also I was ready. I set a goal. A good seat came up. I bowled over the favoured sons, won selection, and here I am.*

## Jenny Shipley

*Traditionally it's been hard to win seat selections in the National Party because the people vote for you. We don't have a council, we don't have any other system. You've got to be convincing so when you do win it gives you an enormous mandate to get on and do the job. The area I represent had already selected Ruth Richardson in the neighbouring electorate so it wasn't a shock. It is interesting, historically, that a number of the women in the National Party have been selected in conservative electorates, like the South Island. Those with conservative values saw that women did have a role and strongly backed both Ruth and then myself.*

## Sandra Lee

*My journey to Parliament's been Forrest Gumpish. I didn't really aspire to ever become a parliamentarian. But my county council got amalgamated with the largest city in New Zealand and I had a significant lift in profile in Auckland. When the Alliance was formed we had a candidate for the Labour Party in Auckland Central who'd been the architect of the new right reforms and there was a strong desire, particularly on the part of left wing and working-class people to get rid of him. So they jackbooted me into standing. I didn't have a strong desire to become a parliamentarian. But I agree with Jenny that when you've served as long as I have in local government, and I've done a long service, you know that to make the real changes you actually have to get at the legislation.*

## Marian Hobbs

*By the time I came in it was MMP, so I'm really different from both Jenny and Sandra. I was on the list. After you look at the first five you have to look for balance of gender and that immediately meant that women were higher. So my first time into Parliament was coming in off the list.*

*There have been women involved in political decisions in this country outside Parliament, outside councils, for a very long time. I think that's actually what gives you the strength. A woman finally wins through the male hierarchy, then they find that in the community there is a huge support for women candidates. That's what happens in the end. It was the women in the rural organisation. I remember lecturing to a group that used to meet at Lincoln University, a fabulous group of rural women activists from all sectors, all political parties. They didn't have a political party sense about them but they were activists for health, education and environmental issues. They were really strong women, not just volunteers, they were activists.*

## Sandra Lee

*What was interesting in our party was that the economic downturn of the early eighties forced women on out of necessity. Women were sick of doing good work and just showing up. They wanted to start getting hold of the thing by the throat and saying, 'We have a view about this and we do have some knowledge about economic issues as well as the social issues that flow from that.' They were being hit socially and were being hit economically, and they wanted to make a difference.*

*I do think that the ability of New Zealand women, because of our colonial past, and the position of Maori women as well for other reasons, was marginalised for a very long period of time. There was a generation of women who just decided that they weren't going to clock that lot any more. Whatever their political colours they decided that rattling the teacups and the pat on the back on an annual basis wasn't going to work. So there was a strong demand, not just in the voluntary sector, to get to the boardroom tables, to lead the charge in terms of activism, to be the people making the submissions, to be the clinicians, to be the professionals, to be the ones who excelled. I think that the larger representation that we have now was a real fulfilment of the aspirations of that generation.*

## Jenny Shipley

*There were some women who had broken so much ice it did make it easier for other women to aspire and become determined and focused, and set goals and say 'I'm going to take this on because I am as good as my male colleagues.' It was women supporting women and men supporting women. Politicians, both party and parliamentary ones, realised it was going to be hard for them to be relevant in this day and age if they weren't seen as able to make decisions with men and women together, bringing the experience and wisdom of both. I wouldn't want to side myself with the view that this is a gender battle. There are some times where sexism is still very prevalent but there's also a reluctant realisation they ain't going anywhere without us, also an increasing respect that able women and able men together can really crack good government and make a difference.*

## Sandra Lee

*There's a certain amount of mythology, largely spread by women, that if you elect people like us we'll be much better than the blokes. Which we are. There was actually no scientific evidence for that but it became a very PC thing to support the inclusion of women. There were blokes running around everywhere who had their fingers crossed behind their backs that sort of said, because it was the right thing to say, we need women in politics.*

*I remember when I was first elected, it was so different. For women to get elected into county councils was the hardest bastion, a wall in my opinion. I remember when I finally became the county chairman, they could never quite change the title. We had a Queen Street solicitor come along to make a submission. He caught me in the chamber during the luncheon and insisted I clear the table and wipe it for him. I dutifully got the tea trolley and wiped the table. Then I returned at 1 pm as chair. He looked up from his books and papers, I gave him a wink – I think he learned a bit that day.*

## Marian Hobbs

*When I left school in 1965 there were jobs but I didn't have a choice. I was a woman. I was heading for either teaching or maybe journalism. But I wasn't really heading to a great and exciting career as head of a finance bank. Not like the young women who left school from my school in the 1990s who are going to be engineers and doctors and psychiatrists and scientists and accountants. It wasn't like that for me. I felt really circumscribed by social expectations.*

*I don't believe that those social expectations really started to lift off for women until about the 1980s. The things that we got excited about and went onto the streets about in the 1960s and 1970s were abortion, about the only social issue that I can remember to do with women only.*

## Jenny Shipley

*I haven't come to Parliament just to deal with social issues. I'm interested in governance. I think my experience and my skills are equally as relevant and a lot of women in my generation who came into politics held that view. It's legitimate for women to come in for social reasons, for particular activist reasons, and that has been a change I've observed since I've been here. The broader base you now observe. But there's one other thing you can't overlook. My generation could control our fertility. If I look even in the early- and mid-sixties the ability to control our fertility and make choices meant that we weren't second class. We were equal with choices. It's wrong to overlook that fundamental change. The second thing was the technology revolution has allowed women to make the choice of coming to*

*Parliament. It doesn't take all Saturday to do the washing. You push the buttons as you rush past the machine. In my adult lifetime that's changed massively from my children and my husband being dependent on me, to all of us being able to expect to be independent and interdependent without compromising each other's aspirations. So technology is why we are where we are today.*

## Sandra Lee

*I don't think that there's been huge changes from my perspective. There's enormous pride in this country that we've had women in the highest elected positions. I haven't noticed any improvement in the behaviour of men in my years in the House. I haven't noticed that women behave better than men anyway. I certainly didn't come here to hold hands and pray. I'm an atheist. But I do think that the fundamental issue is that no woman comes to the House of Representatives because she wants to come and bring her body and her gender into the House in isolation to everything else. But what I do think is important is that every single woman that comes into the House has come and demanded the right not to be disadvantaged from getting there in the first place by virtue of their gender.*

## Marian Hobbs

*Women are in the House because we are human beings and have as much right to be here as anybody else. We bring different perspectives but because I was born a girl doesn't mean I shouldn't be an engineer, doesn't mean I shouldn't be a politician. So those of us who have driven and worked hard to have women in the House come from the view that there should be no block to us. I don't think we'll step back from that, but that doesn't mean that I'm going to accept that only a third should be there. I'd be quite happy if the whole House were women. I don't care.*

The advance of the monstrous regiment has some way to go. Yet women have changed the tone and the substance of political debate and are now well represented, though they find it easier on the lists, where parties try to keep themselves respectable, than in the directly elected seats. Yet success has been an inoculation. More women there encourage more to come and make women the norm, not the exception.

Parliamentary representation is on its way to finding whatever its natural level might be. Yet women are still under-represented in universities, particularly outside the ghetto of Women's Studies, and business remains a largely male preserve still associated with the male characteristics of aggression, dynamism and loud-mouthed boasting (even though none of this has made New Zealand business particularly honest or successful). Women have a real contribution to make in networking and sensitivity in business, but they are not coming forward to master it, and in the most dynamic sector of New Zealand business, the small firm and the family firm, they are the most exploited though partners in decision-making and everything else. Wives keep the thing going but the men like to think they decide, so women's role in the partnership is more behind the scenes and less up-front than it should be.

Yet the pace of advance has been enormous over the last two decades and will increase again as women move out of the caring occupations and up into all reaches of power and decision-making. Once that change has started there is no way it can be stopped or rolled back. It will find, not its natural level, for that is a sexist assumption, but the preferred level for the women themselves.

That deserves to be substantial, even dominant, for in New Zealand the female of the species is tougher and more dedicated than the effete males who have held power for so long only to end up grumbling at the advance of women and carping at 'FemiNazis', or resentfully escaping into the refuges of sports, sheds, and alcohol. The best indicator of the prospect to come is young people. The young male culture is defensive, escapist, even resentful. That of the young women is real and realistic as well as more serious and dedicated. The one looks well geared to progress, the other for regression. So perhaps it's time for the emancipation and radicalisation of young males, but no doubt women will take proper care of that, as soon as they're in effective control.

**Chapter Ten**

# Maori

Maori hardly featured in the *Half-gallon Quarter-acre* because they made no impact on my life in a South Island insulated from racial as from all other problems. The racial problem in Dunedin was Scots, and the colour problem a choice of tartans. Students (all white, of course) once tried to show me how to do a haka but the lesson was cut short by genital injury. People made jokes about 'keeping Maori time' and *Truth* had a column where animals were 'cunning as a Maori dog' and Maori said 'py kori' and were portrayed as idle. For the most part Maori might as well not have existed.

Stereotypes were all I had to go on, though I did interview Maori MPs, who responded to my questionnaires with a sententious ponderousness I thought at the time must have been significant (if only I'd understood it). My only experience of race relations was marching to protest against Maori being excluded from the South African tour, a demonstration as bereft of Maori as the team; and watching an incident in Dunedin's only Chinese restaurant when a drunken, self-proclaimed digger loudly attacked the Chinese owner as 'not one of us' but staggered over to hug an embarrassed Maori delivery man, proclaiming that he was. Race relations don't feature when there are no other races to relate to.

Today racist humour is dead and it would be impossible to ignore Maori as individuals or as a culture. They have a new pride and a new assertiveness, a bigger role, and general indifference has been replaced by a widespread desire to make atonement for past wrongs and to close present gaps. The Maori renaissance has generated a new pride and a new sense of purpose. The rush to the cities has transformed a de facto apartheid, with a rural Maori population in the remoter and less fertile parts of the North Island, into an urban melting pot. The renaissance emphasises the tribe and tradition. The urban drift detribalises, cutting Maori off from traditional structures, and bringing them together as Maori rather than Ngati Kahu or Ngati Porou. They are plugged into the Pakeha market economy but mostly at the bottom end. In the good years high pay and full employment opened the prospect of progress. That didn't happen because sado-economics hit Maori particularly hard.

It took time for the radicalisation which advanced blacks in the USA to develop in New Zealand. Blacks and Asians had been imported into American and British societies. Maori were the first possessors, which conferred rights, status and an automatic right to representation the others lacked. It also brought more support and sympathy from a majority motivated either by guilt and a desire to atone, or from feelings of national solidarity, two races one nation, welded together by war and sport. So discrimination was less harsh and the New Zealand experience more accommodating and harmonious, while Maori have been less aggressive.

The identity is less clear cut. The census has changed its definition of Maori several times and now counts as Maori the quarter of a million who identify themselves as that, plus a further quarter million who describe themselves as Maori and some other race, usually Pakeha. That leaves out the 56,000 who have Maori ancestry but do not identify as such. Only around half of those with Maori ancestry and entitlement plus anyone with an element of Maori blood, or who feels themselves to be Maori, bother to register as a Maori for voting, and intermarriage has been so extensive that most youngsters have a non-Maori parent. Sir Tipene O'Regan, with an Irish father and Maori mother, was Steve O'Regan in his student days and still faces the joke, 'I knew you when you were a Pakeha'. He says, 'When people began to get worried about the extent to which I was Maori I said, "I don't care. I'm Ngati Tahu and you can get bothered as much as you like over that but it's not my worry."' While John Tamihere, whose great-great-great-grandfather signed the Treaty of Waitangi, and whose father married a woman from County Cork, explained his own Maori identity to her:

## John Tamihere

*She found it very difficult and said to me, 'My boy, you're making me feel uncomfortable because everything you come home with and talk about is Maori this, Maori that. What about your Irish and Scots side?' I said, 'Well Mum, if I was in Dublin I'd probably be in the IRA. If I was in Scotland I'd probably be a Scots Nationalist. But I'm a New Zealander so I've taken on a bit more of that.' With that sort of analogy she had a fair idea of where we were coming from. In your genealogical make-up you've got to be respectful of all your bloodlines. You can't put your Maori ancestors ahead if you have mixed genealogical connections, and if you practise your customs properly you are never brought up to stamp on the head of any ancestor. A lot of bad things can happen if you do.*

In other words, you looks at your lineage and you makes your choice. In a survey only half the Maori interviewed described themselves as such. The rest opted for 'Kiwi', 'New Zealander' or some cocktail description. An identity soft at its very wide edges is not going to produce a driving ethnic force to threaten the majority.

The names of the government departments with Maori responsibilities have changed regularly. So have the roles, shifting from the paternalism of the Hunn report to 'by Maori for Maori' solutions. The view that there is a gap between Maori and Pakeha has always been the central preoccupation. Yet even that is questionable. In fact, the gaps appear to be narrowing, not widening. Self-employment rose faster than among Pakeha and the average weekly income rose to $351 for Maori as against $467 for Pakeha. As the exploding Maori birth rate hits the labour market the ratio of workers to dependants among Maori will increase as it falls for Pakeha, reversing the trend for them to be relatively poor because their workforce is so small.

The first arrivals in the cities found easy, well-paid jobs. This created no pressure to improve themselves or their families when Rogernomics destroyed the jobs: Maori homes were not as educationally supportive or as pushy as middle-class Pakeha, because they'd assumed work was easily come by, so Maori kids weren't as motivated. Unemployment created a culture of despair and social disintegration so well chronicled by Alan Duff. People I spoke to deplored Duff, but more because of his right wing politics and his political incorrectness in drawing attention to inconvenient issues, than because of the accuracy of his picture. With forty-four percent of people in prison Maori, there is clearly a problem. In the sixties, the Guide Rangi image of Maori prevailed. There were no Maori studies, no sociology, no history. Until a Pakeha, Michael King, began to write it.

## Michael King

*I began to write about Maori for two reasons. Nobody else was doing it at the time – Maori or Pakeha – and secondly, I had started my journalism career in a Maori area, Waikato, working for the* Waikato Times. *I got assigned what was called 'the Maori Round' and spent my weekends attending events and didn't understand a word of what was going on. So I enrolled in Maori lessons to be able to understand and do that particular job. In the course of it I started to hear the kinds of stories that I felt ought to be part of the New Zealand historical equation but simply weren't being heard.*

*I decided to move from journalism into writing history and biography around Maori topics. They weren't writing it because Maori culture was an oral culture, not a literary one. Shortly after I started doing this the Maori renaissance got into full gear. The things I was writing probably contributed to it, but as it gathered momentum a voice was then heard in Maoridom saying we are the ones who should be writing about it and analysing it and not somebody from across the cultural frontier. The time that that started to be said emphatically was the time that I looked elsewhere for other things to do.*

Maori are no longer a back-burner issue. Their old, tired, tame leadership was docile in the days of full employment, but the Maori renaissance produced a new confidence, and economic problems produced new leaders to lead them forward, transforming Maori from a tourist attraction into a problem.

## Tipene O'Regan

*There are key historical drivers in the reshaping of the Maori consciousness and the strengthening of iwi and tribes. The Second World War was a powerful force, followed by the population explosion.*

*For a short time the Maori birth rate was one of the highest for any ethnic group in the world and that was accompanied by economic structural change in the rural areas. So you had a huge shift of a Maori population not into the heart of the city or into the heart of what makes cities tick, but suburban and characterised by low incomes and huge concentrations.*

*That created a repoliticisation of Maori, driven by a level of concentration, that the Maori population had never had before. With the increased wealth and the increased mobility of the population, cheaper cars and all those sorts of things, Maori people who were retiring or who were doing well in the cities were going back. There was a constant movement backwards and forwards between city and the home territory. People were dying in the city and being taken home for burial.*

*In the rural areas the heartland was being refurbished with urban money and particularly the marae and the homes by repatriated urban wealth. Maori consciousness and Maori cultural capacity grew and flowered. Demographic change had powerful effects.*

In Michael King's view the renaissance was more than this, though he recognises the great benefits it brought.

## Michael King

*The effect of the Maori renaissance has been extraordinary. It's completely rewritten the social contract in New Zealand. At the time that I grew up, New Zealand always thought it had the best race relations in the world and Sir Keith Holyoake would always say that in international forums. But the reason New Zealand appeared to have good race relations was because Maori and Pakeha lived in different parts of the country. Once Maori came into the cities in large numbers and Maori and Pakeha were interacting there was conflict and New Zealand society had to change.*

*It has changed. The judicial system has changed. The education system has changed, the way the public service system works has changed. All those changes have come about as a result of the Maori renaissance. It's produced a degree of backlash but the number of good, solid rednecks in New Zealand is actually very small. Most New Zealand Pakeha want to do the right thing by Maori. They want to understand what they ought to be doing and why things are being done. The resentment I am more concerned about is not the one which suggests that everything has been done for the Maori but the one which suggests that we are now over-emphasising the place of Maori culture in New Zealand life as against the Pakeha cultural ingredient. People are now starting to say, I think with some justification, just as Pakeha don't have the right to demean Maori culture, Maori don't have the right to demean Pakeha culture.*

Maori culture was at last more important to Pakeha than hakas and hongis.

## Tipene O'Regan

*We have an interesting example of the Kiwi village with the Te Maori exhibition in the early eighties. All of a sudden to see this selection of treasures at the Metropolitan in New York with Maori elders opening it, and Americans queuing for it, write-ups in the* New York Times, *suddenly New Zealand glowed. When the exhibition came back and it was moved through New Zealand, there were queues up and down the country in all the major centres. That had a profound effect. There's still a thriving Maori art and culture, particularly in the contemporary area. It's quite stunning. The Maori presence in the national culture is increasingly a very rich one.*

*When we were at about ten percent of the population I remember saying we should have ten percent of television, ten percent of national radio, ten percent of the music space. If you ran that argument right through on a population-based arts funding you would have some pretty dramatic changes. We know that within my own people the group that just come together to sing and go round the tribe teaching it is a very powerful unifying element and it has a presence today that it certainly did not have twenty or thirty years ago.*

The main driver of change was political, the radicalisation of Maori representation, from Ratana MPs to more energetic and able members like Mana Motuhake's Matiu Rata.

## Tipene O'Regan

*I was arrested in the fifties over rugby and the general race relations issue. That issue was largely won. Holyoake and Marshall came to power and just said that non-inclusive Maori teams were over and finished. Marshall wrote that policy because he was that kind of very highly principled liberal. So I regarded the 1959–60 battle as a battle that was won.*

*The battles of the eighties were really about relationships with South Africa. I was restrained but did end up outside Lancaster Park with a group of my Ngai Tahu aunties from Kaikoura who thought we ought to make a stand. Half of the*

*The tree as a national icon. Colin Meads at Te Kuiti*

ABOVE: *Mount Cook, me and friends. Ball Pass*
BELOW: *It's tough to break into women's rugby. Taupo*

ABOVE: *Some sheds are air conditioned: Jim Hopkins, Lyttelton*

RIGHT: *Ab Fab Fashionista: Trelise Cooper, Parnell*

ABOVE: *Artists export too: Grahame Sydney. Dunedin*

LEFT: *An ordinary joker getting old before his time. Taumarunui*

*PTO for further messages from our sponsor. The Edge, Auckland*

ABOVE: *Welcome to Polynesia, Otara Branch. Otara market*

LEFT: *I can't see the Campbells coming. Can you? Tuatapere*

ABOVE: *Smile and say 'Clistchurch'. Christchurch Cathedral Square*

BELOW: *World Famous in Tuatapere: Sausage Capital*

*I think it produces tinned milk. Queenstown*

Ngai Tahu Trust board was out with us and the other half was sitting in the grandstand. There wasn't the unity amongst us in that period.

Bastion Point had a huge effect, not so much on Maori because they are generally pretty knowledgeable about the appalling evil which was done to the Ngati Whatua, the Orakei people, by the Labour and National governments successively. It was bad and it reflected some of the worst aspects of the function of class and racism in New Zealand society. What shocked most New Zealanders was the sight in full colour in their front sitting rooms. Television brought essentially northern concerns into everyone's home. Here were New Zealand policemen, New Zealand soldiers, New Zealand officials reading Riot Acts and forcibly removing other New Zealanders. That went through the nation and had a very marked effect. People started to say how did this happen? A whole bunch of Maori, clearly not violent, nasty, turbulent people, with old ladies singing hymns being carted away in truckloads. It had a profound impact.

There was also the regular television coverage of what I have called 'the Februaries of our discontent', the seasonal marches on Waitangi which were getting more and more violent. There was a huge cross-section of people tied up in those protests. There might have been enormous distances between the most conservative Maori elements of the traditional Maori leadership and the expressions of urban violence at the other end of it. But the one thing they all had in common was their concern about the Article Two rights and the Treaty.

There was common ground about the treaty grievances historically. The genius of the Lange Labour government was to seize on that and diffuse that violence which was growing, by the simple fact of taking what we had advocated in 1975 as Ngai Tahu by simply giving the Waitangi tribunal the authority to investigate various issues back to 1840. Suddenly all of the tribes started to focus on due process research and analysis and *presentation of their arguments. Order was brought about, appointments were made to the tribunal and those who were protesting for the sake of protesting suddenly found themselves without an alliance.*

Jim Bolger's government offered $1 billion, as an 'envelope' not to be exceeded. It was promptly 'returned to sender' by Maori leaders, and trebling or quadrupling is probably essential though it will never be raised to the levels of loss, updated to present-day values of $16–18 billion for Ngai Tahu and $122 billion for Tainui, and so far government has responded to demands to raise the ceiling with a judicious silence. Sufficient to the day is the evil thereof.

Having struggled through all the legislation, the insertion of Waitangi rights into state-owned enterprise legislation, and faced down cries of dismay about the loss of land and rights, the Labour government now considers that the Waitangi process is the way forward.

## Margaret Wilson

*The whole process of the method we chose in New Zealand to address the recognition of past grievances was under the Treaty of Waitangi. It's taking so long because we didn't choose to do the sort of global apology and hand over a vast sum of money to an entity. We chose, because that was the agreement with Maori, to acknowledge the specific grievances where they occurred to people in a particular area. The apology is extremely important in my view because it is acknowledging your history and it's trying to do it in the most honest way you can. Saying sorry is not enough, you've also got to have compensation and the compensation has to be specific to the ancestors that suffered that grievance to their descendants. It's for them to decide what they wish to do with that. It's harder and it's not tidy, but ultimately it probably is the best way to go.*

> *The Waitangi process is not going to produce equality for Maori. It's a settlement of historical claims. But it will be a very necessary part of a continuing process. We have found in addressing the past that it's much more complex than people realised ten or fifteen years ago. But the future can only be addressed through acknowledgement of the past. The transferring of resources is what's happening at the moment. How those resources are used is essentially a decision for Maori. By definition, imposing a solution would be in opposition to the notion of partnership and what the Treaty was about. It would be one partner telling the other what to do.*

The Treaty is a shaky base on which impressive structures are being built. At the time a convenient con to satisfy a home government reluctant to take on yet another colony, that New Zealand was being donated by incumbent authorities while persuading them that nothing much had changed. Since then it has been reinterpreted by historians and more vigorously by judges, taking the injunction not to act in a manner inconsistent with its principles, as a living instrument. Maori began to demand its extension from land to fishing rights to even the airwaves, so the process and the legal industry associated with it don't lack for critics decrying it as a back-door constitution imposed without consent to give one section of the population greater constitutional rights. Bob Jones ridicules the results:

## Sir Bob Jones

*I'm very concerned about this contrived race issue that has been generated. People are very angry about constantly having things Maori pushed down their throats, including Maoris I might add. The history of Maoridom in New Zealand has been to be patronised and treated very well. The Waitangi process has been taken right over the top. The Arts Council recently spent*

*$850,000 on devising a new logo. But it had to be a Maori logo. Why does it have to be a Maori logo? Maoris represent fifteen percent of the population. Did the money go to a designer? No, it did not. It went to flying Maoris in from all over New Zealand to have huis. We get this sort of bloody nonsense all the time.*

*Every time we open a new embassy – and bear in mind we've got a Labour government so we're opening them all over the world, we'll start on the moon soon – this group of Maoris have to be flown in to chant and purify the bloody place. It's an insult to everybody and the cost is enormous.*

*This constant pushing over of this Maori thing at the remaining eight-five percent of the population does cause irritation. Maoris are migrants here, like we are. We're all migrants. Yet now we've selected this race and suddenly every government department has to have a Maori name, everything has to be advertised in Maori. Nobody bloody reads Maori and we all have to pay for this sort of patronising sentimentality.*

A more basic criticism comes from John Tamihere. The Waitangi process delivers direct benefits to Maori still integrated in the kiwi structures, but many aren't.

## John Tamihere

*My great-great-great-grandfather signed the Treaty of Waitangi in 1841 and the rights that he granted me in doing that I don't have to go back to. If I'm a Catholic I don't have to go to Rome to practise. I'm from Tainui and I don't have to go back to my tribal domain to practise the rights that he signed up for me in 1840. A lot of people want us to go back. I don't subscribe to that view. We no longer live in the model that has been settled on. Our tribes don't exist socially, politically and culturally the way they did; eighty-six percent of all Maori are urban and eighty percent of them are under the age of forty. It's a very young demographic, and they no longer live in tribal domains in enclaves. Most Maori are detribalised and the tribal tie is fading. Up and down the country, many have no tribal organisational capacity or infrastructure, and many are excluded from the Waitangi process. Anyone with a brain in Tainui doesn't live there. I don't know whether you've been on the east coast of the North Island or not, but they grow reasonable sheep and gorse, but if you've got bigger populations you've got to move out to where the new economies and the new technologies are. Only ten percent of my tribe live in the tribal homeland, but those ten percent under the new regime have a huge say over the ninety percent that don't.*

Too bad, says Margaret Wilson, urban Maori have to reconnect. In Sir Tipene O'Regan's view its join or lose out.

## Sir Tipene O'Regan

*I don't know who the urban Maori are. You are talking about a group that has been invented. They are Maori people who belong to iwi, some of them live in cities. Their leadership who run the argument that they are excluded are essentially contract social service providers. They are prevented from getting at the assets.*

*The fisheries settlement is not a cornucopia of instant welfare cheques, it's a right to own some capital. It's the equivalent to owning a paddock. You have then got to fence it, plough it, plant it, then harvest it and market your product, then you get a dividend. We are talking about capital here, not a distribution of cash.*

*If you are Maori you must be a member of an iwi. You are entitled to belong. What a citizen does do is a citizen's business but it is not for some group to capture capital assets which belong to collectives of people. If you wanted to break the whole thing up and split it you would get somewhere under two thousand dollars a head for every man woman and child and everyone says well that's over. So is your fisheries. So is your resource.*

Money is divisive. In John Tamihere's view, it's going into traditional politics not where it's needed.

## John Tamihere
*It's hard to engage and participate with people that hold your cheque-book. Even at the best of times they don't listen. They always look at you as if your elders moved out, you moved out, but we sacrificed everything to hold on to what we have got.*

*The second line of the argument is that you're looking to upset the apple-cart because you have got shares in land. I might have a farm. So you're going to upset their societal infrastructure. All this hocus pocus about 'we're a loving, caring, beautiful iwi that love everybody and look after them', I find very difficult to accept.*

*The new tribal aristocracy has done quite well. You can name them on two hands. They drive the best cars and own the best houses. I don't mind that if it's based on merit. I do mind if it was based on my grievances. All I'm trying to do is wake them up to their duties, obligations and responsibilities as fiduciaries.*

The accusation is strenuously denounced by Sir Tipene O'Regan.

## Sir Tipene O'Regan
*Part of the argument is a series of slogans mouthed out of Parliament that the tribes are led by some sort of ageing kleptocracy that has plundered the people. These people mouthing it drive around in big four-wheel drives and participate in a parliamentary model that in 1990 dollars was spending $2400 a minute on the poor. In my thirty-nine years on the front for Ngai Tahu I have only found two leaders who*

*have improperly enriched themselves, and then not very effectively, and I have only known one or two lawyers that I'd put into the same category. If you are a Maori you belong to a tribe or you have a right to belong to a tribe. Whether that person wants to participate in the life of the tribe or whether they want to derive their social services from a contract service provider is up to them. I challenge the concept, but it is a very good drum to beat because the power culture loves to have a model of urban dispossession in order to justify its social policies.*

Margaret Wilson argues that equality is a Section Three issue, the common rights of citizenship available to all. John Tamihere prefers a new political activism.

## John Tamihere

*I'm only a little half-breed out of West Auckland. I'm in the big house and nobody would have thought of that ten years ago. I've got huge support out on the streets where it counts. The organisations that support me are head-down backside-up type organisations that are working day in, day out to keep people's heads above water, and they are good people.*

*Urban activism was led by the Maoris from Bastion Point. It was the return of urban Maori dispossessed and disadvantaged. The improvements came out of urban Maori drivers. They had a lot of vim and vigour, just as expat communities often hold on to their culture more than the home-based ones.*

Sir Tipene O'Regan sees it more as an issue of economic advance.

## Sir Tipene O'Regan

*There are two things. There's the general participation and economic contribution. Some groups, like the Mongatu Incorporation in Gisborne which is over a hundred years old, the Waipareira Trust, Whakatipu Incorporated, the Arawa Land Trust, have been significant contributors to our economy and to our exports for a very long time. No one bothers to notice them, or the exports they earn, the employment they create.*

*New Zealanders cannot cope with the idea of significant Maori economic success anywhere. The lengths they go to avoid the fact that the Whale Watch Kaikoura company is entirely Maori owned and operated is really quite an interesting dimension of the character.*

*I'm optimistic, at the end of the day, biology will determine it much more than public policy and the biology is in favour of the shift to Maori. One of the problems is as the Maori middle class increase they will tend to move, as the Afro-American middle class has done, towards being more politically conservative or at least against the welfare culture. That may mean that the Maori political spectrum will differ.*

Current stars of the American process of advance by enrichment are the Tamaki brothers, who turned an inspired idea for tourism into a multi-million dollar business.

## Mike Tamaki

*About fifteen years ago I used to drive for various tour companies in New Zealand. There was always a real gap in the market for more personalised tours, and particularly those that portray the Maori culture a bit more in-depth. Maori culture was superficially portrayed but it was of a stereotype nature and nothing of any depth was really coming through.*

*When we started we were leather clad, long-haired boys riding Harleys around, and probably not fitting the description suitable for a bank manager to give you a loan. I remember approaching the old bank manager. There he was, you know, bank managers all look the same. They've got grey hair, all swept back, big thick glasses and eyebrows that run right across their heads from one side to the other. He had NO stamped diagonally all across his face and I had a half-page proposal. 'I need a bus to get this thing going', I said. He chucked it back at me.*

*I eventually went and saw my brother. He had a Harley Davidson he used to keep cleaner than his face. It took me three months to convince him to sell his Harley. We did all the marketing ourselves. We didn't have any schooling or education about how to market. We just started building relationships with people and that's how we got going. The company now employs 120 people and we have around about 153,000 people go through every year. We try very hard to create businesses within our business.*

Maori business, Maori television and programme production, support for Maori enterprise, even Maori welfare organisations, liberal councils and the fisheries and language bodies are all viewed with intense suspicion by Pakeha critics eager to detect graft, Canadian con-men or the smell of Tuku Morgan's underpants – as if no Pakeha organisation ever went bust, no Pakeha contract was ever fraudulent and television wasn't peopled by con-artists. Kiwis love to cut the heads off tall poppies, but brown ones are slashed nearer the roots. The obsession is ignoble, inhibiting and shows more than a touch of desire to keep Maori in their place. It is essentially jealousy. Maori have both a right and a need to develop their own culture and interests in their own way. One nation, two cultures is a desirable and exciting outcome as long as each respects, stimulates and learns from the other.

## Michael King

*Biculturalism should go to the extent that people who want to be Maori can do so, and that the facilities and the opportunities for them to do so are there, just as the facilities and opportunities are there for people like me to be Pakeha. I think that the Maori language should not be compulsory but it should be available at every school in the country; if it's not, then you are only paying lip service to a concept such as biculturalism. So I'm still convinced that for most Maori that's the most fruitful way to go, and for the country as a whole that's the way to go because if Maori are content in their situation, if they are living in a way that allows them to be Maori in ways of their own choice, then they are going to be much easier people for Pakeha to deal with. The bicultural equation in New Zealand is only going to work when both peoples have access to their own cultures and both respect the cultures across the cultural divide. Each should be at ease with their own tradition while recognising the validity of the other.*

Merger will go on. Artists blend the cultures but both will develop in their own way to contribute to the new nation.

## John Tamihere

*To be proud of Maori is great. We've taken our culture and we are moving on, we're not leaving it behind. Right now I represent a constituency that has 680,000 Kiwis in it, but 190,000 Maori. It's got 380 schools. When I go to those school prize-givings eighty-five percent of the school is getting up and doing Maori culture. When you look out in the audience to their parents they are beaming, they are ebullient, they are proud. Their children now are developing, after Britain took off to the EEC, a feel and understanding of what it is to be a Kiwi. This is part of the evolution of nationhood. I believe in that. I know it's happening because I can see it and feel it, and it's great. Those kids that will be the captains of our industry by the year 2050 will have a different world-view of what it is to be a Kiwi, and of the Maori participation in the evolution of the nation.*

Chapter Eleven

# Auckland

Auckland City is neither New Zealand nor a city, but an enormous sprawl hoping to be a city when it grows up. Cities have dominant centres. Auckland is a few streets surrounded by a vast suburban sprawl covering an area greater than London. A droplet of city in a sea of suburbia, rivalled by half a dozen mini conurbations all called cities, clustering round like planets of a mini-sun, drawing shoppers, businesses and activity away from the centre, which is left the preserve of tourists, cruise-liner passengers with a day to spare, and hobgobs up for a visit. Shoot a gun (preferably a large one) down Queen Street and you'd bump off more foreigners than natives. Here even the bums are Chinese.

New Zealand is cut off, south of the Bombay Hills. The real New Zealand is agricultural and rural, busily producing what Auckland spends. The GDP, the exports, the production that pays New Zealand's way in the world come from the rest of the country. Auckland imports, consumes and manipulates money. Finance lives here, production further south. Auckland is peopleopolis, a spreading suburban mess trying to be a great city but never quite making it.

Auckland is more pluralistic and cosmopolitan than New Zealand. It houses the largest Polynesian community in Polynesia and is a fifth Asian – Chinese like the urban life and Auckland is New Zealand's nearest approximation to it. Though remote from the preoccupations and lives of most of New Zealand, a remote head-office town somewhere 'up there', the place where those youngsters not committed enough to go into the public service and not smart enough to go overseas end up, Auckland is the commercial, media, fashion and huckster capital. Headquarters to the national TV channels, to finance and markets and those big companies who haven't transferred head offices to Australia yet.

Auckland is the glass of fashion and the mould of form (not now a reference to Spirella corsets), the biggest centre of population, but not quite metropolitan enough to satisfy those young New Zealanders keen for city life, a craving which can be satisfied in Sydney, Melbourne, Los Angeles or London, but not Auckland, which can provide only a diluted form of metropolitan life for those who want to be in bed by ten. It may satisfy neophyte suits and those who don't quite dare to venture into the big pool, but it's third division south compared to the real thing.

Which makes it an amateur version of Australia, constantly trying with its bridge, its tower, its skyline, to emulate Sydney but neither big nor beautiful and certainly not brutal enough to make it. Neither the bridge nor the harbour can compete with Sydney, but Auckland is growing fast enough to make New Zealand top-heavy, scheduled on present growth rates to reach a population of two million by 2020. That will lop-side what was once a four city, federal, balance completely. Because it's growing, Auckland is a property boomtown. Not necessarily a sign of economic health.

If Auckland doesn't quite make it in the big city stakes, it goes far enough in that direction to be different to the rest of New Zealand. Its Mayor is an outspoken populist, John Banks, a former National Party MP and Minister of Police, a health food manufacturer, and passionate advocate of cracked bee pollen. He was triumphantly elected in November 2001 after a long sojourn in redneck radio where the answers are easy and the audience huge, making his transition to local government, with all its complexities, a difficult one. New Zealand's fastest-firing populist, ever ready to shoot from the mouth, now faces up to the problems of its biggest city.

## John Banks

*Auckland's growth is good and bad. It's good because this country desperately needs more population but it's bad because it has a huge impact on the infrastructure and that needs to be dealt with because the population of Greater Auckland will double in the next twenty-five years. It will unbalance New Zealand but the rest of New Zealand is not that important. Auckland is New Zealand. Everything north of the Bombay Hills is New Zealand.*

*This is the powerhouse of the economy. In recent years it*

*hasn't performed that well. Greater Auckland has been dragging the chain and we need to look again here in terms of investment, growth, jobs and economic output. Real New Zealanders do come from the South Island. I appreciate that. But those of us who make things happen live in Auckland because this is where the world begins and finishes. This is the epicentre of the yachting fraternity for the world. This is where the America's Cup belongs. So it should be the greatest city in the world.*

Helen Clark, herself an Auckland member, is prepared to help, though less than Banks might want.

## Helen Clark

*Auckland is very important because it's the only metropolis in the country. It's a tremendous advantage to be an Auckland-based politician. Auckland is a third of the population. It's also a city, which has a tremendous amount of New Zealand's export and import trade flow through it. Good access to its ports and its airports is very important, and over many years Auckland hasn't had its share of the transport dollar out of central government. Auckland didn't get its share of the transport dollar over a very long period of time, perhaps because the previous government had an anti-Auckland bias, but the money didn't go in here when it should have. That's something that's starting to be corrected now.*

*Sooner or later something has to be done for Auckland. If Auckland is working well the country is going well. What's held New Zealand growth back in recent years is that Auckland hasn't been in a position to take advantage of the export-led growth, which other parts of New Zealand have had. What happened with the sudden removal of tariffs was that the industry built up in Auckland and, reliant on tariff protection and import protection, faded away. It's taken a long time for new internationally competitive industries to grow here. So there was that period when Auckland was a big service-oriented consuming economy but not generating much export wealth. Therefore when you go into a phase of export-led growth Auckland doesn't benefit from it.*

However, Auckland is merely the central city in a ring of cities clustered round, restricting its growth, ensuring that it can do nothing on its own. Bob Harvey is Labour Mayor of Waitakere City and a former campaign manager to Sir Dove-Myer Robinson, the dynamic reforming Auckland Mayor whose proud plans were frustrated by the then much larger numbers of tin-pot boroughs surrounding him.

## Bob Harvey

*It was impossible for anyone not to like Robbie. I was his campaign manager. I raced around with him to those bleak, dark halls where a thousand people used to turn up to hear him. I adored Robbie. He taught me everything I know about politics. Robbie was the great visionary and if they had listened to him and done the things he wanted, we would have leapt ahead, but he was stopped by the petty jealousies of the other mayors. They had mayors in Newmarket for God's sake, and Mount Eden, so Robbie was the mayor of a very tiny part of the region.*

*Auckland is trapped. It has nowhere to go and yet it is the very hub of the wheel. So we've got to work with the edge cities. We shouldn't fix Auckland if it isn't broken.*

One conurbation, one authority, one mayor, one focus, is the logical solution. Central government would fear that as creating an enormously powerful rival: an elephant in the cuckoo's nest. None of the local politicians want it. Except Banks, who is prepared for it 'down the road'. Provided he were mayor.

Auckland is a difficult subject to write about for a professional South Islander, a Mainland Mainliner because it's a mess, but a lively pulsing one. Auckland is Life: the lively focus of fashion, music, media and culture. Elsewhere they are scattered like mission stations in hostile territory or spread like aerial top-dressing. In Auckland they're concentrated. Like fashion. Trelise Cooper is one of New Zealand's top fashion designers, Auckland-based and proud of it. Trelise has been a major contributor to the flowering of fashion.

## Trelise Cooper

*What my international audience really enjoy about what I and other New Zealand designers do is that we do something different. There are no constraints, there are no traditional ways in which we are supposed to dress so we can be a little bit whacky. It's original and it's unique and individual.*

*We're great risk takers. I think we're quite a determined nation. We've got that Number-Eight-Fencing-Wire attitude. We can do. I'm untrained, and that makes me unconventional. I say 'we want to do it like this,' or 'I want this,' and they go, 'Well, you can't do that,' and I go, 'Oh I can.' So somehow we make it work, and I think that unconventionality is a freedom.*

*You find the beautiful New Zealand wines on the best wine lists in the world and I believe that New Zealand fashion is headed the same way. What's unique is a lack of constraint, we don't have any heritage constraints. It's a 'can do' attitude. We were old fashioned a little while ago and we are not anymore. We don't have anything we have to conform to. So we can be uniquely original.*

All this is made in Auckland by local workers in a busy Parnell workshop where the detail and the design can be done in a way that wouldn't be possible in a cheaper Indonesian sweatshop.

Fashion is part of the cultural industries' complex of arts, pop, media, writing, theatre, dance, opera and music. All need cities. So New Zealand's biggest supports the biggest concentration. If art sprang from beautiful surroundings rather than hard graft it wouldn't live in Auckland but would wear gumboots. New Zealand would have more culture per acre than anywhere outside the Elysian Fields. That was the hope of settlers, and Thomas Bracken, poet of God's Own Country, put it in worse verse:

*Here the poet might soon gather subjects for a thousand lays*
*Here the artist might discover rich employment all his days.*

Robert Stout said, a century prematurely, that Bracken had 'helped to create a national literature'. It didn't happen. New Zealand was neither big nor urban enough. The backblocks now throng with post offices turned into craft centres, banks into potteries and sheep-shearing sheds into galleries. There are even pottery motels where, presumably, visitors cast their own breakfast bowls. The lower levels of the art chain struggle in the country to live on whatever share of the tourist dollar they can attract. If anyone ever stops. To flourish, art needs cities. There are the concentrations of consumers, competition and cash without which culture wilts.

The infant industry argument, which Dr Sutch turned into a system of economics, applies to culture. It needs funding and nurturing and has been supported by governments, the New Zealand Lotteries Commission, National Film Unit, New Zealand on Air and New Zealand quotas for pop music. Classical music, opera, ballet and the theatre need subsidy. Ian Fraser originally wanted to be an actor and went north from Dunedin to Wellington, to the only professional theatre, after Richard Campion's brave pioneering effort to establish a national theatre company failed when the New Zealand Players had crashed, long ago in 1960.

## Ian Fraser

*I came to Wellington wanting to become a professional actor in 1970 and by 1973 I was working as the Executive Officer for the Performing Arts at the Queen Elizabeth II Arts Council. The job involved my going out to at least five fledgling professional theatre companies and sitting with the incredible believers who'd set these places up. All a kind of imitation of Downstage, because if it could happen in Wellington, why wouldn't it happen in Wanganui or Dunedin? I'd sit with them to write their budgets and submissions to the Arts Council. And during that year at least five new theatre companies came in with a certain quantum of government subsidy. It wasn't very high but then it didn't need to be.*

*We moved from Downstage to having a viable regional network of professional theatres within the space of a decade. You'd see a Stoppard play in the West End with a starry cast, and you'd come back to New Zealand and go to Circa where they were doing a production of the same play, and that production would lose very little or nothing by comparison with the West End.*

Today professional theatre is alive and well and living in Auckland, Wellington, Christchurch, Dunedin and Hamilton on national and local funding. Ballet and opera would not survive without subsidy. Music has had funding longer than most, but rarely enough.

## Ian Fraser

*When the National Orchestra was set up it was a fragile bloom. It was as the creature of Peter Fraser, the then Prime Minister, who said we must have a National Orchestra. For a long time there was a sense that it was a very fragile thing, but it's grown and it's fifty-five years old now. When it began there were no professional or semi-professional regional orchestras. These days there are good regional orchestras. So the taxpayer is paying twice: once so that we can have a National Orchestra and next through Creative New Zealand, so that the regional orchestras can exist.*

*There are two overwhelming arguments in favour of having a national orchestra. One is about the issue of coverage, that the very best music that we can possibly hear live is taken around the country to as many centres as you can make commercial sense of within the reality of the government subsidy. The second thing is the argument about quality. I don't believe that this country is large enough and we don't have the resource base in terms of great players to be able to have more than one team of musical All Blacks. That is what the National Orchestra is.*

Even with subsidy, life isn't easy for New Zealand's crop of professional actors and musicians. Anything beyond a meanly calculated living wage has to be made on the side, via commercials, session music and any other available opportunities. Art is a struggle. The big bucks, like the real professional heights, lie overseas. The unsubsidised arts are flourishing, subsidy-less, particularly in Auckland, but the living ain't easy, putting meat paste on the bread, not caviar. Greg Johnson, one of the most successful local pop musicians, scrimps along.

## Greg Johnson

*I did architecture at university for three or four years and meanwhile I had been doing music the whole time. I decided, to hell with this. I can go and earn five or six hundred dollars a week cash-in-hand playing and singing in the pubs, playing a bit of jazz. No one had ever said you could be a full-time musician. It was not even vaguely considered as a suitable occupation. A career in music is very much battle your own way.*

*If you talk to any artists in any genre in New Zealand it's a beautiful lover but it's not really going to pay your rent. You're going to end up poor if you stay here. That's the problem. So we're trying to break out. Infrastructure is the biggest problem with music. That's slowly developing but the best-selling New Zealand song is still 'Don't Dream, It's Over' by Crowded House, 1986, a long time ago. I'm just hoping that some others can break out.*

*I tend to sell anything between five and ten thousand per album so it's not a living from selling records. I'm lucky, I'm a songwriter, and that's really where my income has always come from. Publishing. You have to be broad. We are jacks-of-all-trades. We do the odd documentary soundtrack, a commercial here and there. I've got a piece of music in the background of a Jamie Oliver commercial at the moment. Those kind of things help your yearly living.*

Elspeth Sandys, a student of mine in Dunedin, became a successful novelist in Britain but found times tougher when she came home.

## Elspeth Sandys

*They will still read a manuscript without it coming through an agent in New Zealand, so there is that advantage of starting off here, in that you won't be totally ignored first off. There are some quite good script assessing people who will help you to place your manuscript with the right publisher. So if you're starting off I would say it's easier here now. There wasn't much being published here in the seventies. Now we probably over-publish. We tend to have lost any notion of judging work by its excellence. So books tend to be chosen for a whole range of other qualities, including, one hopes, some sense that this is good or fine writing, but that isn't necessarily the only criterion, or the main one.*

*There is a market. But it's not a market that can actually make a lot of money for a writer. Sue McCauley in the South Island has just published a wonderful article about how almost impossible it is to support yourself as a writer here. Yet she's regarded as one of our serious mainstream writers. I support myself by still working for the BBC in England.*

*It doesn't encourage writers to be courageous, to take five years to write a difficult novel, and to starve to death. You can starve to death more easily here. It's warmer. If you have an auntie somewhere with a caravan in a paddock you can go and hole up there. The equivalent doesn't exist in Britain.*

Artists find it easier today than they did. Grahame Sydney, who went overseas to train but found he couldn't paint until he came back to the source of his inspiration, Otago, sees the art market as maturing rapidly.

## Grahame Sydney

*The very strong voices, visual voices, like McCahon, were making major statements and hitting home to a small minority, but an influential one, and quite often a wealthy one. The statements being, we don't need to go anywhere else, we can do it from here, and we must. And I think that took root very rapidly in the early 1970s. By the late 1970s there were a lot of dealers. But that ten years was an extraordinary period of change on the art scene anyway. The supporting public, the buying public, got in behind New Zealanders, of which I was very lucky to be one.*

*The New Zealand art community is extremely well supported. For a country this size, literally a city nation anywhere else in the world, the number of artists who are supported and are well supported is extremely high. I think we are very generously treated by our arts interest. We have a sophisticated audience which is keen to buy the best of New Zealand works in the same way as we have a very rich support for authors, and a readership per capita, which I think is one of the best in the world. It staggers me to go to Australia and find that the best of Australian artists are not being as well supported as the best in New Zealand. There are some wonderful patrons here, possibly far more artists than one would ever guess are surviving and surviving very well.*

Yet the real market and the real riches still lie overseas. Overseas challenges. Once it was training and learning. Now it is stimulus and perspective.

## Elspeth Sandys

*If Katherine Mansfield was living today she wouldn't have to go to England but she should go somewhere because you're digging in too narrow a seam. If you're going to be a writer of depth you need to experience cultures outside your own. New Zealand is an island and not attached to another nation, so there isn't that kind of cultural infeed that you get in European nations. I just think, 'Go somewhere, anywhere', it doesn't have to be England, it can be Japan, the States, but go and live somewhere else and reassess your culture on the basis of another one. You understand New Zealand better if you go away.*

*I don't believe that any good writing comes out of a rootless, amorphous existence of moving about all the time. I think it comes out of being rooted. Some of our best writing is very small in its canvas, but it's deeply rooted. I'm thinking of things like the* Plum Trilogy *by Maurice Gee, Katherine Mansfield herself. Her greatest writing, I think most critics would agree, was rooted back here, but she was writing from Berlin, from France, from England.*

The issue is critical mass. Range cultural industries with opera and ballet at the rarefied atmosphere top, pop music at the bottom, and the change over the last forty years is clear. Records, film and publishing give those practising these arts a living. Local writers and musicians can generate overseas sales because record companies and publishers are parts of multinational organisations. Musicians once did cover versions of overseas hits, book publishers concentrated on New Zealand books: colour photobooks, preferably with a minimal text written by famous authors on an off day, books by sporting heroes, and endless books about cities, banks, companies, universities, beekeeping, indeed anything New Zealand, right down to New Zealand lists of disasters, shipwrecks, heroes, murderers, triumphs, rugby teams lists of lists and so on.

All that still goes on. Yet now publishers also pour out quality writing by local authors and there is a living in writing though not, as Michael King emphasises, a good one. Art has to be its own reward.

In my early incarnation as an apprentice New Zealand nationalist, the only one in existence outside Auckland University, which ostracised me as a Pom, our great hope was a literary expression of New Zealand identity. John Mulgan's *Man Alone* and *Report on Experience*, said much that was perceptive about New Zealand. So did Curnow's poetic manifestos and the early modernism of Glover, Fairburn, Baxter and Curnow, some of Maurice Duggan's short stories, and, in a maudlin sort of way, Mason's *End of the Golden Weather*. In music, only Peter Cape's poetic songs rose above Gill Desh, though the cinema screen was blank. After seeing *Runaway*, New Zealand's first full length feature film, I thought it better that way.

The search should now be abandoned. The goal was wrong. The definitive New Zealand won't be anything written, recorded or filmed. That doesn't mean precluding the great New Zealand book, film, painting or music. Many are being produced. The real issue is different. C.K. Stead's imaginary writer, Hilda Tapler, when asked what is New Zealand about her book says, 'That's for you to say. It's a New Zealand novel because I'm a New Zealander and I wrote it.' The test should be work by a New Zealander coupled with real quality rather than about New Zealand. It can be about wine in France, cheese in Ireland, necrophilia in Northumbria, which may be dead boring, but the test is quality and the universals of human experience and relationships are the grist for greatness, not the parochial.

## Greg Johnson

*I never sit down and think I'll write a song about something in New Zealand. I write about stories that have happened there and there are stories that are relevant to a place, but I write about social politics and about human experience. I don't think the location matters at all.*

*If you were to analyse any Crowded House song they are probably about Melbourne or Auckland as well. Universal things are just that. Universal. You don't necessarily have to be singing about Maori place names in order to be incorporated in the New Zealand theme. By virtue of who we are and where we're from we will sound inherently different.*

Better though for local sales to have New Zealand allusions, and fascinating for patriots to have quality work about New Zealand, but not essential. Take the Kiwi big three: Gee, Stead and Shadbolt. C.K. Stead's novels are about New Zealand themes, a colonial education in London, war in Crete, life in Auckland, with the loveliness of Auckland's two harbours as a backdrop. The other two also write about New Zealand. Yet their basic themes are relationships, universals, and for Stead the recurrent theme of old age: *à la recherche des fucks perdus*.

The gain is in both quantity and quality. Good New Zealand books, films and music are available in most genres: romance, mystery, horror, love or war, and children's books. Competition to be published is more intense. So quality is higher. The best is not only world-class but sells there too.

In the earlier generations the best and brightest writers and painters went to overseasia, 'to England, Life and Art' as Pember Reeves put it. Many stayed. This Katherine Mansfield syndrome lost New Zealand Dan Davin, David Low, John Mulgan, Fleur Adcock, Jane Campion, Russell Crowe (a condominium with Australia), Frances Hodgkins, Les Gibbard, and many others. Culturally the New Zealand *Who's Who* isn't a 'Who's Here'. Many others did the literary equivalent of OE, like C.K. Stead, Janet Frame, Colin McCahon, Rita Angus, Robin Morrison, but came back to stay like Ngaio Marsh who lived as an English grande dame in Christchurch but 'came alive' whenever she went back. An increasing number didn't go at all. Their archetype is Peter Jackson, the kid from Pukerua Bay who made it not big but megascopic without leaving, while Sam Neill pursues a successful international career from Otago. Both are examples, which will be followed as critical mass builds and overseas publishers, producers and talent scouts exploit the opportunities arising in cut-price Kiwi culture.

The world has shrunk so fast and the market has globalised so fully that New Zealand isn't now a cultural identity but a province in a global culture and a small, parochial market within it. English-speaking but dealing with the universal human themes rather than the distinctively provincial. The test is now quality. Culture has learned the trick of standing upright here and though we never considered it possible forty years ago, there are now so many standing in the crowd that no one notices any more.

Unless they're legless. The most exciting new culture isn't culture at all but wine, a subject best treated in Auckland because so much is grown there in West Auckland and more is consumed. Restaurant and wine reviews now fill a greater acreage of print than literature, and though Aucklanders might reject the thought that anyone drinks wine to get drunk, it is also true that Auckland is improved by being viewed through the romantic haze produced by a good bottle of chardonnay, which can even make the Horrible Hypodermic look attractive. Indeed, another bottle might blot Auckland out altogether.

The growth of the wine religion, the huge improvement in quality and the almost fanatic importance attached to growing it, touring it, consuming and savouring it, talking and writing about it, is one of the biggest changes since those dim and distant days when I used to buy Department of Agriculture wine from the Dunedin Post Office at two and six a bottle, when New Zealand wine-growers were concentrating on sherry, port and fortified wines.

The industry was pioneered by immigrant families such as the Corbans, the first of whom came to New Zealand from Lebanon in 1892 as a trader on the Thomas goldfields, eventually becoming a farmer and wine-grower, and from Dalmatians like the Brajkovichs. Michael Brajkovich's grandfather came out in 1902 as a gumdigger bringing the rest of his family out between the wars.

Immigrant families had a history of farming and winegrowing, usually for family consumption, on small farms back home. They settled in West Auckland as orchardists, market gardeners and fishermen and began to make wine.

## Brian Corban

*Some European New Zealanders did make wine, and there are examples of that going back to James Busby, the first New Zealand resident in 1840. But most of the European efforts at making wine tended to be an annexe to other commercial activities. For example, the Chambers family in Hawke's Bay regarded winemaking as a gentlemanly pursuit as a support to the main farming activities.*

*The big distinction is that in the case of the non-European winemakers from the Mediterranean, whether they were our family who were Lebanese, or Croatian or Dalmatian, for them it was an economic necessity. They returned to their roots to find a way of supporting themselves and their families. They ended up being pioneers for a very difficult industry which didn't come into its own until much later.*

*It was really from the late fifties onwards that the winemaking industry started to develop quite rapidly. I remember in the case of my family, it was 1958 when we bought the land for our first expansion out at Henderson, and then went to Gisborne and then eventually Marlborough. New Zealand had been through a period of prosperity during the agricultural boom of the fifties from the Korean War onwards, and that meant New Zealanders had more money to buy luxury items. They were starting to travel more. The first wave of New Zealanders who had experience of overseas wine in any sort of mass or volume really was our troops in the Second World War, when they went right through Italy. They came back with some understanding that wine was an alternative drink to beer.*

*The increase in wine consumption, and most particularly table wine as against traditional fortified ports and sherries, really came in the sixties and seventies with younger people travelling and building an appreciation of wine. The traditional techniques were pretty well known, but they were also at a relatively low order compared with today's very scientific techniques.*

*The big boom in the development of more sophisticated, scientific techniques in the winemaking industry in New Zealand came with the later generations of winemakers who were educated more scientifically. A good example from our family is my cousin, Alex Corban, who was a BSc graduate from Auckland University, and attended Roseworthy College in*

*Australia, which is a famous winemaking institution. Alex, because of his scientific background, was able to pioneer a number of new techniques in wine-making in the industry in New Zealand. We produced the first sparkling wine in the country in 1962 – Premier Cuvée.*

*Alex also led the way in stainless steel technology and refrigeration techniques in the wine industry for producing table wines. The first tanks that we bought were obtained from the New Zealand dairy industry as second-hand tanks, but then rapidly we moved on to getting our own fabricated. Our family pioneered exporting. We started exporting to Canada and the west coast of the US in the early to mid-seventies, but it was hard work. New Zealand was a country at the end of the earth with a tiny population and not a great international profile. It wasn't particularly well known for winemaking. So it really was a very hard slog.*

*It wasn't until the eighties, when a lot of other New Zealand wine companies followed on, that New Zealand started to develop some critical mass in exporting. Even then it was still very tiny until well into the nineties.*

New Zealand's land and climate are well suited to wine growing, particularly in West Auckland, around Gisborne, Hawke's Bay and Marlborough, the first wine-growing areas. The big turnaround was stimulated by the ending of import controls, which encouraged growers to stop producing an unsaleable, cheap wine lake, to dig out müller thurgau and leave the cheap end to the Australians (so much better at the cheap). Strength was quickly established in white wine, particularly chardonnay and sauvignon blanc, both as good as any in the world. Reds, which the Australians dominate, came later.

Moving up-market was a risky business. The best way to become a million dollar wine producer is to start with ten. It needs skill and scientific training. Michael Brajkovich took the family business, San Marino Wines, up-market as Kumeu River by getting the best training available.

## Michael Brajkovich

*My father was very forward-thinking and knew that we had to have the expertise. He encouraged me to go and get it and sent me to Roseworthy College in South Australia. Quite a few New Zealanders actually went through that course subsequently. I was there from 1979 to 1981, and a few Australian winemakers who had qualified had come into our industry and brought new skills, new expertise and new standards of winemaking.*

*In New Zealand I was the first Master of Wine. It was an unusual experience because up until 1988 you had to be English and in the British wine trade before you could actually sit the exam for the Masters of Wine. In 1988 they opened the qualification up to international students. So the following year I went and sat the exam and passed. I wasn't expecting to because it is a very difficult exam, but I guess the experience I've had in the industry and also being through a very good tertiary course has helped.*

The wine industry, poised to take off by the 1980s, needed the critical mass to break through. Marketing an unknown brand is difficult. In the competitive, snobbish wine trade it could only be done by riding on the back of the Australians.

## Michael Brajkovich

*The Australians did a terrific job in the mid to late eighties marketing their wine, particularly in the UK, and that's always been our biggest market. We went in there in 1988 at the London Wine Trade Fair where we were the featured nation. Since then it's gone from strength to strength. There have been one or two icon wines that have really led the way and Montana's sauvignon blanc from Marlborough, and Cloudy Bay, for example, have been very successful. But we've been successful in our own way, on a much smaller scale, with our chardonnay.*

*We still have to be very careful about our pricing. New Zealand is the highest average price of any country going into the UK and we guard that jealously, but as our volume increases we may not be able to maintain that. That price does become a very important determining factor.*

New Zealand's is a premium wine product with a price margin of up to two dollars a litre over other wines on the British market. Maintaining that means staying out of the mass market.

## Brian Corban

*Because of the cost of production of New Zealand wines, there isn't a place for New Zealand wines at the bottom two or three price points of the market. The Australians can produce wines that fit those price points a lot more cost-effectively than New Zealand winemakers can, simply because they have such vast production and such vast cost-efficiency in producing the wine. We can't match it.*

Concern for quality has produced the decision by top winemakers to replace corks with screw-tops – a typically pragmatic New Zealand move when cork has a problem with tainting anything between two and ten percent of the bottles. Resistance has been minimal in the UK, but more stubborn in America where the traditional ritual is a fetish. The real problem on the horizon is the threat of over-production. Unless the world's drinkers can keep pace.

AUCKLAND

# Brian Corban

*I think New Zealand is well on the way to a very strong international reputation for specialist, high-quality production. And the future lies at that end, not in making mediocre New Zealand wines for low prices. As long as we aim for the top with top business management, top business planning, top marketing, I believe that we have a place in the international industry, come what may.*

I'll drink to that. So will the rest of New Zealand as wine produces a better and better export return and boosts New Zealand's reputation in a field it never contested before: high-quality production for a top of the range market. Raise your glass, world, and look up to New Zealand, not down.

As for me, drunk or sober, it's time to move on to another piece of Auckland's exciting pluralism: Otara Market, the Saturday morning cross between a Polynesian festival, food and craft market, *son et lumière*, tourist attraction and filmic spectacular. Provided they don't think you're a tax inspector assessing what fell off the back of Polynesia.

I started out at the Dawn Raid stand, christened after Muldoon's infamous raids on Island overstayers; it's now the Islander's revenge. A co-operative of three friends who met at polytechnic, producing outrageous T-shirts with Otara's invented STD code and terms of abuse of islanders, like 'Bunga' and 'Cocoland' turned into slogans of pride to finance CDs and a wide range of music, island and local, produced in their own studios.

*In 1996 we all met together. We had business studies and all that sort of stuff but we wanted to do music and we didn't have enough money to fund it. So we started wearing funny, humorous T-shirts. We got other people to wear them and that generated the cash flow to make the music. There are six or seven companies now and we have our own factory.*

The market itself is an exciting, bustling babble, and a riot of colour from the fruit, the shirts, the mats and materials, the dresses on the crowded stalls, all bringing life and excitement to sprawling South Auckland. Mark Gosche, Minister of Transport, one of three Islander MPs and Samoan City Councillor, Sua William Sio, showed me round.

## Mark Gosche

*This all began twenty-five years ago in 1976 or 1977. The elderly people were discussing how to build the Island community and make money for it because part of the takings from the stallholders goes back into the community. That's the way it's set up. For all the different islands this is the central market where everybody can come and do their shopping. I always say if you're looking for a Samoan in Auckland all you've got to do is come to the market. Sooner or later you'll meet up with him.*

## Sua William Sio

*The other idea is the fact that twenty-five years ago it was difficult to get green bananas, it was difficult to get our fish. If a Pacific person went into a fish market and asked for our kind of fish they would give it to you for free. The crafts are a new development because what the Pacific people normally do with a proper cloth or a mat is they save it underneath their bed mattress for traditional purposes, weddings, funerals and so forth, but today, because of the way of life here, it's seen as a way of earning money.*

*Here in Otara we do function as a community, more so perhaps than other communities. We have had years of struggle, of trying to get along with each other, of knowing the different languages, of knowing the different cultures. That has come as a result of many years of struggle. You had Maori coming from north and south about the 1960s because it was built for low income people, and then you had the Pacific people coming in from the islands, all speaking different languages, all doing things differently, and then suddenly you put them together and there is a lot of fighting – verbal as well as physical. But as a result of that something really good has come. We have been able to make a big contribution in sport and music. There is a wealth of talent here. This is rugby league territory. It's all coming together into something very exciting.*

That excitement is palpable at Otara's Island experience of fun, food, music and colour, slap-bang in the middle of South Auckland's dreary acres. Go. But go early if you're going to get a park.

The antidote to the easygoing, overeating, overweight indulgence of Otara lies at the other end of Auckland in the Academy of Sport and its associated cluster of gyms, testing, advisory and training bodies out at the campus of the university. Traditionally New Zealand played only two sports: rugby union and cricket, which were small-scale on the world scene. That concentration allowed a small country to carry all before it. Particularly in rugby, it is a land of legends, like Colin Meads.

## Colin Meads

*It's our national game and back in our days it was a way of getting away from the farm on the weekends. It was a sport that New Zealanders just liked to play, I think we liked the physical contact, and compared to a non-team sport it brought a lot of friendships. We all started as little kids running around in bare feet in Saturday morning rugby. You go to school, you get into primary school teams, and that was the start of your rugby, and then you just went through the age grades and under 21s then, being a country boy, you played senior rugby at a very early age. I was playing senior rugby here at the age of seventeen.*

*It's a sort of disbelief and shock when you're first picked as an All Black. There's a lot of pride. The family is so proud and you're proud yourself, but being a New Zealander you don't really show that sort of thing but you're terribly proud. You're proud of the jersey, you're proud of everything that goes with being an All Black. But it's always mellowed with the sincerity and doing the right thing and being a good guy. You played for the love of the game. It was our national game, you wanted to play it, you were desperate to be good at it, and every team you played for you played to win because the natural heritage was playing to win.*

*We were never paid. It was purely an amateur game. If you got to the All Blacks you got on tour. We used to get ten bob a day expenses. We used to get paid once a fortnight and looked forward to our seven pound a fortnight. The money came in the mid-nineties. There was a sort of shamateurism coming through. No one was allowed to be paid, but most of the top players were, in a backhanded sort of way.*

*At the end of 1995 and early 1996 it became fully professional and it was all above board then, and a lot more money came into the game through Murdoch. The game throughout the world went professional. It had to come because they were taking so much rugby players' time and players wouldn't stay in the game without the professional element to it, but now a lot of players firstly think money. They look to their future. Other countries are paying more than New Zealand, and we are struggling to hang on to our players. Once they have represented their country for a few years they look overseas for their retirement fund. So it's taken a little bit out of the game that before was purely there for the love of it.*

Chris Laidlaw is equally concerned.

## Chris Laidlaw

*We are slowly adjusting to the reality that we're not going to win more than, say, sixty or seventy percent of these test matches. That's quite hard to take. But that is the reality. The moment the game professionalised we lost our inherent advantage.*

*We've still got all of the qualities. It was partly technical know-how, it was partly a sense that you had to die for your country. When I first went away as a player of nineteen on a tour of the UK, I was told by one of the councillors of the New Zealand Rugby Union that you go with the full weight of three million expectations on your shoulders, boy, and you've got to deliver. I couldn't sleep for the first three or four nights.*

*That's changed. There are so many other expectations that are at work that it doesn't matter so much. An All Black has to deliver for the country but he's delivering for himself, to a much greater extent, and earning his money. There is a certain nostalgic loss there, I think. But it's the way of the world.*

Rugby, once supreme, almost a national religion, is now only one of a jostling scrum of sports. New Zealanders are still sport-obsessed but that enthusiasm is spread over a larger number of sports and more of it goes into the couch potato position so big in America.

Defeats for All Blacks, who'd previously ruled the world, a falling return in other individual sports, the pathetic performance at the 1998 Olympics, where Australia swept the board, were all a bitter awakening. Policy-makers and sponsors all threw themselves into a belated national effort to professionalise and catch up.

The Labour government of the eighties had believed that government had no role in running the economy. That was best left to markets. Not so sport. That government had a

Minister for the Commonwealth Games, later the Minister for Sport, and the clamour for funding made government ever more important.

## Trevor Mallard

*We are naturally good at sport. There's lots and lots of talent in New Zealand. We've got the sort of country where it's good to be a sportsperson. But that's not good enough these days. We're tending to go off the pace in a number of sports, and therefore we need to put an investment in. Even our rugby team hasn't been going quite as well recently as it has been in previous years. We had some wonderful times but we really haven't got much that's setting the world alight at the moment. Élite sportspeople doing well make us feel better about ourselves. New Zealand on a Monday after the All Blacks have won on a Saturday is a much better place to be – we're much more productive, much happier.*

This spending boost is also aimed at building a healthier nation, dragging people away from their tellies watching New Zealand triumphs, and out to exercise. All this produced the National Academy, based in Auckland with offshoots in the other main centres providing a national recruiting and training network. Its head is Alistair Snell and, yes, he is related.

## Alistair Snell

*In 1997 and '98 it was seen that what we were doing in this country before was a bit ad hoc and we needed to be a lot more systematic about it. So the world were starting to do it and we were very quickly starting to fall behind. We needed to get a heck of a lot more sophisticated. So the Academy was established, creating an integrated environment for the athlete to be able to get access to things necessary to help them prepare and subsequently perform. You come in. We can sit down and plan your competition programme, plan your training programme, assess your strength and condition to determine how much extra weight you're carrying, then develop a programme to ensure that your skills can be harnessed in the best way possible. You can do all that close to your own home without having to go overseas.*

The system can't turn a fat slob into a superman. So I didn't try the strenuous regimes. But others were being assessed and tested by John Marsden, a Kiwi trainer recruited from the Australian Academy to develop its techniques here, or measured by Auckland University scientists assessing bowling action. Here, as in business, the universities, and farming, New Zealanders are rising to the challenge of a more competitive world and are ready to spend public money in areas where only a few years back long and loud protests would have greeted any government intervention. Now spending has begun, bars are going to be steadily raised. There is no turning back, whatever the calculus in five years' time of how many medals per million dollars it brings.

My own athletic efforts are strictly confined to tourism of the amiably ambling kind. Most of this is done in the South Island, my tourist mecca, but I have to accept that for some Auckland is equally attractive. Bob Harvey's personal paradise is the rolling thunder of West Auckland's beaches, particularly Karekare, an area he's written about and visits all the time, as one of the elderly team of lifesavers who protect bathers on high days and holidays.

# Bob Harvey
*I first came here when I was fifteen. I biked down from town, and the surf club was having a party and they took me into the lifeguard family that I've been part of for forty-seven years. I just happen to be the mayor right now but I have always been a lifeguard and I have always cared about this place.*

*Karekare is a unique place. It may be because of its deep and ancient Maori history which is very close, it might be the magnificence of the beach and the surf, the ruggedness of it, that has attracted people. It's been attracting people, potters, writers, painters and people who want to get away from everyone else to come here. It's a very enveloping, very holistic community. It's stayed that way and it's still small. It doesn't even have a shop, you can't even buy an ice-cream here, yet people keep coming back.*

*People have always come to the West to escape. They have come out and lived here in the bush, I think the bush attracts people. Maurice Shadbolt, Brian Brake, painters like Dean Buchanan, Anne Robinson are world-class, they come here, work here and they are accepted. There has not been a big gap between rich and poor, I think most people have been average. We have the largest Croatian community in New Zealand, the largest Dutch community, and we've got the largest group of people that enjoy being Westies.*

Auckland is New Zealand's main tourist destination. Yet most tourists won't even get to West Auckland – to Karekare and Piha – unless they're dedicated surfers. They're on a tourist circuit with Auckland the point of entry, the largest single calling-point for cruise-liners and the starting-point for the circuit down to Rotorua and Taupo.

Tourism developed early for New Zealand, with a flow of British aristocrats, journalists and politicians coming on voyages of exploration or social enquiries. At the start of the last century, with tourist numbers just over 5000 a year, New Zealand was the first nation to establish a Minister and a Department of Tourism. Small beginnings to today's mighty industry, steadily doubling numbers and its contribution to the GDP and looking forward to growing exponentially in the new millennium.

Mark Burton, the Minister of Tourism, plans to develop it still further to upgrade its quality and its contribution and to spread it round New Zealand.

## Mark Burton

*Tourism is now getting close to ten percent of GDP for New Zealand. The most recent calculation puts one in ten jobs either directly or indirectly attributable to this industry. So from the time thirty years ago when it was the sort of job that people didn't call a real job, now it is the job, and for growing numbers of New Zealanders it's going to be a long-term employment base.*

*There's some of the finest mountain walks and national park tramps in the world. Adventure tourism is one of the key things that New Zealand can offer, and all within relatively short distances. You can experience virtually every climate and every sort of environment imaginable. That's quite an attractive proposition, particularly for people who have limited time and want to have a diversity of experience.*

Opening up the rest of New Zealand is a consummation devoutly to be wished providing it doesn't mean the Warren Cooperisation of more and more beauty spots. Auckland is a suburban slice of the great universal anywhere and a tourism which does not venture well beyond it short-changes tourists and the nation. What is unique about New Zealand is not sprawling suburbia but its magnificent scenery and the opportunities afforded by a country which has become a pleasure machine for outdoor sport, adventure, fishing, yachting, sailing, cycling and all the less strenuous forms of tourism.

Tourism still has enormous potential in New Zealand. It's beautiful, its thrill-packed, it's convenient, it's friendly, and it's safe. Unlike Florida with its muggings, or Australia with its penchant for murdering tourists, particularly English ones,

New Zealand has no need to advertise: 'Come to Kiwiland. You may not get mugged. Or murdered.' Killing yourself on a DIY basis is the only option. The natives are friendly and adept at taking photographs for visitors, though not necessarily at getting their heads into frame. Its magnificent scenery is conveniently packaged with a wide variety of scenery available within a few hours, from mountains and wild bush, to lakes, coves and beaches; offering spectacular settings, thrills and the more simple pleasures New Zealanders are now making available to the world after enjoying them so much for so long. Greater love hath no nation. But then few have New Zealand's balance of payments problem either. More doesn't necessarily mean worse. In New Zealand it has to mean better for the land, the locals and the tourists themselves. Provided they get the tourist millions quickly out of Auckland and off to the real New Zealand.

## Chapter Twelve

# Ringing The Changes

My senior citizen's tour of the four corners of paradise, plus Auckland, makes one thing clear: New Zealand has changed. Even the South Island, heritage island, where Old New Zealand went to die, isn't what it was. Nostalgia never is. All those I talked to emphasised the changes – revolution in the eyes of the left, not revolutionary enough to the right – to a degree which left me feeling more fogeyish than at any time in a long career devoted to rearguard actions. Yet it would be extraordinary if New Zealand had stood unscathed in a changing world. Whatever their degree of change fatigue, countries like New Zealand must run faster to stand still, in relative terms. The change game isn't one of two halves. Once started it never ends and the new stability is to ride it effectively.

The beneficiaries of change told me how much they'd enjoyed it. Ordinary mortals won't necessarily feel the same. So I barged into caravans and tents at the Mount Maunganui camp site, accosted bathers on the beach – particularly any wearing bikinis – and badgered partygoers at a New Year party in Karekare, asking how New Zealand had changed. It was an imposition, particularly on campers over lunch, but all answered in friendly fashion, though the same approach in Britain would have produced a chorus of invitations to rearrange 'Off Piss' to form a well-known English phrase or expression. Along with loads of 'Who do you think you are . . .?' or even 'An Englishman's caravan is his castle,' albeit a tin one. But everyone replied seriously and on the whole optimistically, certainly more so than the British, who are invariably inclined to think things are going to the dogs. Here's a sampler of their responses:

*Thirty years ago you came back from overseas and you stood on the beach down here at Karekare and looked out and you felt you were at the end of the world, really on the edge of the world. You don't feel that now.*

*Thirty or forty years ago when I was a teenager, I was very insular, very inward-looking. Rugby was important. World affairs weren't so important and the rest of the word was a long way away. Nowadays I'm on the Internet at least half my working day, most of the products I sell I need to know about as soon as they're developed overseas. We feel in touch. Much more so.*

*Personally I think the 1981 Springbok Tour was a major turning point, that was really when New Zealand became internationalist rather than a little piece of Great Britain lurking down in the far corner of the South Pacific. I think we made our mark on the world in 1981, and we have really never looked back.*

*It's good as gold. I mean, okay, there're some people that are on the 'down and out' but the average guy has got a house and a couple of kids and his wife and his car, he's usually got a boat. If he hasn't got a boat, he's got a caravan. If he hasn't got a caravan he's got a holiday bed somewhere. And you can go fishing or boating, it's a good country to live in, as long as they can organise the crime, that's the main thing. Every joker wants to smoke pot or whatever. Well, okay, as long as he's not harming anybody else.*

*People flaunt wealth in a way that they didn't before. My family was poor, that's more than thirty years ago, when I was a child. You didn't have television, you didn't have most things. You thought everyone was the same. Some people were building mansions. It was very discreet. Now people flaunt their wealth. I don't know if the gap is actually bigger but people's expectations are bigger. People aren't as humble as they were. My parents were humble and I was always told to mind my station, not get too big for my boots.*

*We've got more opportunities than we did years ago. Our family mostly come from the sawmill and the forestry side of things. Years ago it used to be redundancies and lay-offs. But Asia has opened up. Where I work in the sawmill our main market is China and all round Asia. Years ago it was just the local economy and that was it. So it seems to be getting a lot better. The lifestyle is better and you've still got places like these camping grounds. Over here you've got the modern New Zealand and you've still got the everyday New Zealand.*

*We've been through a period of being more concerned about the individual. Now the pendulum is swinging back to a more community attitude. It's almost as though we've reached the depths of individualism so now we're going to promote a much better level of community. I hold the view that every day that goes by gets better, but people have come out the other side of the individualists period with a bit of certainty about what they want to do now.*

*Thirty-plus years ago, longer than that, we used to come out West and get a half-g and get it filled with sherry or Mr West's red, which he kept just for the family, which was as rough as hell but it was the nearest thing to European red wine that my grape friend could possibly contemplate. Thirty years ago my youngest child was just two, and just in her lifetime technological developments have just opened up the entire universe, the way we, even at the bottom of the world, can enjoy.*

New Zealanders have coped with change. Many find it exciting, though older people were a bit fearful about crime, teenagers, or a world leaving them behind. Hardwick Knight, at eighty-five the oldest person I talked to, voiced this.

## Hardwick Knight

*I can tell you one thing, that it hasn't changed. The first thing to be noticed on arrival was the corrugated-iron roofs as we came on the train from Lyttelton into Dunedin. That hasn't changed. When I was first here there used to be a pile of the* Otago Daily Times *at the side of the road and you threw down your money and picked up your paper. They've completely disappeared now. The papers disappeared without the cash. I think that is symbolic of a major change. We never troubled to lock the door at night. Now it's very worrying to go to bed and think, oh, we left the front door open. It is a very big change.*

Change flowed in from overseas as the spread of the American suburban lifestyle, the triumph of consumption over production and of economic liberalisation over intervention, affected all the advanced industrial countries. The Maori renaissance wasn't imported but still parallels the revival of indigenous populations in Canada, the US, Australia and elsewhere. The techniques of protest and the resistance which highlighted the problem were all developed overseas well before indigenous pride mobilised them in New Zealand.

Most changes were imported willingly, and in the case of the younger generation, enthusiastically. The changes of lifestyle, fashion, consumption and attitudes poured in through the media and via travel and were all inevitable. No advanced society, particularly one dependent on tourism, can cut itself off from the changes in the advanced world. Tourists didn't want to come to a time warp or a rural slum. Even if the Mondo Kiwi of C.V. Smith and Sid Holland had been preserved it would hardly have been a marketable tourist proposition. Only the ideological changes imposed by New Zealand's élite for their own benefits were more questionable and less welcome.

A small, insulated society cut off from the world, as New Zealand was, is characterised by dislike of difference, by uniformity and by pressures to conform because differences frighten. So the biggest change, itself the agent of further changes, has been the death of distance. New Zealand has been fully plugged into the wider world by burgeoning media, news channels, the Internet, and the two-way travel explosion. Kiwis go overseas and learn. Incoming tourists demand modern facilities and menus more varied than pies and pavlova.

Open up the doors and diversity, pluralism, new ideas and new lifestyles pour in as old barriers and inhibitions crumble. Conformity begins to look old-fashioned and the coercion which maintained it repressive. Resistance and dissent become easier while the end of the Cold War removed suspicion of radicalism, even of socialism while it also undermined opposition to change, weakened the case for an attack role for the RNZAF and made it difficult for ACT to destroy opponents by calling them 'Communists'. Not that that stopped them thinking it.

All this impacted on New Zealand more than on most countries, but with typical Kiwi ingenuity New Zealand adjusted more quickly to its outward-bound course. Change no longer had to be fought for but it flowed into every nook and cranny of life and everyone, even those who really hated it, began to praise its benefits. Diversity and liberalism triumphed. Rule by the grey and the RSA ended. The days of protest were over and those of rapid adjustment began ushering in an age of pluralism, biculturalism, sexual tolerance, diversity and simple hedonism.

New Zealand's Grundies went into full retreat, their dominance broken by abortion, trial marriage, pink power and sexual emancipation, all of which lost their power to shock. The *New Zealand Woman's Weekly* became her regular right. Sex, once a repressed obsession, was relegated to hobby status somewhere behind sport and wine in the hierarchy. Those still suffering from the intermittent fret of tumescence could turn to massage parlours for the practice and the back pages of ever-shrinking *Truth* for the theory. Not very dirty book shops appeared under plain cover.

The older generation didn't like a bar of this new world but, being Kiwi, they confined resistance to grumbling. Their weapons and power had been abolished. Only the sound of air sucked in through false teeth, or raised eyebrows and disapproving looks were left. So they either redoubled their escapes to Queensland, gardened more vigorously as a form of protest, became silver surfers on the net or put their faith in New Zealand First, which promptly let them down. Grey Power was restricted to the fight for a better super. Even that became less vigorous as warnings multiplied of a growing and cripplingly expensive pensioner population doddering ahead of an actuarial shiver.

Pleasure and hedonism, long-prohibited immigrants to New Zealand, where self-improvement was preferred, were soon being pursued more happily than virtue. Wine snobbery in its major denominations, particularly white, became the new religion. The great unmentionable became all too frequently mentioned. Self-improvement is less important than home improvement. Hints on how to save money which had been a staple of New Zealand literature, magazines and conversations became less numerous than advice on how to spend it. A market developed in books telling Kiwis how to enjoy themselves, how to drink, make love, keep fit and cheat at tarot.

When I arrived in Auckland in 1959 there seemed to be only one restaurant called, for some reason I couldn't understand, 'The Gourmet'. There I was introduced to the wonderful world of BYO, a mysterious routine of going down to a bottle store, buying something undrinkable disguised in a brown paper bag, putting the bottle in the restaurant's fridge, then opening and trying to drink it (which was the hardest part). In Pleasure City, a.k.a. Dunedin, restaurants were few and far between: stomach-filling stations for those who didn't particularly like food. The most exotic was a Hungarian restaurant which survived, three-quarters empty, for several weeks, and a Chinese restaurant, which was an offshoot of a greengrocery business, with cabbage in every dish. If we never ate out it wasn't only because as a mean Yorkshireman I begrudged spending any money on things a good wife should provide for free (though I did), but because it was a major expedition to find anywhere to do so. If you did it was usually closed.

All is changed, in Dunedin and everywhere. Restaurants abound. There must be two per tum-tum. Cookery and wine books and magazines outsell sport. City streets have every style of cooking, from Thai to pie, though I've yet to find a Yorkshire Grub pub. There's music in the cafés at night, though no revolution in the air, streets are lined with restaurants, café-bars, wine bars, and coffee bars producing a quality of latte froth which indicates that New Zealand cows do continuous aerobics. Cities are alive and gay with gays advertising where to find Gayness. Every city and town has its arts, wine, Pelmanism, music, aromatherapy and literary festivals. Décor has become for women what sport is for men, with each sex taking refuge from the other in its chosen activity.

In half-dead country towns banks are now bars, post offices restaurants, railway stations craft shops, boutiques or anything that pays a rent, though not yet massage parlours or drive-in brothels. Country people know each other too well for that and need reasons to drive to town occasionally. The national bedtime must have gone back by a full quarter of an hour to fit all this hedonism in.

The consumer society has triumphed. Not as completely (or as expensively) in the South Island as in Auckland. Not as colourfully in the small towns as the large cities, yet it still laps everywhere. Even the countryside, once a place to drive through or wait for the AA, is now livelier, with people from the city coming to dude ranches, health farms, farm hospitality, or even buying their own lifestyle mini-dude ranches where they can see themselves as Hugh Hefners, with sheep. Farmers run restaurants, food critics prowl the land and wine tours trundle busloads of trainee alcoholics into the wop-wops to soak up the surplus and allow wineries to cut out the middle man by pouring their product straight down the gullet of the consumer. All the barricades have fallen to the general satisfaction of all.

Once Kiwis went overseas to escape provincial dullness, the constrictions of conformity and the snores of the fretful sleepers. Then they got a little excitement and a vision of what they were missing in New Zealand. Now they're no longer seeking something they can't find at home, just getting a more expensive version of the same lifestyle. They can find more ethnic varieties and exotic lifestyles, many specially preserved for *National Geographic* – or climb heights not available at home and discover the delights of cities which are far too large to live in but exciting to visitors. Yet at the end of the day, they don't return with dread, as if to a form of captivity as Bill Pearson and so many others did. They see that New Zealand isn't so bad after all and has an ambience as good as most and more cheap than any. Been there. Done that. Time to settle down, enjoy the pleasures of domesticity and settled relationships after the hurly-burly of the chaise longue, and produce a new generation of Kiwis. Who may not even want to go overseas if improvement goes on at this rate, and if the dollar goes on falling to ensure that they won't be able to afford it.

The imposed reforms tell another story. The gaps between rich and poor had never been wide and the perceived gaps even narrower in an egalitarian society where even the wealthiest have to pose as men of the people, one of the lads, and ever willing to buckle down on the shop floor. Roger and Ruthonomics widened them. The underpinning of full – or as its critics claimed 'over full' – employment which had made Jack proud and as good as his master because he could always tell him to get stuffed and find another job, was kicked away. Public provision was made meaner and benefits cut.

At the other end of the scale, the reforms and, more importantly, the greater opportunities for speculation, fiddling, living on the company or even looting it, plus rising asset and property prices all generated a wealth explosion, some of it new and nasty. They removed the inhibitions of money. Once shy and reclusive, wealth began to display, even flaunt itself. Not the coronation economic liberals felt was its due but at least a public preening.

Wealth can't segregate itself in New Zealand as it can in the US with its guarded mansions and gated estates. Yet New Zealand's richest individual, Graeme Hart, isn't exactly easy of access in his $17.4 million Glendowie mansion – New Zealand's most expensive – or on its costliest boat the Ulysses, which cost $40 million to build and $2.5 million a year to run. Michael Fay and David Richwhite bought their own island, Great Mercury, a 1718-hectare spot on the map, off the Coromandel. Lesser lights had to rest content with second homes in Wanaka, which has more millionaires per acre than any other town. So the Marshals of Money were more inaccessible than any holder of political power.

New Zealand's most expensive street, Wairangi Street in Herne Bay, has an average valuation of $4 million per house, top price $6.5 million. Four other North Shore streets – O'Neills Avenue, Clifton Road, Audrey Road and Minnehaha Avenue – have average valuations of over $1 million, which is a form of segregation which Old Wealth areas, like Remuera, were never capable of. Wellington's most expensive streets, Bayview Terrace and Carlton Gore Road at Island Bay, have average valuations of $1.2 million. At these prices people build lavish architect-designed houses different from the ticky-tacky boxes appropriate to Nappy Valley or Mangere. Compared with them, Dunedin's dearest – Tolcarne Avenue, in Maori

Hill, with an average valuation of $298,000 – is Cheapsville itself. Indeed, in Dunedin wealth could be offered: 'Buy one. Get Five Free', compared with Auckland prices.

Much of the wealth so splendidly housed is new. In old New Zealand fortunes were built on old money, government-conferred monopolies or cornered markets in construction, manufacturing, or motors, benefiting Fletchers, Jeffs, Fishers, Paykels and Todds; or the great basics of booze (Myers, Kelliher), media (Horton, Kerridge), and basic industries such as extraction, dairy, timber and shipping. This settled world of money was shaken up by corporate raiders, unregulated markets and asset-stripping as predatory capitalism was turned loose in cowboy company country with its endless opportunities for quick acquisition and accumulation or spectacular collapses and casualties, such as Allan Hawke (Equity Corp), Colin Reynolds (Chase Corp), Bruce Judge (Judge Corp), all of whom managed to put the 'SE' on the end of their spectacular corp; while later Michael Fay and David Richwhite (labelled 'Rich, White and Fay' by David Lange) took refuge abroad when their sharp practices were exposed, though they at least kept their money.

Suddenly New Zealand was treated to 'Rich Lists', themselves a manifestation of the new preoccupation with money. They changed more quickly. Flashy names fell out. New Masters of the Kiwi Universe muscled in. About half the 2002 list of top wealth is new money. Three-quarters of the 1996 list had earned their fortunes themselves and two-thirds of New Zealand's wealth came from competitive industries. This is not a list of idle rich. Most of the people on it work hard to acquire more. Yet nor is it worthy respectability given the incidence of asset strippers, property developers and the number who have either taken the money and run off abroad or cashed in their chips like John Spencer, Peter Masfen, Trevor Farmer, the Plowmans, Robertson Stewart, Chino Mace and many others.

Primary production isn't heavily represented, except for fishing with Talleys, Skeggs and Valas well up there, while Howard Paterson is busy in technology as well as the world's largest deer farm. But the range has widened. Media, with Peter Jackson a Tolkien millionaire, Lucy Lawless, a.k.a Xena, the Warrior Princess, estimated to be worth $11 million, and Paul Holmes not short of a bob or few. Sport is there with Jonah Lomu's fortune reduced from $8 million to $5 million by divorce. So are Maori, with the Maori Queen estimated to be worth up to $9 million.

Not much of all this trickles down to the people in the way the monetarists promised – though John Kenneth Galbraith described the process as dropping horse manure onto the road for the birds. The big fortunes shade down to the growing number of millionaire farmers, more and more of them as land and export prices rise, and IT and new technology millionaires, who lost out in the dot.com debacle, recover nerve and money. New Zealand has become a land fit for millionaires to multiply in. They may be working millionaires, more egalitarian millionaires, smaller in fortunes and numbers, millionaires overseas. But they are dollar millionaires nonetheless and well apart from the mass of the people.

The poor, sadly too numerous and too many to list in a national 'Poor List', are too noble to flaunt their status as the rich can. They are now more numerous and less mobile because job losses, particularly long-term unemployment hitting older manual workers hardest, low wages and the benefit cuts designed to help them avoid the Dependency Culture (an economic version of ME) have made their lives worse. Privatisation, hitting the strong of back hardest, destroyed a near subsistence economy living cheaply on the backblocks where timber and railway workers were housed.

## Sam Neill

*There was a little town between here and Dunedin, a little forestry town. It was a sort of microcosm of New Zealand really; just a few families, it was a forestry centre. They had a little school, a little post office and a little store, and maybe eight or nine houses. Nine little families, everybody knew each other, nobody was well off but nobody was poor, all their kids had an opportunity to go to university and do something else. Then it got sold like the rest of the forestry. Everybody lost their jobs and now there is no community. Nobody is there. Nothing. It's gone. They didn't know what they were doing. They didn't realise the consequences.*

The world's great Food Economy, where once everyone had been able to claim rural or small-town roots, became overwhelmingly urban as small towns shrank. Tim Shadbolt laments the process in Invercargill:

## Tim Shadbolt

*We ask ourselves over and over again: why are people leaving the city, what are the attractions that other cities have got? A big part of the reason was the restructuring that happened in government. There was an enormous pressure to centralise into the big urban centres and we were terribly disadvantaged – all the big government departments we had, like the railways and the post office, literally thousands of civil servants and middle-class Southlanders left our city overnight when restructuring took place. That created some of the real disadvantages that we have.*

Post offices, bank branches and railway stations closed. Railway housing was sold off, services were provided by outreach instead of locally, insurance, fertiliser, stock and station repair and maintenance jobs, all dependent on farming, contracted. So did the schools. The state had built New Zealand's small centres in the nineteenth century. It undermined them in the late twentieth.

Yet the process did develop local resilience and produced political changes, like the election of Tim Shadbolt or Georgina Beyer, the world's first transsexual mayor, a former sex worker (as prostitutes are called by a generation too PC to use them), who moved even further up-market to become an MP.

New Zealand became colder, harder, and more urban. Everything was run, pushed and driven harder; slack, and the old easygoing ways and jobs, were taken out. Soup kitchens and clothing banks returned. Charity shops blossomed. So did car boot sales and 'fell off the back of the pa' markets. The New Zealand dream: a job, a home, a car, a bach and a boat, once available, or at least aspired to, by all, was less accessible and denied those at the bottom of the pile. The few have it chromium-plated with ever bigger boats, super-cars, huge houses and second palaces, often at company expense. The many who had caravans, baches or boats watched them appreciate in value while the next generation was being locked out of the market, unless it inherited. As for the new underclass, the bottom five percent – to whom ACT claims to devote its whole strategy of making the rich richer as the best way of helping the poor – struggled for even one of the two basic essentials of New Zealand life: a bed and a banger. National's decision to charge market rents on state housing was disastrous for this section. Until Labour reversed it.

Segregation came in healthcare by insurance, dental care by dosh, schools by area. So a classless society became more of a layer cake: top Kiwis with wealth and property, usually financed out of the business, not the pocket; the middling class pawkily comfortable and living more meanly; those right at the bottom, the excluded, struggling to get onto the first rung of the New Zealand ladder, and struggling to stay there.

The excluded are grounded. Middling folk holiday in New Zealand by camping or caravanning or staying with relations. Kids and better-off oldies go overseas, usually to Australia rather than the real world. The élite travel wherever they want by air via the Koru Club, which is New Zealand's élite at the airport, segregated from those who struggle to pay their own fares, and in punishment for this are relegated to sweat, struggle and hamburgers downstairs, until all can be herded into the same plane where they sit, paid for passengers at the front, self-paying behind, plebs and sporties right at the back.

This graded society is still not a class one in the British sense. The differences are economic, not those of accent, breeding, education and class. Good tailoring has no place where casualness rules. Quality isn't recognised, even if brands are, particularly in trainers. The differences are economic, which means the ability to claim expenses as well as salary; a power difference which enables the better off to control and manage their own fate, live where they want and do what they want, while the inability to spend someone else's money means more struggle.

Those at the top enjoy more of the blessings of consumer society, better brands, up-market products, more expensive housing, and these differences could become self-reinforcing in the bigger cities as gaps widen between the private and the élite state schools, drawing pupils from the better off in the better areas, and the bog-standard schools struggling with the disadvantaged and those from poorer areas. These beginnings of a class society are clear in Auckland and, to a lesser degree, in Christchurch.

In the segregating city something approximating to 'society', though flashier and nastier, has also emerged, with a glitterati whooping it up at 'charity' dances and dinners and an exhausting calendar of Gloss Balls, 'Ski Your Heart Out' Balls, lots of balls plus Witches and Warlocks parties, Gallery Openings, Awards Dinners and enough cricket, rugby, yachting and sporting balls to supply the world with testosterone. The obsession with location and display are flaunted in yachting, wine, restaurants or housing, where wealth is lived in decent seclusion.

New Zealand has no *Tatler* and *Bystander*, but Auckland has *Metro*, where glossy lifestyle meets long-winded journalism and good serious articles mix with celebrity gawps and gossip. A national glossy magazine market has emerged, opening the palaces of the rich in *New Zealand Homes* to allow the rest to emulate and envy. *New Zealand Gardens, New Zealand Boats, Cuisine* and *Travel* all highlight other aspects of their lives, though anything called *New Zealand Society* is precluded because only sociologists would buy it. Pretentiousness and parody are also out because, mercifully, New Zealand isn't big enough to support *Hello* or *OK* or their chronicles of tacky fame and crude celebs. New Zealand's élite may be crude, even tacky, but they've more sense than to parade it too proudly.

Wealth can show off and strut, albeit not on the same scale as in lands where money doesn't just talk it swears, but it's no longer relegated to Hawke's Bay or Canterbury, or a tweedy squattocracy, enjoying long trips abroad, the only place where New Zealand wealth could be flaunted. When wealth was the state that durst not speak its name it hid its processes of accumulation because there was nothing to spend big money on except private education or perhaps a swimming pool in which leaves would accumulate and sheep might drown. Now wealth is urban not rural, and flaunted not quiet, with more to flaunt it on in a consumer society where everything is for sale, and the world is New Zealand's shopping street.

In an urban consumer society the rules change. Wealth has

more outlets and power and can be more lavishly housed in Minnehaha Avenue (what wealthy London street would survive with such a ridiculous name?) and other streets too expensive for real people to live in, unless born there. The North Shore moves up-market, the sections of the rich get bigger, those of the rest shrink, particularly in Auckland, but New Zealanders remain relaxed about wealth and display. The growing graduations are the butt of jokes, not bitterness, because segregation on American lines in wealthy ghettos can't happen in a small society. Smallness has its benefits.

The consumer society is the froth on top of a changed New Zealand. Farmers are more enterprising in what they grow, and in seeking new markets. The Great Food Economy provides the world with a whole new range of dishes, far more tempting than the old basics, all produced because the consumer wants them. Business is more innovative and better at selling rather than fiddling shareholders. Look at Fisher and Paykel's drawer dishwashers, the self-sealing jars, the educational software exported round the world. The cultural scene bubbles with exciting new writing, art, drama and films. Torpor has turned into ferment as New Zealand fizzes where once it slept amiably. The change is almost as widely shared as it's praised and proclaimed.

New Zealanders have not only accepted change but are proud of their ability to cope and ride its accelerating pace with their characteristic ingenuity. All except the poor, for whom ingenuity is a criminal offence. This less equal society holds out more opportunities, offers more variety and is more interesting than the old, which makes it a better place to live for the majority and exciting in ways it never was before. The old joke – 'I went to New Zealand but it was closed' – is hardly applicable today. Which won't stop it still being used. The old ones are the best ones, as Winston Peters says.

New Zealand can never be a class society like Britain. No

sane country outside caste-ridden India could. It is well protected by prevailing myths, to which wealth must conform: equality, fairness and the belief that Jack is as good as his master. The good boss still mucks in with the lads rather than building distance, and must still act the good bloke even if he or she manifestly isn't. Most Kiwis aren't really interested in status, merely what money can buy. Nor are they particularly greedy or envious. They certainly aren't blessed with any great sense of deference. That can be left to the English, or at least those who still have forelocks to tug, because far too many have gone for the bald-headed, Phil Mitchell, thug look. New Zealand lacks a recognisable upper class to tug them to. Doug Myers isn't worth the effort. New Zealanders merely assume that if some are daft enough to spend money on status symbols, yachts, over-priced real estate, or lavish houses, more fools they.

This isn't the replacement of an egalitarian society by a class one, merely a move to the norms of other advanced consumer societies. Its suburban man and woman live their average lives in the best and most pleasant location, the Pacific Basin, and in one of the least populous parts – New Zealand, Tasmania or Northern California – which are the best.

New Zealand's diet of change has made it like everywhere else. No longer special. Another part of the great suburban anywhere. Old-style New Zealand lives on only in Crumperature and the Man of the South image. Reality is less unique, more polished and more cosmopolitan and no longer isolated. Indeed, New Zealand's strength is to be well plugged into the world but still able, because of smallness, to sustain the best lifestyle on offer in it, more cheaply than anywhere else. Snobs may still dismiss New Zealand as not living in the real world. That's its greatest advantage, the USP of the better society: much closer to the world but still a better place to live, no longer a joke, as Tom Scott points out:

# Tom Scott

*New Zealand used to have the worst eating in the world. Our food, our dining out, was just dire. John Cleese and his people came here to do 'Beyond the Fringe' and they were in a hotel in Timaru. John Cleese asked for an omelette with three eggs. So they brought him out an omelette with three fried eggs on top! I remember watching the Monty Python sketches and someone would have a drink of wine, 'Mmm, mmm, New Zealand wine, faint aftertaste of lamb.' Barry Humphries said, 'New Zealand is a country with seventy million sheep, three million of whom think they're human beings.' New Zealand was just a sort of joke. In any British or American sitcom, when you wanted to mention the name of an obscure, irrelevant, dopey country, you tossed in New Zealand, and you hoped that your audience was sufficiently literate to even know where the place was. We were the butt of overseas jokes because we were so remote. Kipling said we were the 'last, loneliest and the most loyal'.*

*But now our food and wine is astonishing. I think it's a combination of soil and climate and our food is now fantastic. I remember going to Australia and having a latte, thinking, 'Oh, how sophisticated.' I went to Britain recently and I couldn't get a decent cup of coffee anywhere in London. The best restaurants in London are now run by Kiwis.*

*On the international market we can add freshness. We don't know how good or bad we are. We do some really atrocious things and don't realise they're disgraceful. We also do astonishing things and don't realise how good they are. It's like Darwin. All sorts of strange flora and fauna grow in an isolated environment and I think we do produce some astonishing oddballs.*

*I do a bit of speaking and lecturing and talking – schools and stuff – and wherever I go round the country I'm staggered at the range of interests and the kind of creativity in this country. For a tiny wee place at the bottom of the world, it is an incredibly creative place, and there are people doing extraordinary things everywhere. I'm incredibly proud of it. The country you describe in your very funny but depressing book years and years ago, even you would have to admit that it now bears very little resemblance to that little book.*

The new New Zealand retains many of the advantages of the old but is well adjusted to the new and therefore able to offer the best combination of benefits, coupled with excitement, and boosted by the adaptive ingenuity which once repaired tractors, but is now applied to survival. The desperate search for an identity can now stop. New Zealand has found it as the Adaptable Nation, successful surfers on oceans of change.

Chapter Thirteen

# Back To The Future

New Zealand was a good society built by individual effort and the state, that derogatory word for the community in action. Together they settled and developed Britain's overseas farm and built the post-Depression settlement of insulation, managed marketing, social security, fairness between sections and people, and the scaffolding of a new nation. All that sustained the good society with one of the highest living standards in the world.

The settlement may have tilted balances too far from the individual to the state, been too egalitarian, based on a corrupt deal between capital and labour, giving each other an easy time and the right to be economically inefficient, but it supported a good society and it endured, eventually failing not because of any inherent faults but because of British betrayal and the protectionism of agricultures far less efficient than New Zealand's much derided 'welfare-economy'.

This generated and justified an overreaction the other way, as New Zealanders took it out on themselves for the sins of others, dismantling the trusted and tried structures, with no consideration of what was good or bad but because all of it was unacceptable to the new ideologues, who preferred a system of economics appropriate to a huge continental economy and imposed it willy-nilly on a small vulnerable one. New Zealand had long ago rejected laissez faire and free markets as inappropriate to a small vulnerable economy. In the eighties and nineties they were reimposed.

It didn't work. Instinctively wiser than the politicians, the people disliked the demolition of the world they knew. When sado-masochist economies failed to deliver, the people took their revenge, putting the politicians on a tight leash to ensure that they did the job consumer democracy demands of them: pleasing, not punishing, the people.

In 1984, 1990 and 1999 New Zealand governments had won power by promising stability and a return to normal from the excesses of the previous government. Labour in 1984, National in 1990 had betrayed the promises by plunging into agendas of change. The rot stopped first with the party which had begun it. Ejected humiliatingly in 1990, Labour lumbered on for a period unsure whether to recant and apologise for what it had done, or to claim credit for any glimmers of improvement as the product of its reforms. Initially half-hearted and sotto voce, the apologies became louder and more sincere, as the ideologues dropped away, and economic success inconsiderately failed to show. New MPs and members unscarred by the eighties came in as leaders tainted by guilt and failure moved out into the limbo dumped leaders must inhabit in a country with no House of Lords to give them custodial care and no useful role to distract them from what they most want to do: snipe at their successors. Opposition is a great inculcator of virtue. Nine years of it were a full dose but showed Labour just how much its voters felt betrayed and how far it had to go to get back in touch with them. National's own unpopularity helped out and, after a succession of disposable leaders, Helen Clark climbed out from under the monetarist rubble to rein in market liberalism.

Time eliminated the need to defend what had been done just because Labour had done it. Rogernomics had produced no real benefits in either growth or employment because the perpetually promised pay-off never came. The only recovery was of the type available when lunatics stop banging their heads against brick walls. It was time for social democracy to come out of the closet, but not too far, and for Labour to return to type. In policy development for the November 1999 election and in its pre-election coalition with the Alliance, the preserving jar of social democracy, Labour took on the job of tilting the balances back.

## Tom Scott

*Helen was a terrible Leader of the Opposition. I thought when I was watching things in the House she hated being Leader of the Opposition. She's not suited to Opposition, that kind of rough and tumble. She's too clever, too self-conscious for the rugby league brutality being in Opposition requires. Having become Prime Minister she's been a revelation. She's been astonishing. That is what she was born for and what she's trained for, and she's been an extremely able Prime Minister. I'm at a loss to work out why she was so bad as Leader of the Opposition and so good as Prime Minister. It's almost a mystery. But the change has been astonishing. Labour is now a more modern version of what it was. They've copied lines and tones and aphorisms and marketing skills. They have the focus groups working non-stop, night and day, working out what people want. They listen carefully to what the focus groups are saying and modify their rhetoric accordingly. But they have shrugged off Rogernomics, there's no doubt about that.*

*Cullen, who was one of the people least enamoured by Roger Douglas, is one of the brightest people who I ever covered in politics. Sometimes he's a bit short on the charm front, but Michael is definitely hugely intelligent. Helen and Michael have managed to pretend they were just minor players in the Roger Douglas revolution, and now the party is much more responsive to the Labour electorate.*

The National Party followed more slowly, having been taken over by ideologues more recently. Jim Bolger, a political compromiser, couldn't stop the rush to folly. Ruth Richardson rampaged on, and when she was disposed of, Bolger was damaged by the messy coalition with New Zealand First, and the even messier way it fell apart in a frenzy of waka-hopping. Jenny Shipley overthrew Bolger to resume the march down dead-end street.

For it too, opposition was the educator. In 2001 Shipley was overthrown for Bill English, who recognised that the Party had to return to caring conservatism and the centre ground even if he wasn't sure either how to get there, or whether he should jettison new right politics and tax cuts.

# Bill English

*When you get beaten in an election a certain amount of water has to go under the bridge. The public have to see you fulfil the obligations of an opposition, which are to understand why you got kicked out, and to reconnect with all those people who voted you out. That's the process that we are going through. It's something you don't enjoy to start with, but it's a very necessary part of being a decent government when you get back in.*

*People had had a decade of social change, economic change, we changed our whole electoral system. My party came to be seen as disconnected from the reality of people's lives, too narrowly focused on a few issues, and people wanted a break. So now you've got a country which is like someone sleeping off a hangover. They want a bit of peace and quiet for a while, but the real issues will be back.*

Temporarily or permanently, the Taliban had been forced back into their caves because New Zealanders wanted a return to stability, an end to restless change. The new Labour Government began to repair the worst damage.

## Helen Clark

*There's certainly a feeling in New Zealand that governments just ran away with the election mandate, did things they never foreshadowed at all, and people started to wonder why it was worth turning out to vote at all. The main enemy we had in the last election was cynicism and apathy, because people were getting to the point where they wondered whether anybody could make a difference. And we've had to show that we had a clear programme, would implement it and would make a difference.*

The programme was carefully portrayed as 'third way' moderate and unideological so as not to frighten anyone. Yet the spin could not hide the differences. In Britain New Labour kept social democracy in the closet and came to power with a huge majority to do not very much. Helen Clark came in on a similar percentage share of the total electorate and with no majority at all to do a great deal.

Parliamentary life has always been more interesting for New Zealand MPs than for their British counterparts because smaller parties mean more consultation and more influence, and every MP who's neither a total lunkhead nor an alcoholic has a good chance of being a minister, which is usually more of a threat than a promise. But from 1999 that gap widened for Labour MPs. With huge majority, minimal programme British Labour MPs are kept busy doing nothing. Kiwi counterparts, with a more radical programme but no majority at all, find life more interesting. Fortunately for them, Helen Clark is tougher than Tony Blair. The first act was to increase direct taxes, a blasphemy in the eighties and nineties and something which took British Labour five years. It returned Accident Compensation to the public sector, the first check to the tide of privatisation, then re-nationalised Air New Zealand. It scrapped National's employment legislation, tilting the balance back to workers and unions, and Darien Fenton saw the unions returning to life.

## Darien Fenton

*Labour's put us in a stronger position. It's improved the situation. From the moment they were elected it changed the climate. Almost a day after the election people were ringing the union office and saying we're allowed to join a union now. So there is a much kinder feeling around towards unions and a much stronger feeling on safety. They have introduced new labour laws which I think if they were introduced fifteen years ago the union movement would have said they were sell-outs but we see them very much as organising tools. It's still our job to actually organise workers, so they don't provide the answers and they don't try and do the job for us but they give us the opportunity. They've improved the minimum wage, they've brought in paid parental leave, which was a great victory for women because we've fought for ten years to get it.*

*I'm an optimist, always an optimist. What keeps me going is the union members, many of them are Pacific Island and Maori workers who had so much courage and so much bravery through the nineties when I saw them stepping out and still being union members when it wasn't safe to do so. The quality of people now that we are seeing coming through into the union movement reflects very much the workforce of New Zealand which is increasingly Polynesian. It's very exciting but it's going to take us a long time to rebuild what we've lost.*

*Returning to compulsory unionism isn't on. The big lesson we learned from that is that we stopped doing our jobs. It did deliver for people who got pay rises, but I don't want to ever see the union movement in a situation again where it was so vulnerable that within a year or two it could be almost completely wiped out by a new government.*

Investment in the public service, particularly health and education began to check the deterioration from two decades of low growth. Helen Clark had started on a Sisyphean task.

# Helen Clark

*The most enjoyable has been being able to back the rusty old vehicle of New Zealand out of the no-exit, neo-liberal street and get it on a different track, which is much more identifiably socially democratic, and puts New Zealand in the mainstream of Western political systems and thought, not out on some crazy extreme adventure. Then you keep moving in that direction. There's a lot of things you can start in your first three years in government, but you need a much longer period to make the kind of impact you come in to politics to make. So we will be campaigning again on the next set of objectives for a second term, based on the direction we've established.*

The revival of the economy made it easier. Two decades of balances tilted from production and exports to finance and imports by high interest rates, and a dollar kept far too high, had weakened the production economy because the fundamental lesson of competitive trade had been ignored. All the productivity gains and the improved efficiency in the world are no use if the exchange rate is too high to allow domestic production to sell its goods in ever tougher markets, at a price the world is prepared to pay. Piddling percentage productivity improvements mean nothing against an overvaluation of ten or twenty percent.

Price is crucial and price overseas is determined by the exchange rate. In ignoring that lesson monetarism defeated itself. As that great democrat Rob Muldoon had pointed out, economic policy should be decided by government for the purposes of the people not by unaccountable central bankers playing one-club golfing in a one-hole game. Central bankers see inflationary threats everywhere. The two sacred principles of their craft are high interest rates and an overvalued currency, which is a virility symbol for them when it's hard. Don Brash, the former Reserve Bank Governor, was supertypical of the breed. People grow up fearing whatever nightmare most terrified them as a child. As a neophyte National Candidate, Don had endured the horror of being defeated by Social Creditor Garry Knapp. New Zealand suffered the consequences of this terrible shock to the Brash psyche in interest rates far higher than they need have been, an obsession with inflation long after it was dead, and a dollar so high it strangled an economy which either lives by exports or dies. The one area where the free market was not allowed to apply was the most crucial: interest and exchange rates.

Because New Zealand is a price taker not a price maker, the war on inflation punished its productive sector for crimes it had never committed. Today inflation is dead nearly everywhere, killed by the weakness of labour, intensifying world competition, the spread of efficient, just-in-time distribution systems and huge new productive capacities coming on stream. No one can now dictate, even manage, prices. So why waste so much time and effort defeating a dead enemy as Brashnomics did, compounding an appreciation of the dollar produced by the inflow of money to buy the privatised assets in the Roger-Ruth Fire Sale (Everything Must Go!) further by the excessive borrowings by the banks to stimulate the housing boom and stock market speculation both of which then compounded the problem by pushing up interest rates.

The dollar stayed cripplingly high up to the late nineties as Don detected the inflationary beast behind every gooseberry bush. Then it fell as foreign investors cooled. The Bank was 'persuaded' by government from 1999 and frightened by post-September 11th economic fears in 2001. It didn't react to the dollar's fall and the growth it stimulated by raising interest rates.

## Sir Bob Jones

*The straitjacket had gone on the economy because house prices in Auckland were going up, so all the overdrafts went up. This was not the market economy. This was absolute centralism and statism. It was crazy. Now the Reserve Bank have learnt the error of their ways. They keep their heads down. They don't go out talking about it, and they let things happen. I know that Cullen in Opposition subscribed to the sort of thing I was saying. He told me. I think he and Anderton have just told them to just leave things alone.*

*I'm enormously optimistic about New Zealand now on the economic front. Economically, things are going along very nicely, with a little bit of luck, too. The exchange rate will rise as we prosper but that doesn't matter. Just leave it alone. Let it be a true market rate.*

A competitive exchange rate produced the boost that two decades of monetarist economics had failed to provide. The exchange rate converts New Zealand costs into prices on international markets. A low dollar makes domestic production attractive and competitive, a high one penalises it, making imports cheap; so exports revived, imports were held back by price (the only barrier permitted in a free trading world), tourists poured in, investment grew. The growth which had eluded New Zealand for two wasted decades began.

The same key had once boosted the initial growth of all the dynamic economies from Germany and Japan to the new dragons of South-East Asia. New Zealand finally turned it, making the export sector profitable and boosting the whole economy, a trick which still eludes Britain, the European Union and Japan in its present misery. A competitive exchange rate is particularly crucial for a small nation which has to be super-competitive. Those for whom a hard exchange rate is a cross to repel the vampire of inflation might want it super-cautious but only growth builds investment, new markets, innovation and new skills, and if those compounding benefits are maintained, New Zealand can take its place on the growth escalator so many others have ridden for so long. A low exchange rate shifts the whole dynamics of the economy, liberating enterprise, stimulating the new opening markets and providing the opportunity for ideas, new products, services, initiatives, all of which flourish as growth bubbles.

Yet the growth has to be sustained to work its compounding magic, meaning that the low exchange rate must be too. That's easy for a small nation which doesn't have to face threats of instability or the institutional constraints of size. It's more difficult for central bankers, who prefer the stability of the graveyard to the excitement of growth. Don Brash showed that he'd learned nothing and forgotten nothing, raising rates in 2002, on the grounds that growth of just under three percent was 'potentially' inflationary and an intolerable strain on the economy, even though it had been restructured, reorganised and put on a long and painful outward-bound course to clear the way for growth. This was folly when the New Zealand economy needs four percent growth stretching into the foreseeable future to make up the ground it has lost and put it into a virtuous cycle of improvement.

Whatever the prospect, growth came like rain on the monetarist desert, creating a new world of opportunity which the adaptable, inventive, ingenious Kiwi was built by God to seize. Agriculture was helped by Britain's decision to kill six million livestock. Farmers rushed into every available niche market. Entrepreneurs built yachts, boats, self-sealing jars, made cosmetics, developed health foods, specialised software, or did specialised radios, new IT systems, programmes for all kinds of needs, in fact anything New Zealand ingenuity could devise to sell overseas. Heaven knows. Anything goes. With the competitive exchange rate it went.

New Zealand was coming to mean something more interesting than dead sheep and butter, though the wide variety of exports made transaction charges greater. Costs on penny packets to diverse markets often by air are higher than the old system of selling bulk through settled channels, but any return was good after years of low returns. The stimulus to ingenuity and inventiveness was considerable. The diverse, exciting economy generated growth and jobs, and a growing tax take after a decade of higher unemployment, spending cuts and low growth.

New Zealand has long tried vainly to diversify out of agriculture. Dr Sutch provided the formula of the fifties in protected industry and import substitution. By the seventies it was Think Big projects in energy and steel and Closer Economic Relations with Australia. Then it was the free market suck-it-and-see. Finally IT, upgraded skills and education. Yet none replaced the dependence on agriculture, most proved ephemeral.

The late nineties pointed a better way ahead in a recognition that agriculture will always be basic, but grows if it and the whole economy are kept competitive by a low exchange rate. Kiwi ingenuity has great scope for developing new crops and markets, and new ways of adding value, and spin offs in a world agricultural market which is less flexible because either big scale or peasant traditionalism. The key, therefore, is not diversifying out of agriculture but to diversify agriculture and use its success as a stimulus to all the spin offs which will develop in the rest of the economy, keeping the food economy as the powerful drive motor and letting the non-agricultural economy respond to market opportunities and develop what comes naturally. With a little help from government.

Growth needs a more responsive and better regulated stock market, better corporate governance and an end to New Zealand's predilection to invest in houses, not businesses.

# Brian Gaynor

*We've got one of the most laissez faire, unregulated share markets in the world. Now, the rules are being tightened up. The new Labour government has certainly brought in some new rules and regulations, but they only take us on par with the rest of the world. It's not as if we're becoming a regulated economy. We're still well below. There has been a lot of instances where companies have been raped by the major share holders or by the directors. Less and less in recent years, but certainly in the late eighties and right through to 1996, 1997, 1998, there were a lot of examples. When you have publicly listed companies raped by directors and major share holders, investors lose confidence. So they take a while to come back.*

*New Zealanders, more than ever, have a preference for bricks and mortar. All the statistics show that a New Zealander would prefer to buy a house, and would prefer to own a house, and would prefer to have a second house and a third house and a fourth house, rather than invest in the share market. That trend has accelerated in recent years, there's been a huge amount of money invested in housing. We know well-known rugby players who, when they make money these days, instead of investing in businesses, they own more than a dozen houses. That's the way they invest their money. So we're not creating the kind of wealth generating new companies. We're not getting people willing to invest in the kind of companies that will create the wealth and jobs in the future. You don't create any exports by building an extra ten houses, you do by creating a business that makes software and exports that software to the UK or to Australia, or elsewhere.*

A competitive exchange rate and investment structures more adept at providing venture capitalism are preconditions for the growth New Zealand needs, but both need to be supplemented by strategy.

Economic liberals and the business community dislike government, but government can develop consensus on where the economy should go and guide and assist it to get there by encouraging innovation, venture capital, export sales, clustering and regional development so as to reboot the economy. Government must encourage and sustain, not control.

# Brian Gaynor

*In the past we had no economic policies to create growth so we brought people in in the hope that they'd do it for us. But that's a silly thing to do. You've got to have the basis there and you've got to have established who you want to be. Then, say for example, if you want to be very good at research and development in biotechnology you try to get people who've got skills in that area.*

*The lingering mistake from the reforms is the feeling that government can't pick winners. So you can't have any kind of government policies that decide we'll be good at electronics, or IT, or biotechnology, because governments can't make decisions like that. So we don't have any policies to be good at this, or divert some resources into that. So we're still just floundering around hoping that some day something will come out of the sky and deliver some kind of an industry to us that we will become very good at and prosper as a result of that.*

Growth builds national strength and confidence, which in turn become the bases of an effective foreign policy. New Zealand's long search for a new rock appears to be over. Small is flexible, free and effective in an open, multi-centred world which is no longer divided into blocs by Cold War. A small smart country can pursue its own interests as well as fulfil the hopes of the people, which in New Zealand have a more direct influence than in powerful countries where mass electorates are there to be led rather than listened to. When they don't give the answer their élite wants they are asked to think and vote again until they do.

In New Zealand it's the other way round as the élite changes policy to suit the wishes of the people who think not in diplomatic, or balance of power terms, but of basic values: nuclear-free, clean and green, independent, pacific and a defender of international morality. New Zealand's choice is not between rocks or blocs, but between greater or lesser degrees of independence. Bill English is cautious.

## Bill English

*We're probably a limpet heading away from the rocks at the moment. For a small country at the end of the world it's vital that we stay connected to larger intellectual and economic influences. You could call it global fluency. How can we make sure we can talk to the world? We did depend on Britain for that, and that was terrific. They were at the heart of a worldwide empire. That's faded. I believe we should be looking for what I call inter-dependence. That is to have a closer relationship, particularly with the US and Australia.*

*You can be inter-dependent without being subordinate. New Zealand's still a wee bit much in the mode of saying, look, you either do everything President Bush tells you, or you're totally independent of him. That's silly, we can have a mature relationship that's a bit more equal and benefit from the closeness of it. The nuclear ships case has been an impediment to the full alliance, particularly at a military level. But New Zealanders see that as a core value. They don't want to see the anti-nuclear legislation changed and we're not going to set out to change it. So we have to put in more of an effort to build all the other aspects of the relationships, because New Zealand needs those relationships, probably more.*

Helen Clark prefers an independent New Zealand to be its own woman playing a part proportionate to principles and integrity rather than alliances or military strength. For her, smallness is strength, provided it's skilfully used.

# Helen Clark

*As a small country we haven't exactly got a lot of muscle and power to throw around. So our role is one of trying to get the greatest possible multilateral dialogue. That's why New Zealand, from day one, was a very strong supporter of the United Nations, why it gets in behind regional groupings like APEC, why it works through the UN system to the widest extent possible on a great range of issues. There's no power, so you've got to use influence.*

*So we have an interesting role in today's world. While we're clearly a First World Western country with Liberal Democratic values, we also have a position in the South Pacific with a strong, indigenous minority population which leads us to see issues a little differently from a lot of other First World Western countries. You see New Zealand at conferences like the World Conference on Racism, for example, able to bring a rather different perspective than Northern Europe.*

*We have to be our own rock. We have to be confident in our own values, our own position, where we seek our friends. This year I've led a number of missions to other nations, to Latin America, to North Asia. Generally I think New Zealand is perceived as a country with a mind of its own, one which is outward looking, which takes interesting positions on disarmament, the environment, human rights, the great range of international issues of our day. When we speak, we speak for ourselves, not for anybody else. That gives you a little more influence than you might imagine 3.8 million people have.*

Assessment of national prospects are always subject to fashion, but there is no doubt that at the start of the new millennium New Zealand's look good. It's not that every prospect pleases. New Zealand still has to live on the edge. The world could sour, making small craft vulnerable. Biological threats, sabotage, or even epidemics like foot and mouth or BSE, could be devastating to an agricultural producer. The youth exodus could accelerate as prospects open up in ageing societies overseas.

Yet these threats are remote against the better prospects of a world and its markets opening up, the decline of agricultural protectionism, the new pluralism of a multi-centred, blockless world. All of it very different to the stability of settled allegiances and guaranteed markets, like surfboarding after sunbathing, but all holding out exciting prospects if growth is sustained. The new world belongs to small nations, not big. Provided they seize its opportunities.

## Brian Gaynor

*I'm an optimist because New Zealand has huge potential. I'm frustrated because it hasn't reached that potential, but the optimism is there. We're right next to the fastest-growing area in the world. Asia has had its ups and downs but it's still the growing area of the world. In the next ten years 400 million people will move from the rural areas to the cities in China. The potential that has for us, in terms of education, tourism, being able to export certain products – for example timber products – and added values, is a huge potential. We haven't realised it because we got led astray in the eighties. This government is not totally popular with the business community. There's a better feeling that we're making progress in the right direction, but we still have a long way to go.*

Maintaining the growth path will allow a small country to exercise an influence above its weight, and make a principled contribution to the world, particularly the undeveloped islands in New Zealand's Pacific backyard. Failure to grow would reduce New Zealand to irrelevance. Smallness is a benefit but only if it is used properly to build the good society and ensure that it contributes to the world.

## Helen Clark

*I'd like to see New Zealand leading the world and getting that combination of a fair and just society and an innovative and prosperous economy. That's got to be at the heart of the social democratic mission to blend the two together. I came in to make a difference and to preserve the essential characteristics of New Zealand society, which were around that fairness, opportunity, Jack's as good as his master – a secure New Zealand for old and young and families.*

*Over time I've also got very involved in the economic issues and how New Zealand can regenerate its economy, because it had got pretty lacklustre, pretty old-fashioned, stuck in its ways, and it has to step out of that and use the advantages we've got of this incredible education, science, communications infrastructure to leverage a lot more value. The challenge now is to fund the kind of society we want because if we kept falling down the living standards tree, as we did for a steady half century, we would end up falling to the ranks of the Second World and out of the ranks of the First World.*

That means accelerated population loss to a richer world outside, less ability to provide a future for young people, a declining influence in an advancing world. New Zealand would be relegated to the backblocks. To avoid that New Zealand needs to maintain the growth that has lifted it out of the slough of despond and use it to shape an identity as a dynamic nation on the move. Look at Ireland: another small nation that has made a big contribution of talent to the world. Ten years of high and continuous growth, mostly over four percent, have transformed a sleepy backwater into a Celtic Tiger – sucking in skills, industries, investment and talent instead of losing all four. Its dynamic economy boosts a lively cultural renaissance. After twenty years of self-flagellation, New Zealand needs the same and can only look to the same compounding growth to get it.

Chapter Fourteen

# Global Kiwis

New Zealanders have long been a people in search of an identity, their country a nation needing a nationalism. Since the 1940s New Zealand intellectuals – a description one of them told me was as much an oxymoron as military intelligence – have scanned the horizon looking for an identity and a nationhood to emerge. Observing the moa skeleton in the Canterbury Museum poet Allen Curnow mused:

*Not I but some child born in a marvellous year*
*Will learn the trick of standing upright here*

New Zealanders are learning it and donning the confident identity which comes with it. War memorials, which in other countries speak of patrie, fatherland or motherland, here spoke of the empire, of which New Zealand was a province. The South African War Memorial in Auckland records troops as dying for 'their country' though that country's interest in South Africa can't have been huge. The two World War memorials recognise them as dying for 'King and Country', the euphemism for empire. When the Japanese captured Singapore, Australia wanted out of the North African and European theatres. Kiwis stayed on.

It took a century for 'God Defend New Zealand' to join 'God Save the Queen' as national anthem, and alienated intellectuals have long been ashamed of their Philistine nation; in fact, no other country outside Russia has come in for such a litany of abuse from its intellectuals – Bill Pearson writing of the 'Fretful Sleepers', Harold Innes of the 'Status Quo Seekers' and Gordon McLauchlan of the 'Passionless People'.

New Zealanders don't get on particularly well with Aussie neighbours because like repels like and there's no desire to go waltzing with Matilda, yet abroad Kiwis hide behind Australians, as half-pint Aussies or even 'half-baked Poms' in Australia. Before my Pavlova Pilgrimage began, Kiwis warned me that their country had gone to the dogs. Greedy materialism, engulfing globalisation and Gradgrind economics had destroyed national niceness and the feeling for equality, to relegate the beloved country to a pathetic version of Australia without the culture. Others, who couldn't escape, called it a banana republic without the bananas.

National identity emerged quite late in New Zealand. It has no dominant capital like London or Paris to give character, identity and focus to the nation. It has no large Irish population to endow it with Australia's assertive inferiority complex and grudges. It has two cultures, Maori and Pakeha. Curnow had viewed it as the land where European restlessness broke the surf-filled Polynesian dream, but others asserted that both populations had fallen asleep on the beach fulfilling the promise of neither. Kiwi dreamers dreamt of the good society or a 'Better Britain', not a nation with an assertive pride.

Nor is there a history of struggle, or rebellion. The most recent substantial history of New Zealand, Belich's *Paradise Reforged*, argues that New Zealand opted for 're-colonisation' and was regressing back to the maternal breast just as others threw away their colonial yokes. It never rejected Mummy. Mummy rejected New Zealand before weaning. Others seized independence, the condition was forced on a reluctant New Zealand by British betrayal. Ever since the Second World War New Zealand has been let down by British failure, for its pathetically low growth rate dragged New Zealand down the international league tables from second in the fifties to worse than umpteenth. Had New Zealand been Germany's overseas farm or Japan's it would have shared their miracle.

To add insult to this injury, when Britain's comparative decline finally threatened to become absolute, Ted Heath panicked, clutched at salvation in Europe, and rewarded New Zealand for all its cheap food and for giving priority to Britain's products, however shoddy, in return, by a kick in the sheep cods. He instructed his chief negotiator, the appropriately named Sir Con O'Neill, to jettison anything which stood in the way of entry: New Zealand's trade access was among the commitments chucked overboard. The overseas farm was told to find new markets in a world where agriculture was universally protected. Those proudly described on their passports as 'New Zealand Citizen British Subject' found that they were no longer welcome. Unless they had a return ticket.

Britain benefited less from its betrayal and is less happy in its adulterous relationship with France, Germany, and the entangling aspirations of Brussels, than the jilted innocent it left with neither alimony nor compensation. Footloose and fancy-free, New Zealand is belatedly having the time of its life and the challenge has forged a new identity; the first, possibly the only one, born of rejection, though it's early to judge what will happen to the Falklands, Gibraltar and St Helena. This was neither easy nor without pain, but over the years the world has changed. It suits New Zealand better and New Zealand has changed to better suit the world. Out of these processes a new identity has been born: the Adaptable People.

The world is more open as protective barriers fall, opening up export opportunities. It's less divided with cold war over and blocs breaking, offering more scope and a better hearing for a little country with big principles, a positive Goody-Two-Shoes and unselfish to the point of altruism. In a pluralistic world limpets no longer need rocks. The world is smaller, so the loneliness of the long-distance food supplier becomes the convenience nation just round the corner. Enough distance to be different in seasonal production, and to permit the development of more varieties and products, from nashi to zestfruit, from milk derivatives to better-bred sheep – but damn quick to market and well aimed at the consumer.

In New Zealand, the monetarist outward-bound course at least made people and economy more resilient, encouraged survival of the fittest, pared the flab, cut costs and made New Zealand poorer, hence keener to fight back with more to fight for and more incentive to grab opportunity wherever it came. Exposure to a colder world put a premium on Kiwi characteristics: flexibility, adaptiveness and ingenuity, particularly in the agricultural sector where competitors were either big, flabby agribusiness or protected peasants producing for subsidy. New Zealand ran rings round both. Being more nimble and flexible, it switched from market to market and product to product, ever ready to please the consumer. The scale of New Zealand enterprise also helped. Where necessary, as in Fonterra, that was big enough to compete in oligopolistic markets. Elsewhere smallness was the key. Flexible family farms, small businesses and one-man bands are nimble enough to fill niches, produce premium product like wine while consistently adding more value. They grab opportunities where big-scale competitors lumber.

Small means quick and clever for nations, farms and businesses, and the overarching impression left at the end of my Pavlova Pilgrimage has been not only affection, but respect for the pragmatic and adaptable. My liking for the quaint, which is still there, has been eclipsed by the excitement of a country in ferment, bubbling with the new, the innovative, the good, the simple idea which sells and the creative energy thrown up by Kiwi ingenuity.

It's exciting to see Southland changing so fast and thronging with new ideas, from boats to cars, and chocolates to Internet chemists; to see Dunedin leading the world in filming the wild; Otago students hampstering to develop and market new ideas to sell to venture capitalists, where we once sat around grumbling at the University Grants Committee. Stimulating too, to see new crops from farming, new ideas in tourism, exciting computer graphics and software programmes for lucrative but niche markets. To share this excitement is impossible in bigger countries, where development is within monoliths and behind closed doors, where it doesn't involve the initiative or energies of the mass of the people whose only role is to gawp in bemusement, where far more Kiwis are involved in what is a national effort in a nation which is a real democracy and has long been a home for the quirky, the offbeat, the crank, and devoted enthusiasts working away in sheds to produce ideas from pool cleaners to nuclear fusion. Now it can reap the benefits.

New Zealand papers are filled with reports of this inventor developing a programme for restoring old photographs likely to bring millions of dollars in Internet orders, that educational software developer producing unique programmes for niche markets for the deaf, blind, or the disabled, of that technician with a new global positioning or radio system. Designers, developers, inventors, visionaries, clever fixers and DIY technical geniuses have always been there, but with New Zealand plugged into the world wider horizons open. Some will fail, some will be cons or cranks, a few will triumph. That's how markets work but a lot of bread is being cast onto the waters. Six and a half thousand of New Zealand's 9000 exporters contribute less than $100,000 a year. That number is growing because smallness, ingenuity and the ability to respond quickly are the keys to success in a world which wants the new, the innovative. The world will buy, take over, invest, back or co-operate because New Zealand is not only a good place to have ideas, but a good place to implement and produce them with costs so low.

When this lively undergrowth of small firms and new ideas was watered by the dew of a low exchange rate, boosting exports, it began to bubble. With that came confidence as more came forward and one set of developments stimulated another. Peter Jackson's success will become the basis for a strong feature film sector with skilled technicians producing for New Zealand, and for the world. The Kiwi characteristics of adaptability, hard work, ingenuity, and the touch of desperation produced by an underdog position are bringing success. Starting from behind is an advantage in a world of challenge; New Zealand has lots to prove.

From all this the new national identity emerges in the characteristics New Zealanders are programmed with by the process of growing up in a small, still simple, and still comparatively equal and open society. New Zealand is a society shaped for people and the whole country a pleasure machine, both run to maximise their happiness.

As New Zealanders have learned the knack first of surviving then of succeeding on their own, so a new confidence and purpose emerge, fragile at first but building all the while. Other nationalisms are rooted in the soil, the capital, the loveliness of the land, or in taking on the negative tones of hooliganism, racist soccer thug nationalism. New Zealand is not immune from these kinds of influences when it comes to battle with Australia. Yet they aren't part of an identity which is bred in the bone, a portable identity which goes with the Kiwis wherever they travel.

Which is often a long way. These are a restless people, a gypsy nation with travel in the genes. Almost as many New Zealanders go each year as visitors come in to enjoy the National Pleasure Plant; and travel completes the Kiwi. Overseasia adds the experience of metropolitan life, Fairburn's Megalopolis and of other cultures, primitive or advanced. It provides the experience of diversity, culture, sweetness and light. The world is New Zealand's finishing school to round off the adaptable Kiwi – a people at home anywhere, able to mix with anyone, put down roots and contribute their skills anywhere. They go. They see. They conquer. Then most return. New Zealand is a country of choice. Coming back is a deliberate preference, a demonstration of commitment. After experiencing and being improved by the alternatives.

## Greg Johnson

*New Zealanders are well travelled and I certainly am. I've always maintained that I can live in New Zealand as long as I can escape twice a year and get a dose of the things I can't get here. I think change is good as well.*

*You can take the New Zealander out of New Zealand but you can't take New Zealand out of the New Zealander. We feel like we're members of a fairly small and slightly exclusive club. I always have this idea in my head that if I was on the Trans-Siberian Express and I saw my least liked New Zealander two seats ahead of me – someone I just did not like – I guarantee we would find common ground and would talk about something in that isolated environment.*

Young people I spoke to on the beach at Mount Maunganui felt the same:

*Home is always home. Whenever you've been, over to Australia, up in the Islands, or Sydney, Melbourne and Brisbane, they're all good to go and visit. But when you get on the plane and come home it's always home. It's just more relaxed and it's home. A good place to be. I'd like to stay there, maybe for a couple of years, but most people end up coming back in the end. You've got familiar surroundings and you know what happens. It's a good spot.*

Students in Dunedin agreed:

## Charlotte Clifton

*You go overseas and you see someone who's from New Zealand and you've immediately got quite a connection. My sister was walking down the street in London and a guy was coming the other way and she thought, 'Oh my God, I know that guy.' And he looked at her and said, 'Dunedin.' She said 'Yeah,' and they smiled and kept walking. You feel you've got something because there are so few of us really.*

Being ever-easier to satisfy, the travel lust poses the problem of brain drain. Locally-made people have long been New Zealand's best export, losing its brightest and best by investing its taxpayers' money in raising, nurturing, training and educating Kiwis, to go to work for more money in other countries: which get Kiwis without costs.

In the eighties and nineties low domestic growth and high unemployment produced a net population loss to Australia, with over a hundred thousand going Ozwards in some Muldoon years, causing that great man to joke that it raised the IQ of both countries. This was a safety valve, a same drain rather than a brain drain. Younger New Zealanders go, and will go when Australia is doing better, as it was for most of the eighties and nineties. They come back when the New Zealand economy picks up, as it has more recently.

Yet higher wages, greater specialisation, greater challenges and more excitement and competition overseas can become addictive, and young Kiwis go abroad just at the traditional age of marrying and settling down. Stay and they'd settle to the joys of Oamaru or Dannevirke; meet partners overseas and it could be Osaka or Denmark.

Overall, New Zealand probably gains by bringing in more and better qualifications than it loses, though it doesn't always use this brain-gain well enough. But to go or stay are personal decisions. Young New Zealanders find London, and the United States – to which they are now just as likely to go – exciting and stimulating. They also find both overcrowded, expensive, over-pressured and less desirable to live in compared with New Zealand, where the unique quality of life is a huge non-monetary compensation. What's the pleasure of living in an over-priced flat in London, trying to cope with a job, and possibly a baby, as well as have a life?

In New Zealand, life expands to fill the space available. Overseas it contracts, and living is a pressure not a pleasure. The choice between metropolitan excitement but squalor and sitting in a house on the Port Hills looking over to the mountains, or in Devonport looking out to Auckland, with space, fresh air and freedom, all at a much lower cost, is difficult only for the really big earner. Or the snob. Once on the London house-price ladder it's tempting to stay, particularly for Kiwis who buy houses, do them up, sell at a profit, then buy another on the ladder to millionaire status. Yet it's also sensible to come back and buy, say all Tokoroa on the proceeds from a London semi. Émigrés like Paul Beresford MP and dentist, or Judith Mayhew – a senior City figure – have built careers in Britain, where it's easy for classless Kiwis to get on because they relate to all, where no one's sure which box to classify them in. Others will follow. Yet the numbers are small, and probably falling and émigrés still make a contribution to New Zealand.

Others go to test themselves against foreign competition and return more confident having won. As soon as Tom Scott had got a letter from *Punch* offering to employ him and use his cartoons, he came straight back to New Zealand to draw them for the *Listener* and the *Evening Post*, becoming New Zealand's first media polymath.

Sam Neill, too, wanted to match himself against the competition.

## Sam Neill

*Growing up in New Zealand when I did, we had the idea of England being the place of excellence where you would go and measure yourself against some kind of template of what was good in whatever field, but particularly in the arts and in drama. I never had any money to go to RADA so I was not trained there, but I wanted to go and see if I was any good standing beside English actors.*

*I found that I was all right in that field. That was great affirmation for me, particularly when I did a television series called 'Riley Ace of Spies'. It was seven or eight months' work, all at Ealing Studios, and every day there would be a handful of really top-flight English actors. I found that I was completely comfortable in their company, and anything they could do I could do, if not better, then just as well. That was really good for me.*

The great majority of those who go for experience, for romance, or to work out their travel bug will come back. They'll find no one's missed them and by going they've provided others with opportunity. The jobs they leave are quickly filled and the churning workplace offers more people more opportunities to learn, do, experience and train, than in static societies where 'in death there is hope' because everyone sits around waiting for someone else to die. Those who return come back improved, more sophisticated, experienced, and better qualified to make a contribution to New Zealand. Churning improves societies as well as butter.

The clinching argument for doing nothing to halt the trend is that nothing *can* be done. Nothing can stop young people travelling, specialists specialising, or the talented wanting to climb taller trees. Even big countries like Britain suffer a brain drain of top talent to the United States, because every English-speaking nation is drawn into the American nexus: look at the nationalities working in the World Trade Towers. Which is why some want to build up the New Zealand population by anything between one million and six million.

## Chris Laidlaw

*There are economic arguments which support the view that we need somewhere in excess of five to seven million people here for pure reasons of market science. So that you get the dynamism of small enterprises that have a sufficiently viable domestic market to get themselves up to the starting line to compete on the international stage. There are all sorts of other social reasons but I would like to see a New Zealand with ten million people in it.*

Millions would want to come. Yet in an overpopulated world, protecting New Zealand's uniqueness by not making it as people-ridden and as unpleasant as bigger nations becomes more important. Mass Asian immigration would be unacceptable and do little to relieve population pressures back home. It would also eliminate the benefits of smallness and the relaxed lifestyle and easy access to the good life it sustains. Nor is there a consensus on who to bring in or on what mix of races, age groups and skills New Zealand needs. Restricting entry to designated skills and specified wealth levels would not be a high expansion but anything bigger than this is pointless until decisions are made on which way the New Zealand economy should develop. For instance, demands for nuclear physicists might not be quite as high as that for plant biologists, animal geneticists or those able to develop health-food products or drugs from milk.

Australia and Canada are much bigger. Yet they too suffer from brain drain. The problem will always be there in an open world where talent and special skills are marketable. Indeed, any reduction of Kiwi migration is more likely to come from the short-sighted closing of doors in Britain and Europe than any local restraint on exit. An open world will stay New Zealanders' oyster. Yet as a more complex and varied society emerges, and as economic growth provides more opportunities and jobs, more will stay and more return, to make their contribution to New Zealand rather than just being proud of it at a distance. Kiri Te Kanawa belongs to the world. Her future counterparts will go as she did. Yet Peter Jackson and Sam Neill have shown that it is possible to be a world talent working in a world market whilst retaining roots and a base in New Zealand. More will imitate their example.

Kiwis abroad, whether as visitors, long-stayers or residents, are useful for New Zealand. They constitute a sales force promoting tourism, New Zealand wine and other products, from Vegemite to anoraks, boots, and the Swanndris, which are carted up hill and down dale as mobile billboards for the land they come from. This Kiwi Diaspora is available for mobilisation, via the Internet, where information can be put out for them to spread the word and receive back their news of opportunities, markets, benefits and the tricks of survival. This will sustain their identity and keep them in touch, ensuring that the Diaspora gives each other a leg up, not just a leg over, giving exporters a market, and New Zealand a world of contacts and not-so-secret agents.

Kiwi is a global brand and a portable sense of identity, independent of the place which nurtured it but strong enough to last a lifetime. New Zealand is wherever they are, as the proud penumbra spreads round the world. The standard joke that the Kiwi eats, roots, shoots, and leaves is true. New Zealand is anywhere they are, an arboreal slum, at the top of every tree, or as the devoted delvers and fixers toiling at the bottom or the hob-gobs touring, photographing and videoing it. Wherever they are, Kiwis benefit themselves, their country, and the one they're in.

This new (extra-mild) nationalism has developed just as globalisation erodes other national differences. Being a cosmopolitan bird, the Kiwi is well suited to the new age, with an identity less subject to erosion because it is bred in the bone by the process of growing up in New Zealand and sustained, now that diffidence and the colonial cringe have gone, by the quiet confidence born of success. Kiwis are part of the world and the future, not a remote land cut off from the one and fearing the other. They know who they are and what they are and they're happy with both identities.

## Sir Bob Jones

*The reason I stay is I was born here, so my roots are here, and I'm perfectly content here. I'm quite comfortable living here. I enjoy living here. Even in Australia I feel slightly different. People go on about Cuba, with ten percent of their population living abroad, we've got ten percent of our population living in Sydney, and I do notice New Zealanders there tend to gravitate towards one another. Because there's an affinity, there is still a difference between us and Australians. In America I feel distinctly foreign.*

## Bob Harvey

*I think that this country has huge potential. It's safe. It's wonderful. It gives to New Zealanders as much as they want and as little as they want. If they flee I don't care. If they go overseas I think they're marvellous ambassadors.*

## Greg Johnson

*I'm absolutely proud to be New Zealander. We have a lifestyle here. I've just been up in East Timor playing to the New Zealand troops in the UN zone up there and that really altered my perspective on New Zealand. When the troops did the haka for us when we arrived into this devastated country, it really struck home. It was the most moving experience.*

## Michael King

*People who belong on the other side of the globe had been transplanted here and felt a bit frightened by what they called the tyranny of distance, the over-bearing nature of the forest and the hostile Maori. In my lifetime all that has completely disappeared. For myself and for my generation New Zealand is in the marrow of our bones.*

## Sam Neill

*It wasn't that I meant to come back. I was spending more and more time back in the country, and then one day I actually realised. Well, here I am. I'm living here and I am very pleased to be here. Every time I would go away I would feel more and more homesick. It was really something that was an imperative. This is what I am and this is what I'm part of, and I wouldn't swap it for anything.*

These voices, like so many others I heard, speak of a confident sense of identity, the emergence of the feeling of difference and nationhood that intellectuals have looked for for decades, pulling each fragile new shoot up by the roots to pronounce it inadequate. Now, belatedly, it has emerged out of the combination of the characteristics instilled by a small, intimate society, hardened by the economic ordeals of rejection, excessive liberalism and the slow build back to normality, then energised by globalisation.

Bigger countries saw their industries undermined and their identities eroded by globalisation but New Zealand was plugged into a shrinking world which opened up opportunities for Kiwi inventiveness, ingenuity and creativity. The adaptable nation was well-placed to succeed in a world opening up – in which the small could enter into their own.

So my pilgrimage became a voyage of discovery The best bits of the old, the sense of fairness and equality, the openness, the benefits of small-scale and universal access to the good life are still there, supplemented now by the new dynamism and confidence of a nation which feels itself to be going somewhere. At last. Dullness and conformity have been replaced by excitement and pluralism, slow growth by fast adaptability, dependence by independence and comfort by challenge. The future we'd looked forward to in the sixties has arrived but by a route we couldn't possibly have conceived of then.

It's sad not to have played any part in the struggle to defend the good society or to blend the best of old with the new. Sadder still to be too old to begin over in the new New Zealand as I once did in the old. Yet there is the consolation of ending this pilgrimage by concluding that although New Zealand is less unique, a part now of the great universal anywhere, I can still write of it as I did in the *Half-gallon Quarter-acre Pavlova Paradise* – that it's the best part of an overcrowded world in which a uniquely privileged section of humanity has an exciting prospect of creating the good society, shaped not for the élite who can take care of themselves anywhere, but for the ordinary people who have the benefit of growing up in an extraordinary country.